RESOLVING TREATMENT
IMPASSES

RESOLVING TREATMENT IMPASSES
The Difficult Patient

By Ted Saretsky, Ph.D.

Adelphi University
New York, New York

With Contributions from

GERARD FROMM
VIOLA BERNSTEIN
NORMUND WONG
JUNE BERNSTEIN

HUMAN SCIENCES PRESS
72 Fifth Avenue   3 Henrietta Street
NEW YORK, NY 10011 ● LONDON, WC2E 8LU

Printed in the United States of America
123456789 987654321

Editorial/Production Services
by **Harkavy Publishing Service**

Library of Congress Cataloging in Publication Data

Saretsky, Ted, 1932-
    Resolving treatment impasses.

    Bibliography: p.
    Includes index.
    1. Impasse (Psychotherapy) 2. Psychotherapist and patient. I. Fromm, Gerald, joint author. II. Title. [DNLM: 1. Mental disorders—Therapy. 2. Psychoanalytical therapy. WM 460.6 S244r]
RC489.I45S25   616.89'14   80-24661
ISBN 0-87705-088-0

CONTENTS

CONTENTS (Cont'd)

CONTRIBUTORS

Dr. Fromm is currently Staff Psychologist and Community Program Coordinator at the Austen Riggs Center in Stockbridge, Massachusetts; previously he was associated with St. Elizabeth's Hospital in Washington, D.C.

Viola Furst Bernstein, CSW Supervisor and faculty, Washington Square Institute for Mental Health, Senior Staff, Postgraduate Center for Mental Health, Group Department, author of Narcissism, An Overview, private practice.

June Bernstein is a modern psychoanalyst in private practice in New York City and Larchmont. She is on the faculties of the Center for Modern Psychoanalytic Studies in New York City, The Boston Center for Modern Psychoanalytic Studies, and Boston State College. She is also on the editorial staff of the journal *Modern Psychoanalysis* and author of *On Being a Successful Patient.*

Normund Wong is the Director of the Menninger School of Psychiatry, is on the faculty of the Topeka Institute of Psychoanalysis, and is a visiting Professor at the Southern Illinois School of Medicine, Mayo Clinic and the Institute of Living. Dr. Wong is a Fellow of the American Psychiatric Association and received the Master Instructor Award in 1976 from the American Group Psychotherapy Institute.

Ted Saretsky is a Training Analyst and Clinical Professor at the Adelphi University Postdoctoral Psychoanalytic Insitute. In addition, Dr. Saretsky is the Director of Group Psychotherapy at the East Plains Mental Health Clinic and is a psychoanalyst in private practice. Dr. Saretsky is a Diplomate in Clinical Psychology, is author of the book, "Active Techniques and Group Therapy," and has published over 30 articles and chapters in psychoanalytic books and journals.

PREFACE

Early in his career, Freud's genius enabled him to make transference a paradigm of psychic resonance related to past trauma, revived in the present. The projection, reenactment, and perpetuation of introjected and incorporated attitudes of the family belief system in the analytic setting was thus established as the major frame of reference for classical analytic inquiry. Within this orientation, the analyst was clearly defined as a mediating instrument. By means of a working alliance and interpretation leading to insight, the patient could be assisted to dissolve his distorted perceptions and faulty thinking, organize an ego along more mature lines, and deal with life more realistically and effectively. The course of treatment was typically viewed as a linear phenomena with the patient presenting his problems and the analyst responding. Under this aegis, the issue of countertransference was dismissed as an auxilary by-product of the treatment process. At first, the analyst was advised to gain better control over these reactions, to seek further treatment if these responses continued, and finally to discharge the patient if the countertransference was found to be a recurrent interfering influence. Along similar lines, this orthodox viewpoint discouraged analysts from systematically investigating another frequent occurrence, the misalliance existing between patient and analyst as a consequence of collusive interactional patterns. Mutually arrived at homeostasis, played in concert by both parties for unconscious gratification of narcissistic interests, hampered a thorough scrutiny of the unconscious needs served by the successful imposition of roles projected upon one another. This circular complementarity of pathological interactional patterns could be maintained and could exist for years, and produce stalemate, discouragement, and failure, and yet would not be commented upon or even noticed owing to a series of "gentlemen's agreements."

Recent advances in theory and technique have exploded many of our previously held comfortable assumptions. An increasing amount of clinical experiences in working with patients with primitive ego states has had the effect of heightening interest in the interface between patient and analyst. The input of patient and analyst and the major interactional mechanisms that join them have become a significant source of current inquiry. The patient's tendency toward denial and splitting and projective and introjective identification (and the symbolic and actual meaning of these enactments) together with the analyst's capacity to contain, metabolize, and interpret these factors has come to be regarded as the pivotal dimension in treatment success or failure. This adaptational-interactional approach places a great deal of stress and responsibility on the analyst as a good object. In order to modify or revise the psychotoxic vicissitudes of early double binds, mystifications, projections, misidentifications, deceptions and rejections, the analyst is challenged to present himself in such a way as to establish enduring cathexes. The equilibration and regulation of the analytic frame coupled with measured dosing of phase-specific, growth-enhancing frustration and gratification help to promote a slow process of internalization and structuralization in the patient. The completion of developmental subphase needs hopefully contributes to a gradual segregating of the ego as a relatively more autonomous center of psychic activity, thus contributing to the differentiation process and a more cohesive sense of identity formation.

The shifting focus of the therapeutic enterprise places increased emphasis on the analyst as participant-observer. The collaboration of the analyst in a dual capacity, the protector (providing a good-enough mother, an adequate holding environment, a strong container of primitive projections) and the observer (communicating understanding) emerges as the most prominent variable for effecting profound patient change. It is of interest to note that the various viewpoints expressed in this book which in some cases come from authors working from quite different theoretical frameworks, all converge on the necessity for demystifying inner reality and diminishing the "immutably private" sector. The explication and translation of object relations in terms meaningful to the patient represents the fundamental premise of this book and the analyst's highly idiosyncratic and creative use of his own experiences become the driving force that makes cognitive understanding come alive during each session, in terms of the patient's own immediate reality.

In effect then, this book is a guide, a schema for clarifying treatment dilemmas in terms of the phenomenological and intrapsychic experiences of both participants. It is hoped that a careful reading of this book will enable the analyst to more quickly recognize the complex patterning of patient resistance to genuine relatedness and, more precisely, to identify the analyst's own tendencies to erect pathological barriers between himself and the patient.

Ted Saretsky, Ph.D.
Adelphi University Postdoctoral Institute

ACKNOWLEDGMENTS

I want to express my gratitude and appreciation to my wife, Dr. Corelle Saretsky, for her patience and kindness while I was so self-absorbed in writing this book. I would also like to thank Drs. Larry Epstein and Arthur Feiner of the William Alanson White Institute for their friendship, support, and enthusiasm, which helped me to see this project through. Sandi Messinger also deserves acknowledgment for her editorial assistance and typing skills.

A PATIENT'S REVERIE

Don't be fooled by me.
Don't be fooled by the face I wear.
For I wear a thousand masks, masks that I'm afraid to
take off.
And none of them are me.
Pretending is an art that's second nature to me.
But don't be fooled, for God's sake, don't be fooled.
I give the impression that I'm secure,
That all is sunny and unruffled with me,
Within as well as without,
That confidence is my name and coolness my game,
That the water's calm and I'm in command,
And that I need no one.
But don't believe me, please.
My surface may seem smooth, but my surface is my mask.
Beneath this lies no complacence.
Beneath dwells the real me in confusion, in fear, and
aloneness.
But I hide this. I don't want anybody to know it.
I panic at the thought of my weakness and fear of being
exposed.
That's why I frantically create a mask to hide behind,
A nonchalant, sophisticated facade,
To help me pretend to shield me from the glance that knows.
But such a glance is precisely my salvation. My only
salvation.
And I know it.
That is if it's followed by acceptance, if it's followed by love.
It's the only thing that will assure me of what I can't assure
myself . . .
That I am worth something.
But I don't tell you this. I don't dare. I'm afraid to.
I'm afraid your glance will not be followed by acceptance
and love.
I'm afraid you'll think less of me, that you'll laugh at me,
And your laugh would kill me.

I'm afraid that deep down I'm nothing, that I'm no good.
And that you will see this and reject me.
So I play my game. My desperate game.
With a facade of assurance without and a trembling child
within.
And so begins the parade of masks. And my life becomes
a front.
I idly chatter to you in the suave tones of surface talk.
I tell you everything that is really nothing.
And nothing of what's everything,
Of what's crying within me.
So when I'm going through my routine, do not be fooled
by what I'm saying.
What I'd like to be able to say,
What for survival I need to say, but what I can't say,
I dislike hiding, honestly.
I dislike the superficial game I'm playing, the phony game.
I'd really like to be genuine and spontaneous and me.
But you've got to help me. You've got to hold out your hand,
Even when that's the last thing I seem to want.
Only you can wipe away from my eyes the blank stare of
breathing death
Only you can call me into aliveness.
Each time you're kind and gentle and encouraging,
Each time you try to understand because you really care,
My heart begins to grow wings, very small wings, very
feeble wings,
But wings.
With your sensitivity and sympathy, and your power of
understanding
You can breathe life into me, I want you to know that.
I want you to know how important you are to me.
How you can be the creator of the person that is me, if you
choose to.
Please choose to.
You alone can break down the wall behind which I tremble.
You alone can remove my mask.
You alone can release me from my shaking world of panic

and uncertainty.

Please . . . do not pass me by.

It will not be easy for you.

A long conviction of worthlessness builds strong walls.

The nearer you approach me, the blinder I strike back.

I fight against the very thing I cry out for.

But I am told that love is stronger than walls,

And in that lies my hope.

Please try to beat down those walls with firm hands,

But with gentle hands . . . for a child is very sensitive . . .

Who am I, you may wonder. I am someone you know very
well.

For I am every man you meet and I am every woman
you meet.

I am you and I am me.

Part I
Analytic Strategies in Working
With Inaccessible Patients

INTRODUCTION

Throughout its history, the field of psychoanalysis has approached the issue of treatment impasse from many different perspectives. The various interpretations and conceptualizations range from the continuous interest of Freud in chronic resistance patterns and negative therapeutic reactions, to Horney's elaboration of these early formulations in terms of the patient's hostile defensiveness against "good interpretations," and the more recent Kleinian approaches that emphasize the institution of narcissistic omniscience through contempt and devaluation of the analyst's efforts to protect against regressive dependent vulnerability and helplessness. These increasingly sophisticated accounts, although providing continued fresh impetus for reevaluation of classical theory and technique, have come to be seriously questioned in the past decade. The new emphasis on the vicissitudes of static, preexisting disruptive intrapsychic forces leading to stalemate has now shifted to a more dynamic interactional, contextual understanding. Margaret Mahler's investigations into the separation-individuation process within the framework of symbiotic attachments has stimulated the deeper comprehension of the revival of crucial early experiences through primitive transference. Winnicot's concept of the holding environment and Bion's explication of the maternal container have alerted us to the evocation of these regressive reactions as a rudimentary adaptive response to traumatic variations in the analytic frame. The ego psychologists and object-relations theorists have established the principle that object relations effect in a major way the structuring of the psyche. The intertwining and interdependence of object relations and ego structure point the way to the notion of an interpenetrating, unified system emerging from the patient-analyst relationship. Robert Langs has extended this conception by characterizing the analytic relationship as an interactional "bipersonal field" held within a secure frame provided by the structure of the psychoanalytic situation itself. The misalliances that result

2

has the consequence of silent collaborations, destructive acting-out, intensified acute and chronic resistance patterns and reciprocal role inductions have been illuminated by the elaboration of projective and introjective identification processses passing back and forth between patient and analyst. The subtleties of treatment-destructive transference and countertransference entanglements has shed further light on the value of the analyst's continuously monitoring and attending to his own input in order to overcome protracted blockages. Gorney has summarized this recent trend of thinking by suggesting that the persistent communication of entrenched negativity can best be understood as only one-half of a more inclusive process.

The papers' in section I elaborate upon and extend these new formulations and demonstrate how they can be applied clinically in many cases which were formerly regarded as intractable. Fromme's chapter on *Impasse and Transitional Relatedness* discusses the phenomenology of impasse as it relates to different phases of treatment. By concentrating on the pathologically transitional status of the analyst during impasse, Fromme shows how the analyst, by allowing himself in Winnicotian terms, "to be used by the patient," can unleash rage and establish the basis for a successful working through process. Saretsky's chapter on *Masochism and Ego Identity* focuses on the separating function of symptoms in working with border lines. Saretsky suggests that pathological symptom formation often conceals an adaptive attempt to preserve a fragmented ego in the face of losing oneself in the other. This chapter and the following one on *The Resolution of Impasses* are consistent with Fromme's theme on the crucial importance of the analyst's availability as the developmentally appropriate object. The analyst's measured relinquishment of omnipotent and omniscient power assigned to him and his steady support of the ego-building efforts on the patient's behalf are singled out as particularly important aspects of treatment progression. The final chapter of Part I, *Mending Affective Splits Through the Use of Projective and Counterprojective Identification Processes,* indicates how the

3

fragmented self can be solidified and integrated by the working through of affective splits and projective identification. Two alternative treatment intervention models are suggested in accordance with whether the patient's split transference creates adhesive attachments to all-good and all-bad object images or whether an arrest in ego development causes fluid, stormy, chaotic alternations of contradictory emotions in relation to the same object.

Chapter 1

IMPASSE AND TRANSITIONAL
RELATEDNESS
M. Gerard Fromm, Ph.D.

INTRODUCTION

Throughout its history, psychoanalysis has necessarily and usefully concerned itself with problems related to impasse—for practical clinical as well as for theoretical reasons. Impasse is a situation of no movement, and hence of a failure or at least a partial failure of therapeutic results. The patient remains, in some fundamental way, unchanged in his suffering. The analyst* is disappointed, frustrated, doubting, fatigued. In this culture of narcissism the analyst may feel more than passing disillusionment and more than passing concern—for the patient's continuing troubles as well as for the way those troubles seem to accuse him, as if their existence, in and of themselves, is the enduring responsibility of the person who at one point wished to help in understanding them.

*The terms "analyst" and "therapist" will be used interchangeably throughout this paper; it is to be understood that both refer to the psychoanalytic psychotherapist.

On the other side of the coin, it has indeed been the experience of impasse in analysis which has provided the clinical data and impetus to push our understanding of human development beyond whatever its then current confines might have been. An early example comes directly from Freud (1905), whose review of the impasse in and the unexpected termination of Dora's analysis led him to see the centrality of the transference, at first as a major if now recognized obstacle to the treatment. Here, knowledge—of the transference as resistance—evolved from impasse. Bird's (1972) discussion of this issue emphasizes Freud's redoubling of this process; that is, with further reflection, Freud turned the impasse of transference-resistance into the knowledge of the transference as the major vehicle of the treatment.

> Then, in what seems like a creative leap, Freud made the almost unbelievabe discovery that transference was in fact the key to analysis, that by properly taking the patient's transference into account, an entirely new, essential, and immensely effective heuristic and therapeutic force was added to the analytic method. (Bird, 1972, p. 269)

There are innumerable examples of this dialectic process, of impasse leading to discovery, throughout the development of psychoanalysis. There are also ways in which this dialectic seems to divide the analytic community; for example, around the issue of analyzability. Should analysts risk the inevitable experience of impasse, failure, perhaps harm to the profession that eventuate from working at or beyond the borders of clearly understood psychopathology? Rather, should not analysts conserve themselves and their standing in society by accenting psychoanalytic work with patients whose pathology has been documented to be clearly accessible to analytic investigation and influence (Rangell, 1975)? On the other hand, how are we to learn about and help those deeper troubled areas of human experience if not by risking ourselves and our methodology in an effort to bridge the communicative gap between two people (Green, 1975)?

These are some of the questions which flow from the experience of impasse (A. Freud, 1976). Data with which to address them have been accumulating slowly over the past few decades, as analysts, sometimes overly optimistic, sometimes out of sheer necessity, have found themselves presented with patients whose suffering was intense and yet whose ability to engage in analytic work, as traditionally defined, was severely limited. One pervasive trend in this work has become quite clear: that an interactional dimension, defined very broadly, must be taken into account in understanding the power, and therefore also the vicissitudes, of clinical psychoanalysis (Winnicott, 1965; Greenson & Wexler, 1969). Andre Green (1975), in a major paper outlining his understanding of changes in analytic practice as reflective of the severe psychopathology currently seen in clinical work, makes this point emphatically:

> Problems of indications for analysis [can] be approached from the point of view of the gap between the analyst's understanding and the patient's material, and from that of the evaluation of the mobilizing effect of the analyst's communication of the patient's mental functioning, i.e., on the possibility...of forming an analytic object [a symbol] by the meeting of the two parties. (p. 18)

Consistent with this effort to illuminate the dyadic nature of psycho-analysis is the concomitant effort to illuminate impasse as an interactional phenomenon. Langs (1976) has emphasized this point of view in his work on the bipersonal field, as has Gorney (1979) in his thorough discussion of a particular kind of impasse, the negative therapeutic reaction. Will's (1977) definition of chronicity fits equally well the interpersonal phenomenology of impasse: that is, that a stereotyped presentation meets a stereotyped response. Casualties to this stereotype are curiosity, revelation, and change itself. Nothing new seems to happen. Both parties to the treatment seem fixed in their image of the other. The fundamental processes of the analytic relationships—attachment, revelation, change, separation—are aborted. Indeed, the impasse may have to do with the particular phase of the patient's relationship to the analyst and to the treatment; that is, the impasse may have as its major motivating force the avoidance of a particular experience, with its fantasy elaborations, in relation to the analyst. One thinks here of the paranoid patient for whom beginning feelings of attachment produce intense turbulence, or the patient for whom the idea of termination assumes catastrophic and growth-inhibiting significance, a domino effect in reverse.

To the extent that an impasse in fact aborts a treatment, one sees a progressive insidious devaluing of the analyst and the analytic experience by the patient. When the treatment comes to an actual end, there is no process of separation, no grief. Rather, there is only the depleted termination of a tiresome non-experience. Nothing differentiates this treatment from the amalgam of the patient's life so far; hence, there is nothing new to be lost. To the extent that the analysis once held hope for the patient, there is, after the aborted treatment, only the defensive warding off of its absence and the dissociation of whatever in it might have mattered. The all too frequent outcome of unresolved impasse is an elision of the patient's entire experience of the treatment.

FRAME AND MEDIUM

If we consider the psychoanalytic impasse from an interactional point of view, rather than solely in terms of the patient's intrapsychic structure, the question of the analyst's contribution to it is necessarily raised. Apart from a simple intrapsychic (that is, countertransferential in the more strict sense) focus on the analyst, one might approach the analyst's potential contribution to impasse by considering his contributions to the entire treatment. The technique of clinical psychoanalysis can be described in any number of ways. One such description would accent two primary functions for the analyst: the establishment and maintenance of the frame, and the offering of a medium. These important concepts have been developed elsewhere (Milner, 1952; Khan, 1960; Balint, 1968; Langs, 1976; Gorney & Fromm, 1979), and can only be sketched briefly here.

The frame refers to the boundedness and structure of the analytic situation. It has to do with all those technical prescriptions and "arrangements" for the treatment which securely establish the rhythm of the work, the privacy of the setting, and the constancy of the analyst. Insofar as the establishment of the frame presupposes the analyst's knowledge (for example, of the conditions for benign regression and for transference development), this action reflects the analyst's authority and professional identity.

The offering of the medium differs from and complements the concept of frame. The analyst-as-medium offers himself, his empathic responsiveness and total mental functioning, to the patient. His purpose is the receiving of the range of impressions the patient is trying to convey, the range of self and object images and of affect that at any given point constitute the experiential transferential level of the treatment. The concept of medium therefore connotes the process level of the treatment, the level of resonance. As the frame of the treatment fades into the background, the analyst-as-emotionally-responsive-medium becomes its foreground. Countertransference in its broader sense has its place here, in that the feeling-reactions of the analyst can be seen as primary data with regard to the unconscious communication of the patient. The crucial factor in the treatment becomes the analyst's apprehending these countertransference feelings, that is, containing them, analyzing them, and in some way imparting their significance to the treatment.

It should be clear at this point that the analyst's dual functions correspond to two modes of relatedness between analyst and patient. In establishing and maintaining the frame, the analyst deals with the patient at the level of everyday reality (for example, of fees and schedules). The mode of communication is linear, logical, informative, individuated. The analyst is, in a sense, the emissary of reality, the professional solver of problems. Expertise is a factor, and the distribution of authority is clearly imbalanced; the analyst leads in setting the arrangements and the method which the patient accepts, more or less, and follows.

The analyst's actions in setting the frame, however, mark off a space in which an entirely different kind of relatedness may occur. The patient's efforts to contract and integrate the dissociated parts of himself require a different communicative mode—associative, empathic, merged in some way with the analyst as alter-ego. Again, the distribution of authority is imbalanced. The patient leads in his effort to communicate, or to evade, himself; the analyst follows. Ultimately, the accuracy of the analyst's interpretive activity rests with the patient to, often unconsciously, confirm or not. This form of relatedness, called into play via the analyst-as-medium, occurs, in Winnicott's (1953) terms, within an area of illusion. That is, the question of the reality status of the patient's imaginings and constructions of his experience, including his experience of the analyst, is set aside unasked; in its place is only the search for its personal meaning. From one perspective, this can also be seen as the area of transference experience, called into play as a transitional phenomenon (Modell, 1963, 1968; Greenson, 1974) to comfort and to bridge a gap between present and past—so that the patient can be someone and be with someone that he is no longer and is no longer with.

I would like now to approach the problem of impasse from this dual angle. My thesis is that impasse in the analytic situation may at times best be understood as reflecting a pathology of relatedness between analyst and patient, and that this pathology may occur in one of two forms, deriving to some extent from the analyst's two technical functions. Pathology is perhaps too strong a word, for the pitfalls that I mean to discuss are inevitable and importantly a part of the ongoing work of the treatment. I do mean to convey, however, the truly debilitating impact on the entire treatment, *if* they are not grasped by the analyst and worked with. I shall take as a guiding conceptual structure for this discussion Winnicott's work on transitional phenomena (1953) and his more recent discussion (1969) of the distinction between relating to and using the object.

Preliminary to considering the two kinds of impasse I am hypothesizing, a brief review of Winnicott's remarkable work on transitional phenomena is necessary. Beginning with his observation about the perhaps universal phenomenon of the infants attachment to a special object, like a blanket, that becomes vitally important at times of separation or deprivation, for example at bedtime, Winnicott elaborates a rich hypothesis about a kind of relatedness, the crucial outcome of which is the integration of the inner psychic life with external reality. Winnicott (1953) describes this process in the following way:

> The mother, at the beginning, by almost 100% adapation affords the infant the opportunity for the *illusion* that her breast is part of the infant. It is, as it were, under the baby's magical control....Omnipotence is nearly a fact of experience. The mother's eventual task is gradually to disillusion the infant, but she has no hope of success unless at first she has been able to give sufficient opportunity for illusion. In another language, the breast is created by the infant over and over again out of the infant's capacity to love or [one can say] out of need....From birth, therefore, the human being is concerned with the problem of the relationship between what is objectively perceived and what is subjectively conceived of....The intermediate area to which I am referring is the area that is allowed to the infant between primary creativity and objective perception based on reality-testing. The transitional phenomena represent the early stages of the use of illusion....[They] start each human being off with what will always be important for them, that is, a neutral area of experience which will not be challenged. Of the transitional object, it can be said that it is a matter of agreement between us and the baby that we will never ask the question: "did you conceive of this or was it presented to you from without?" The important point is that no decision on this point is expected. The question is not to be formulated....It is assumed here that the task of reality-acceptance is never completed, that no human being is free from the strain of relating inner and outer reality and that relief from this strain is provided by an intermediate area of experience which is not challenged [arts,

religion, etc.]. This intermediate area is in direct continuity with the play area of the small child who is "lost" in play....Essential to all of this continuity [in time] of the external emotional environment and of particular elements in the physical environment. (pp. 11—13)

DEFEATING PROCESSES

There are some treatments that seem to come to a particular kind of impasse. As described thoroughly by Cooperman (1969), this impasse has two distinct clinical characteristics. First, the progressive development of the treatment and of the treatment relationship is interrupted or even reversed by the behavior of the patient. Secondly the therapist "experiences a loss of good feeling" (p. 7). In place of feeling cautiously optimistic, the therapist feels "thwarted, often anguished, helpless, frustrated, lost, angry, hurt, and even, when the interference is precipitously introduced, as though physically struck" (p. 7). In short, the therapist feels, and in fact is defeated in his wishes for and efforts toward the growth and development of his patient. He is hit by the patient where he, to some degree in fact, is vulnerable, that is, in his basic identity as a therapist. That the patient is also defeated in his defeating of the therapist, is both true and beside the point. For the moment, change toward more satisfying ways of living has become an irrelevant consideration (perhaps also an impossible one, given what will be discussed later as the precipitant for the attack); it is more important for the patient to have his illness than it is to have his therapist.

Dr. Cooperman offers several detailed clinical vignettes to illustrate his essential point that "a patient may destroy the therapy in order to defeat the therapist, regardless of the price he pays in doing so" (p. 27). Others (Langs, 1976; Searles, 1975; Fromm, 1978) have noted the patient's effort to set right a treatment course thrown off by the misunderstanding or the personal reactions of the therapist; it seems only logical that, under certain circumstances, patients feel inclined to destroy a treatment course as well. The degree to which this is a conscious versus an unconscious effort is a secondary issue; in fact, Dr. Cooperman's data are quite striking for the awareness and articulateness his patients displayed about the defeating process. One patient reported:

> That I was right about feeling about to be struck, [that] he had been debating about whether to strike back at me by continuing to come to sessions, going through the motions, not making any progress, and leaving after several months. He then went on to note that he had done this to his previous therapist. (p. 9)

Another patient responds to Dr. Cooperman's formulation of his manic regression and its consequences as an attack on the treatment by gleefully noting "that I was exactly right...[that] to his wife and family he was now viewed as the sick person to be cared for and I was an incompetent and uncaring doctor." (p. 17)

Dr. Cooperman goes on to describe three interrelated elements of the defeating process: first, that it represents an act of vengeance for a specific hurt felt by the patient to have been inflicted on him by the therapist; secondly, that without attention to this hurt, the defeating process escalates into a full-scale power struggle which may both diffuse and escalate further as "splits" within the treatment organization; finally, that his patients' mode of being in the defeating process mimicked behavior of their mothers that they had felt to be hurtful to them in their growing up. In effect, in getting back *at* the therapist, they also seemed to be getting back *to* their mothers.

This description of impasse highlights what might be thought of as the willfulness of the patient (whose diagnoses in Dr. Cooperman's report range from characterological, depressive, to psychotic conditions). Certainly, an adversary situation is being described—in reality, as opposed to in the patient's transferential life. The therapist is being defeated in the only way he *really* can be, that is, via his real, appropriate, understandable stake in the therapy itself. Two elements in this mode of relatedness are exceedingly important: the reality level of the exchange and the separateness of the two parties.

Dr. Cooperman notes the latter to be the primary precipitant for the defeating process.

> Each patient...described feeling hurt, humiliated, or badly used [narcissistically wounded], and rendered helpless by a considered and concrete act of mine which directly affected the arrangement of the therapy....With each, I had arbitrarily forced into focus our separateness. (pp. 18-19)

In this context, willfulness is exactly the point. The patient falls back on individual will, a separate will, for several reasons. In hurting because hurt, he both avenges himself on and mirrors the therapist. The injury is the therapist's separateness; the response is a display of the patient's separateness. At a deeper level, the patient's willfulness confirms the continued aliveness of a jeopardized self, a self that had been cautiously but necessarily giving itself over to the process of the therapy until being abruptly forced into separateness by the therapist.

In other words, the patient reacts with a form of primitive omnipotence to the therapist's individuating actions, ordinary as those actions might seem. The function of the omnipotence is the reassertion of the delusion of control, when in fact there is an underlying panic that the therapist has gone and taken with him the nuclei of ego functioning and evolving self-representations that had begun to develop within the therapeutic matrix. Here, there is a fear of psychic death, followed immediately by the assertive reinstatement of the symptoms as both a comfort and a weapon. I once heard of a young man, the youngest of a large family, who, at a point in his adolescence when his ever tenuously held together family was finally fragmenting as was his own psychic functioning, leaped in front of a subway train to his death. His motives, as best those could be reconstructed, seemed to have to do, not so much with a wish to die, but rather with a wish to stop life. He seemed to need desperately to put himself in the path of events and of time itself, in a delusional effort to halt the inexorable. In doing so, he dramatized the killing impersonality of his life experience; he became a casualty in and of the real world.

The therapist's separateness, in effect, ruptures the area of illusion forming ever so subtly in the treatment (Winnicott, 1953; Khan, 1971); in Searles (1976) terms, the therapeutic symbiosis is damaged. The patient is forced to operate on either the level of delusion, that is, on the level of a brittle denial of the injury and an assertion of magical command, or on a totally depleted reality level. It is a reality into which the patient now feels helpless to deliver himself. Whatever was being brought to life in the treatment—Winnicott would encourage us not to ask by whom—left with the individuating therapist, leaving the patient feeling without any capacity to create, from within himself, anything which would join him in a living way with the external world.

In another language, this form of impasse having to do with defeating processes can be described as following from an action by the therapist along the frame of the treatment, which has as its primary negative effect a severe perturbation in his offering of himself as medium. There is an assertion here: the therapist has exercised his legitimate authority—to be the separate person he is, to set and manage the arrangements of the treatment. But this clear shift in a mode of relatedness disturbs, even shocks, the other mode of relatedness having to do with the medium of the treatment. Action on the medium has been given over to the initiative of the patient. Hence, there must be a note of betrayal in the patient's response to the therapist's initiatives. It is as though, in Lewin's (1954) terms, the therapist has jarred into painful wakefulness and harsh reality a patient who had been, until that moment, using the therapist and the therapeutic situation to move toward a state of quasi-sleep and a necessary dream. If the therapist misunderstands or devalues the importance of his patience in allowing the patient the use of the medium, then that phase of hesitation (Winnicott, 1941), preliminary to the patient's comfort with the illusional aspect of the treatment and requiring the initial constancy of the therapist, cannot come to completion. Once the area of illusion has been established, traumatic disillusionment becomes a possibility, from which the treatment cannot recover without the considerable turmoil of the defeating process.

The way out of such an impasse seems to be the way in. Winnicott (1953) puts it in the following way for the abandoned child:

> It is a matter of days or hours or minutes. Before the limit is reached the mother is still alive; after the limit has been overstepped she is dead. In between is a precious moment of anger. (p.22)

Drs. Cooperman (1969) and Bird (1972) concur that the hope for the resolution of the impasse (and for its transformation into crucial analytic gains) lies in helping the patient get hold of, and allowing oneself to receive, the deep and live anger toward the therapist for the perceived injury. Bird (1972) puts the technical issue very clearly:

> Significant success, however, can be counted only if the response (of the patient) leads to some rather detailed "chapter and verse" discoveries as to how and why the patient's malicious intent against the analyst was actually developed and carried out. This might include gaining some idea of how much the patient's attack was simply a matter of transference, how much it was caused by the analysis mobilizing his destructive impulses, and, finally, how much it was retaliation for attacks made on him by the analyst. (pp. 292-293)

In essence then, the kind of impasse typified by the defeating process reflects an abrupt and premature separateness of the therapist and a disturbance in a healthily developing transitional relatedness. The frame of the treatment intrudes arbitrarily on the function of the medium. The logical consequences to disturbance in the transitional sphere threaten delusional power or psychic death in vacuous reality (Green, 1975). Reparation and resolution can occur if the rage within the relationship can be contacted, contained, and worked through openly and specifically. The hoped-for outcome here is renewed trust, in the engineering sense; that is, having to do with a new appreciation of, and perhaps a new level of, the therapist's and the relationship's capacity to withstand stress. Such a capacity can now become an important background variable for the continuing and deepened analysis.

A CASE OF DEREALIZATION

There is another kind of interactional impasse, the characteristics of which can be described along the dimensions of relatedness and technique just discussed, though with quite a contrasting configuration. In order to do so, I would like to offer as clinical data a vignette reported in the literature several years ago. In 1955, Dr. Victor Rosen published a paper in the *Journal of the American Psychoanalytic Association,* entitled "The reconstruction of a traumatic childhood event in a case of derealization." In essence, the paper is a marvelous illustration, as Rosen had intended, of the importance of the reconstruction of the traumatic fixation, in this case occurring at about the age of three and a half. A colleague of mine sometimes refers to Dr. Rosen's clinical intervention as a "psychoanalytic hole-in-one." Along the way, Rosen also makes the point that identification may serve as a means for the binding of the overwhelming affect associated with the traumatic experience. I would like to summarize the vignette in some detail because it seems to me to additionally offer a striking illustration of an impasse and its resolution.

The patient, a professional man in his late twenties, came into treatment having recently begun to feel depressed, suicidal, as though he were fragmenting, and full of bizarre bodily sensations. Dr. Rosen describes the patient's feelings of "fullness in the head," "twisting" and "choking" sensations, and "feelings of being transected through the diaphragm." (p. 212) The symptoms appeared after the patient's fiancée, upset with his unpredictable and often violent fluctuations of mood, broke their engagement. The patient lost interest in his work and embarked on a series of casual affairs, during which he developed the obsessional fantasy that his sexual partner would subsequently be found strangled and he would be accused of the murder.

The patient was the younger of two brothers. His father was a successful businessman, unhappy with and bitter toward his sons for not coming into the family business with him. He alternately bestowed and withheld money in an effort to control his sons. He also suffered from a paralysis of his lower limbs during the patient's early childhood. The patient's mother is described as jealous and possessive. She would at times become seriously depressed and at other times violently rageful. The children were put in the middle of the marital strife and expected to declare their loyalty toward one or the other parent. The patient complained about both his mother's seductiveness toward him and her depriving him of maternal care.

This patient was seen by Dr. Rosen on a tri-weekly basis and vis-a-vis for approximately four years. The underlying diagnostic picture was thought to be schizophrenia. A particular technical problem in the therapy had to do with the patient's feelings of unreality and his negating of all interpretations.

> He did not feel that what was said really applied to him. He felt that the therapist confused him with other patients. He said in this regard, "I never know whether something belongs to me or to someone else." . . . . Occasionally, during treatment, he could not tell whether some idea had been transmitted from him to the therapist or vice-versa. (pp. 213—214)

During his second year of therapy, a series of puzzling but critical developments occurred.

> The patient began to recall incidents surrounding the discharge
> of a beloved nurse in his early childhood . . . the only one who
> had "understood" him . . . " the one witness in my behalf"
> . . . . There were recurrent references to recollections of "some
> horrifying experience which occurred while I was looking
> down the long dark hall of our home as a small boy." . . . .
> The patient felt that he had been "a witness to something that
> changed my life." . . . . At the same time he increasingly
> neglected his job. He felt that earning a living was unreal and
> that the money he was paid was "make believe." He began to
> neglect his bills and finally stopped paying for his treatment
> altogether. (p. 214)

Dr. Rosen describes the patient at this time as manifesting "a sullen glowering expression," as "in moody silence," as "provocatively disparaging the treatment," as "slyly destructive," and as "making attempts at intimidation." (p. 214) At one point the patient, in an apparently menacing way, spent some time opening and closing a large clasp knife, leading the therapist to comment that he was indeed being made to feel anxious by this behavior; at that point the patient put the knife away. The patient would not discuss the failure to pay for treatment. "His behavior seemed to indicate a hostile determination to prove that the treatment was all 'make believe' and that it would continue whether paid for or not. This determination was impervious to interpretation." (p. 215) Finally, Dr. Rosen decided to discontinue the treatment until the patient paid his now three-month debt. Payment was made in two installments over the next month and, while waiting for treatment to resume, the patient wrote what Dr. Rosen describes as "bitter letters." "I did not believe you really meant what you said, I thought that you would get the money from my father . . . I know now that I must help in the solution of my problem . . . If I must wait too long, my faith in you will again be shaken." (p. 215)

When treatment began again, the patient produced provocative data, leading eventually to Dr. Rosen's bold reconstruction. In reporting a stiff neck, the patient said, "it felt as if my head were being twisted from my body." (p. 215) He became depressed and suicidal. He had the fantasy that venetian blinds he had been playing with were really "hangman's ropes," and he also felt that he was being given "permission" by his therapist to recall something. Following his report of a dream having to do with "a small chest like a trunk lying on the floor," Dr. Rosen had the feeling "of many loose pieces in a puzzle falling into place." (pp. 215-216)

"I felt quite certain that the patient's mother must have made a suicidal attempt during his childhood which he had witnessed . . . . It also seemed likely that the neck symptoms, references to the rope . . . and the earlier fantasy of the strangled girl, refer to an attempt by hanging." (p. 216) Dr. Rosen's offering this hypothesis to the patient released "a remarkable and violent flood of affect. He was racked with convulsive sobbing in a most dramatic scene lasting about ten minutes. This session was a turning point in the treatment." (p. 216)

Following this reconstruction, the derealization symptoms decreased and the patient showed an increased ability to use the therapy. For example, he was able to analyze the meaning of his withholding the fee in terms of his "identification with his father's punitive and seductive uses of his money." (p. 216) He was also able to bring into the work at this time complicated and disturbing feelings about masturbation. With his father, he confirmed the fact of his mother's suicide attempt, which indeed he had witnessed during his third year, and which indeed had been made by hanging.

Dr. Rosen writes:

> The discharge of the nurse a year later was connected with this episode, because the mother had experienced her presence as a constant reminder of the incident. Both the father and the nurse had treated any mention of the event on the part of the patient as something that he had imagined or as a "bad dream." (p. 216)

He also adds, "when I had suggested the possibility of his mother's suicide attempt in his childhood, the patient had felt as if I had not restored the memory but had merely given him permission to talk about something he had known in some way all along." (p. 216)

THE CAPACITY TO USE THE ANALYST

The impasse in the treatment just described was clearly a very serious one, yet resolution occurred as well as striking analytic gain. From one angle it looks as though, and in fact it may have been the case, that Dr. Rosen's reconstruction was the crucial move in breaking the stalemate, releasing the impacted affect, and crystalizing important memory and insight. From another angle, the way for Dr. Rosen's reconstruction seemed paved by the patient's unconscious effort to represent the traumatic memory (for example, in the venetian blind fantasy and in the dream about the trunk). Moreover, the patient had felt a strange new permission to discover something and had found a startlingly new ability to use his own and the analyst's words. Critically important developments seemed to have been occurring in the patient and in the relationship *prior* to the analyst's reconstruction. The question arises as to how these changes might be described and how accounted for.

Following Winnicott (1969), one could argue that Dr. Rosen's patient came to make the critical shift from relating to the analyst to using him. The former implies a subjective experience, a cathexis toward the other, the operation of projective and identificatory mechanisms, and some movement toward physical excitement and discharge. The latter implies the capacity to use the other for the properties of the other and not as a figment of the patient's subjectivity. In other words:

> The object, if it is to be used, must necessarily be real in the sense of being part of shared reality, not a bundle of projections . . . usage cannot be described except in terms of acceptance of the object's independent existence, its property of having been there all the time. (Winnicott, 1969, p. 712)

Dr. Rosen's patient became able to find his analyst's independent status in the real world. In this new place, the analyst's interpretations, previously negated with hostility or diffused as unreal and as the analyst's misidentification suddenly had compelling power. Furthermore, in this new place, the self-comforting, self-sufficient, self-aggrandizing aspects of his masturbatory activity could, for the first time, become part of a two-party discourse. This level of relatedness, that is, a relatedness reflecting the analyst's separateness and therefore his availability for use for his own properties, is in marked contrast to the level of relatedness earlier in the treatment. Prior to the analyst's achieving reality status for the patient, he occupied what might be thought of as a pathologic transitional object status. In other words, the pathologic relatedness cultivated by the patient included dedifferentiation of self and object, a level of primitive omnipotence, a diffuse and pervasive aura of "make believe" without grounding in reality, and a talismanic possession of the analyst for purposes of comfort rather than work (and rather than genuine play as well).

The impasse, therefore, that is being described here in terms of pathologic transitional status, has as major features to its configuration the properties of unreality (for example, to words, fees, feelings, bodily sensations) and of merger, or lack of separateness between analyst and patient. This is in clear contrast to the impasse characterized by defeating processes, the main properties of which seemed to be its reality level and the traumatic separateness of the two parties. The defeating process attacks the reality of the analyst for his perceived role in the premature loss of an illusion. Pathologic transitional relatedness forces an illusion to the point of delusion, and cannot contact reality.

From a Winnicottian perspective, Dr. Rosen's patient worked with him, and vice versa, in such a way as to accomplish the reality groundedness necessary and preliminary to the capacity to use the analyst's reconstruction. In other words, "[t]his interpreting by the analyst, if it is to have effect, must be related to the patient's ability *to*

place the analyst outside the area of subjective phenomena
[italics mine]. (Winnicott, 1969, p. 711) For Winnicott,
the means of this accomplishment is the patient's destructiveness, and the accomplishment itself reflects "the positive
value of destructiveness." (p. 715) If the patient destroys the
transitionally held other, *and that other survives,* then the
other exists in a world outside the projective inventions and
omnipotent control of the patient. Hence the other is real and
available for use.

To put it paradigmatically, if the child tears the teddy
bear to pieces, the life of that teddy, invented by the child in
first place, comes to an end. If the child acts similarly toward
the mother, the mother will eventually say "Stop it now. That
hurts." The mother's invented life will come to an end, in
both the child's wish *and* in the fact that something will survive, intact. That something is the mother's real life, a
property of her own, now discovered by the child, though
there all along, and potentially to be used and loved as a
genuine other.

Dr. Rosen's data offer compelling evidence for Winnicott's formulation, for it does indeed seem that the gap between the relating to and the use of the object, or between the
pathologic transitional status and the reality status of the
analyst, was bridged by the patient's destructiveness and the
analyst's survival without retaliation. During the second year
of the treatment, anxious memory fragments begin to occur
followed by an increased living out of feelings of unreality in
his work life and in the analytic situation. There develops
then a mood of unmistakable aggression and destructiveness.
Words, for both parties, are useless (relatively), and action by
both parties follows. The patient plays with the knife; the
analyst responds with his actual feeling. The patient refuses
payment and refuses analyzing his nonpayment; the analyst
eventually discontinues the treatment. After payment and
prior to the resumption of the analysis, that is, prior to the
analytic work leading to the reconstruction, the patient writes
in his letters that words, in effect, have finally acquired
reality status for him and that "faith" in the analyst is a new

and tentative development.

I am suggesting that the termination of the treatment was a critical event to the subsequent developments in the treatment; that the patient's push toward representing his trauma, the analyst's capacity to grasp it, and the patient's capacity to use a reconstructive interpretation might well have failed to develop entirely without the event which "place[s] the analyst outside the area of omnipotent control, that is, out in the world." (Winnicott, 1969, p. 714) This event is Dr. Rosen's limit. It limits the patient's destructiveness, and it also recognizes the limits of the analyst's tolerance and technical ability. It affirms a separateness that tells the patient that his fantasy of "murder" will not become real with the analyst, that the analyst will survive the patient's actual destructiveness. Indeed, from another angle, the patient has in effect compelled this separateness as if to find the "witness," who might separately and credibly testify to the reality of a past event, and also perhaps on the patient's behalf. This witnessing follows in the reconstruction and in the patient's confirming with his father the fact of his having seen his mother's suicide attempt.

The pathologic transitional relatedness prior to the event of the limit can be seen, *to some extent only retrospectively,* in transference terms. The patient does indeed subsequently analyze his withholding of the fee as reflecting his effort to control the analyst through money, just as his father had done to him. Only after the reconstruction, however, can one also see the additional transference meaning of the patient's nonpayment and the analyst's allowing of a debt: that is, that the analyst-father is buying the patient-son's silence about the critical event; hence, the patient's feeling of "permission" to remember following the limit. It is clear in this material that the patient suffered a dual trauma in his early childhood: one in witnessing the horrible event of his mother's near suicide, the other in damage of his developing reality-processing ego functions through his father's denial of the event (and its meaning) as the child's "bad dream."

Similarly, one can *in retrospect* see the pathologic transi-

tional relatedness as having as its pervasive background a diffuse maternal transference. In effect, the patient's withholding of fees says to the analyst: "you will not leave me; you are
mine," as well as "your life (your livelihood) does not depend on me." The transference implications with regard to
the mother's potential death and the son's sense of dread and
terrified self-accusation are clear. Also, one can now see the
significance of the precipitating event to his illness, that is, his
fiancée's breaking the engagement, and to the memory
precipitating his destructive mood, that is, of the discharge
of his childhood nurse. The point I wish to emphasize, however, is that the transference could not be grasped for its
genetic meaning until the analyst and patient could ground
the treatment in reality. Until such a development, the data
did not seem to exist for, nor did words seem capable of
establishing, an understanding of the patient's behavior in
transference terms.

It might, however—at this point in the development of
clinical psychoanalytic theory—be argued, perhaps accu-
rately, that the data indeed existed for an understanding of
the impasse in transference terms, and that the data was the
transference itself, as perceived through the aid of the
countertransference; in other words, that the transference
itself was the patient's best effort at remembering. It might
also be argued that the analyst's use of the countertransference data in actual interpretive work might itself have
effected the development considered to be the key to the
thesis under discussion: namely, the analyst's coming to existence outside the patient's subjectivity while still in contact
with the patient. What Dr. Rosen effected in action (though,
and this is very important, not through intention) might now
be possible in words, through a disciplined yet imaginative
use of the countertransference.

The disturbed form of transitional relatedness described
in Dr. Rosen's clinical vignette is pathologic insofar as it *must*
be; there is no leeway within it, no play in the system. The
area of illusion, in which true play may occur, has become an
area of delusion. The patient does not keep the agreement not

to ask a basic question that may take a number of forms; for example, did you (the patient) create the analytic situation or did you find it? Rather, the patient poses the question and insists that his subjectivity is its only answer. This solipsism is clearly not without its own anxiety; nevertheless, it effectively denies object-loss by denying the object existence. To return to the analogy of sleep (Lewin, 1954), it is as though the patient is caught and catches the analyst in a "bad dream" diffuse in time and space; the analyst's function as awakener becomes eventually imperative to the establishment of an object relation and a reality in which to continue the treatment.

A healthy transitional relatedness facilitates an imaginative mastery and integration of the experience of absence. Pathologic transitional relatedness does not allow absence to be constituted as an experience. Rather, the object is totally present (totally possessed by the omnipotence of the patient) and simultaneously nonexistent, as a *distinct* other. There is never absence, as such. It may be that the patient cannot integrate the experience of absence prior to his analyst's making a similar integration. Applied to Rosen's data, this hypothesis would suggest that Rosen's integration of his patient's absence from him (his terminating the treatment) might have been necessary to his patient's developing a similar capacity, a capacity to constitute in himself an experience of genuine absence, the traumatic precursors of which had been so devastating. As Green (1975) has reminded us, the capacity for thought depends upon an experience of absence. It is only after the absence that Dr. Rosen's patient can allow thought to develop toward the memory of many real and potential absences.

To return to the technical language elaborated earlier, pathologic transitional relatedness represents clearly a diffusion of the medium in a way which erodes or otherwise breaches the frame of the treatment. The technical problem becomes the restoration of the frame. The analyst can only offer himself as medium within some frame; outside the frame, the patient is unprotected, as is the medium itself since the analyst's feeling-reactions to the demand come into play.

The analyst-as-medium can be offered, but not conquered—at least not without extensive damage to the reality
which surrounds the treatment and hence to the treatment
itself. Once the frame is restored (accomplished practically in
action, as Rosen did, or perhaps by interpretation from the
countertransference), anxiety deescalates and the medium is
available again for development and communication at the
experiential level.

SUMMARY

I have attempted to discuss in this paper two forms of
impasse which are interactional in nature. The two forms of
impasse can be described as (a) the defeating process and (b)
the incapacity to use the analyst. Both reflect a disturbance of
transitional relatedness. In the former, the patient attempts,
consciously or unconsciously, to defeat the treatment because
of the analyst's premature and injurious disruption of the
area of illusion. The patient is traumatically separate from
the analyst and stuck in a depleted reality. In the latter form
of impasse, the patient cannot use the analyst-as-analyst
because the analyst has not come to be placed outside the
range of the patient's omnipotence. The patient is traumatically merged with the analyst and stuck in delusion. In a
language having to do with the technical functions of the
analyst, the defeating process reflects a traumatic withdrawal
of the analyst-as-medium via his arbitrary action along the
frame of the treatment. The incapacity to use the analyst
reflects an erosion of the frame of the treatment via the
patient's burgeoning demand on the analyst's capacity as
medium. Aggression is central to the resolution of both forms
of impasse. In the first situation, aggression recontacts the
separating analyst and discharges the panic that otherwise
would be deadened internally and at great cost to the patient.
In the second situation, aggression is the vehicle for finding
what, if anything, is left in (or better, as) reality after the invented object has been destroyed. Clinical illustrations of

both forms of impasse are presented. It is important to keep in mind that the two forms of impasse described in this paper develop naturally—at some basic experiential level and outside the conscious intentions of both parties. Impasse, in itself, must neither be simply a strategy of the patient nor a technique for the analyst. Any gains that may come from the mutual work of resolution of the impasse hinge upon that fact.

REFERENCES

Balint, M. *The basic fault.* London: Tavistock Publications, 1968.

Bird, B. Notes on transference: Universal phenomenon and the hardest part of analysis. *Journal of the American Psychoanalytic Association,* 1972, *20,* 267-301.

Cooperman, M. *Defeating processes in psychotherapy.* Unpublished manuscript, presented at a meeting of the Topeka Psychoanalytic Society, Topeka, Kansas, 1969.

Freud, A. Changes in psychoanalytic practice and experience. *International Journal of Psycho-Analysis,* 1976, *57,* 257-260.

Freud, S. Fragment of an analysis of a case of hysteria, (1905). *Standard Edition, 7,* 3-122. London: Hogarth Press, 1953.

Fromm, M.G. The patient's role in the modulation of countertransference. *Contemporary Psychoanalysis,* 1978, *14* (2), 279-290.

Gorney, J. The negative therapeutic interaction. *Contemporary Psychoanalysis,* 1979, *15* (2), 288-337.

Gorney, J., & Fromm, M.G. A model for contemporary technique. In: *Current clinical psychoanalysis* (1979) (work in progress).

Green, A. The analyst, symbolization, and absence in the analytic setting (on changes in analytic practice and analytic experience). *International Journal of Psycho-Analysis,* 1975, *56,* 1-22.

Greenson, R., & Wexler, M. The nontransference relationship in the psychoanalytic situation (1969). In: *Explorations in psychoanalysis.* New York: International Universities Press, 1978.

Greenson, R. On transitional objects and transference (1974). In: *Explorations in psychoanalysis.* New York: International Universities Press, 1978.

Khan, M. Regression and integration in the analytic setting (1960). In: *The privacy of the self.* New York: International Universities Press, 1974.

Khan, M. The role of illusion in the analytic space and process (1971). In:

The privacy of the self. New York: International Universities Press, 1974.

Langs, R. *The bipersonal field.* New York: Jason Aronson, 1976.

Lewin, B. Sleep, narcissistic neurosis, and the analytic situation (1954). In: *Selected Writings of Bertram D. Lewin.* New York: *The Psychoanalytic Quarterly, Inc.,* 1973, pp. 227-247.

Milner, M. Aspects of symbolism in comprehension of the not-self. *International Journal of Psycho-Analysis,* 1952, *33,* 181-195.

Modell, A. Primitive object relationships and the predisposition to schizophrenia. *International Journal of Psycho-Analysis,* 1963, *44,* 282-292.

Modell, A. *Object love and reality: An introduction to a psychoanalytic theory of object relations.* New York: International Universities Press, 1968.

Rangell, L. Psychoanalysis and the process of change: An essay on the past, present, and future. *International Journal of Psycho-Analysis,* 1975, *56,* 87-98.

Rosen, V. The reconstruction of a traumatic childhood event in a case of derealization. *Journal of the American Psychoanalytic Association,* 1955, *3,* 211-221.

Searles, H. The patient as therapist to his analyst (1975). In: *Countertransference and related subjects.* New York: International Universities Press, 1979.

Searles, H. Transitional phenomena and therapeutic symbiosis (1976). In: *Countertransference and Related Subjects.* New York: International Universities Press, 1979.

Will, O.A. Personal Communication, 1977.

Winnicott, D. The observation of infants in a set situation (1941). In: *Collected papers: Through pediatrics to psycho-analysis.* London: Tavistock Publications, 1958.

Winnicott, D. Transitional objects and transitional phenomena (1953). In: *Collected papers: Through pediatrics to psycho-analysis.* London: Tavistock Publications, 1958.

Winnicott, D. *The maturational processes and the facilitating environment.* New York: International Universities Press, 1965.

Winnicott, D. "The Use of an Object." *International Journal of Psycho-Analysis,* 1969, *50,* 711-716.

Chapter 2

MASOCHISM AND EGO IDENTITY IN BORDERLINE STATES*
Ted Saretsky, Ph.D.

This horror of waking—this was knowledge . . . . He tried to
fix it and hold it; he kept it there before him so that he might
feel the pain. That, at least, belated and bitter had something
of the taste of life. — Henry James, *The Beast in the Jungle*

Not long ago, a new patient reported to me that he had
seen the musical, "Jacques Brel is Alive and Well and Living
in Paris", 25 times since the death of his wife, two years
before. I had trouble understanding how anyone could sit
through the same play so often for any reason. Besides that, I
wondered what could be making this man so morbidly attracted to words and music that were so bittersweet, cynical,
and dysphoric. A few weeks later another patient described
his fascination for Bette Middler. "I go to see her every
chance I get and every single time I get depressed, but I love
it. She represents something raw, primal, screaming, ranting,
fuck-it-how-I-look. She magnifies her flaws; she's gut. I want

*This material is an expanded version of an article that appeared originally
in *Contemporary Psychoanalysis,* Vol. 12(4), October, 1976, 433-445,
Journal of the William Alanson White Institute and the William Alanson
White Psychoanalytical Society, New York. It is reprinted here with
permission.

to swallow her up and be her or at least be part of her life. She has power and pain; I want to share some of that." About the same time, still another patient described how a close friend told her something cruel and cutting. My patient was hurt but when the friend apologized the next day, she was vaguely disappointed. "I don't know why but I hate to have to surrender my bad feelings. Just because she was making up to me made me feel I no longer had the right to be upset." And still another patient described the following fantasy: "I wish there was a cause I felt really strong about. A fantasy I have over and over again is that I'm the last Jewish soldier between the Arabs and Tel Aviv and I know I'm going to die for a purpose. I have a smile on my face."

These little vignettes lend themselves to many different interpretations. Most striking, however, is the underlying thread of self-destructive, possibly masochistic attitudes. The recurrent search for pain and obsessional thinking about situations that can only result in suffering seems to defy any other explanation. Yet, I find myself in agreement with Menaker (1953, p. 205), in that "It is often the study of the anomalous, the atypical that points the way to the discovery of deeper truths." The hypothesis that suffering satisfies some masochistic need does not seem sufficient to account for such complex and paradoxical behavior.

Following Freud's conceptualization of the death instinct, various unsatisfactory, incomplete formulations regarding masochism have been offered by Reik (1941), Reich (1933), and Fenichel (1945), among others. Although their emphases differ, each of these contributors is almost exclusively concerned with the libidinal meaning of masochism. As Menaker (1953) has pointed out, the major focus of interest in the literature has been how gratification is achieved for the individual through masochistic behavior rather than examining how it serves the ego.

The recent upsurge of interest in the treatment of borderline conditions, where self-destructive patterns are commonplace, has given fresh impetus to the theoretical and treatment value of viewing the problem of masochism from the standpoint of the self-preservative functions of the ego (Giovachinni, 1972; Kernberg, 1975; Khan, 1960). The conceptual model that this paper is based upon suggests that in the case of borderline patients, masochistic behavior is an important dimension of ego identity and that masochism is related to an adaptive function of the ego. It is proposed that masochism is unconsciously used to bind an ego that "feels sick" (Guntrip, 1968), fragmented, and empty. From this point of view, self-inflicted intensification of painful affects is employed as a primitive attempt to pull together the threads of a definitive though faulty self that is separate from primary objects. Winnicott (1965) has approached this issue from a different standpoint. Describing the latter stages of a successful course of treatment in borderline states, Winnicott maintains that the patient needs to maneuver the therapist into failing in ways that are reminiscent of failures in the patient's original environment. These failures are seen as essential, providing the patient with a chance to reexperience, be angry about, and work through a past situation in the present, and finally to separate.[1] The therapist must not defend himself, otherwise the patient will miss an opportunity for being angry about a past failure just when anger was becoming possible for the first time." Winnicott's observation might perplex those who do not view borderline patients as having any special problem accepting their anger. On closer examination, however, many borderline patients report a curious detachment and "thinness" regarding their feelings much of the time. They tend to discuss their anger, sadness, and hurt as though they knew they felt that way but they're not really sure they're entitled to it. The ego strength necessary to deeply give oneself the right to be entitled to feelings that are not justifiably reasonable, is lacking. The central thesis of this chapter is that borderline patients set up unbearable situations where they are bound to fail, get hurt, or become very disappointed in order to feel their feelings

[1] In a personal correspondence, David Schecter suggested that "often the search for angry release must be justified by ensuing pain."

and own them. This supports a brittle ego-structuring process, and an unstable, but somewhat improved, crystallization of an amorphous ego identity. The cost is great, but the psychic gains in terms of feeling temporarily whole and solid seem to outweigh the suffering that takes place. Although masochism is a complex phenomena that manifests itself throughout the range of many diagnostic categories, the use of masochism in the establishment of a momentarily stabilized ego identity, occurs most frequently in patients with severe ego defects.

Kernberg (1975, p.5) suggests that the term "borderline" should be reserved for those patients presenting a chronic characterological organization which is marked "(1) by typical, systematic constellations; (2) by a typical constellation of defensive operations of the ego (e.g., splitting, denial, primitive idealization, omnipotence); (3) by a typical pathology of internalized object relationships; and (4) by characteristic genetic, dynamic features." All of the patients referred to earlier in this chapter fall within the borderline range according to these criteria. Although the outward behavior and symptom pictures vary widely, the feeling states and self-image of borderline patients have some distinct similarities. Most apparent are pervasive feelings of loneliness and emptiness, the lack of a stable ego identity, chaotic interpersonal relationships, and the presence of very powerful aggressive feelings that give rise to unpredictable mood swings (Grinker et al., 1968). Contemporary psychoanalytic theory accounts for this clinical picture as follows: One essential task in the development and integration of the healthy ego is the synthesis of early and late introjections and identifications into solid sense of self. When splitting occurs, the ego is protected from conflict by means of dissociations. Anxiety is diminished, but the integrative process is retarded and the stage is set for the possibility of identity diffusion. A heightened fear of regression, the partial refusion of primitive self and object images affecting the stability of ego boundaries, a growing sense of depersonalization, and vague feelings of nonexistence occur. Under these circumstances, the experience of pain and depression can actually be a comforting one. The primary gain is to be able to establish a stable "body ego" feeling ("this pain is really mine; this is really me"). It can be reassuring to own oneself, even if the feeling of certainty ("this is my pain") is based on agony.[2]

One of the themes that I will develop later is that borderline patients typically surrender pieces of their ego bit by bit so as to avoid still greater loss. Sullivan (1953) referred to this when he introduced the concepts of "malevolent transformation" and "malevolent integration." Berliner (1947, p.459) has dramatized further the ego's need to cling for the sake of survival to the introject of the hated parent. "Ego then, rather than be an orphan, hates the self in the name of the parent, and even accommodates by being a hate-provoking object." I believe that in the case of borderline patients, the chronic tendency to give oneself up for another is counterbalanced by the reclamation of oneself through self-destructive acts.

A borderline woman who was responding well to treatment, accounted for her earlier provocative behavior as follows: "I've lost myself in other people so much during the course of my life, it feels good to control things and do and say what I damn feel like once in a while. I don't know how to explain it, but even if I know my habits are bad, I feel that I'd be losing a part of myself if I changed. My habits are me."

The proliferation of books and articles in the literature in the past decade on the feasibility of working with borderline patients probably reflects a growing belief that the usual clinical symptoms of depression, anxiety, and guilt frequently cover over or mask more pathological processes. It may be that borderline, schizoid, and narcissistic patients represent a large part of our present clinical population. The

---

[2]Mahler (1971) suggests a similar formulation for autoaggression seen in psychotic children, stating: It is probably directed at a self-object representation connected with the body. The autoaggressive activity, like some autoerotic activities, is probably also an attempt at defining the body-self boundaries, an attempt to feel alive, even at the price of enduring pain. (p. 416).

awareness of this possibility has stimulated experimentation with, and modification of techniques, and shifts in theoretical orientation that may be necessary to deal more effectively with these patients. I will present first a few key hypotheses concerning the development of borderline personality organizations, and how this transmutes itself into adult behavior. Then I will propose parameters that I have found particularly useful in coping with emerging treatment problems.

One of the fundamental fears of the borderline personality is an almost claustrophobic reaction to close relationships (Giovachinni, 1972). This fear can manifest itself through the dread of "being smothered," "possessed," "dominated," "absorbed," or even "making a commitment to something." Many writers (Guntrip, 1968; Fairbairn, 1952; Winnicott, 1965) have suggested that the basis for this anxiety originates within the context of very early symbiotic experiences in the mother-child interaction. The specificity of early separation problems is unique for each person; however, several predominant trends can be detected in the case of individuals who grew up according to a borderline developmental pattern. (1) These people began their lives in an environment that was extremely intrusive and impinging. The availability of cherishing validation and love were unduly contingent upon the irrational values and expectations of immature, self-centered parental figures who had great difficulty seeing their children in anything but ego-extension terms. There was serious lack of respect for the integrity and individuality of the child (Kohut, 1966; Khan, 1960). (2) As the children got older, such normal acts as self-assertion, the keeping of secrets, and the wish for privacy gravely threatened the parents because these capacities all represent ego autonomy and apartness. Behavior that ordinarily would be construed as depicting progressive mastery and growth (being exploratory, putting fingers in the mouth, shouting, touching things) in the eyes of average parents, would be seen by these parents as defiant and bad. Pearce and Newton (1963) have speculated that the malevolent parents' need for manipulation and aggressive control has to do with a reactivation of ambivalent, unresolved symbiotic ties with their own parents. (3) It is further suggested that the parental figure has an unconscious stake in promoting the fear of disorganization, pathological dependency, and a gradual loss of self in the child. The child comes to feel that not even slight divergencies of opinion can be expressed, unless the parent can be convinced that it is acceptable. The rich secret life that the child develops retains an unreal quality because it can be exposed only in sporadic and fragmented form to contemporaries. The net result is that the validating love object and reality tester is the very same person who originally fostered the unwholesome dependency.

With enough reinforcements, this arrangement creates a very tenuous and tentative feeling in the child. On the one hand, the child must repudiate many basic aspects of his own being when feeling engulfed by the parental need-gratification system. This dissociation and subsequent splitting of feeling outside of consciousness leads to a relatively stable but sometimes terrifying level of adjustment within the nexus of the parent-child dyad. Kernberg (1975) put it this way: "Clinically, the child who is going to become a borderline patient, lives from moment to moment, actively cutting off the emotional links between what would otherwise become chaotic, contradictory, highly frustrating and frightening emotional experiences with significant others in his immediate environment" (p.165).

The extent of panic and ego terror that the patient constantly lives with is difficult for the analyst to grasp (Kernberg, 1964). Unbearable conflicts and terrible loneliness are dulled and drained of their affective valence by primitive defensive operations so that much of what emerges appears detached, hollow, and ultimately boring. One gets a sense of a slow, steady deterioration of vital self. This "secret essence" (Reik, 1952) represents the core being, the "living, breathing me." When this central structure is coopted and coerced into capitulation, nothing is left. To check this regressive trend, patients will resort to any method that will preserve some shred of personal identity. What we usually think of as "craziness" is very likely a compromise formation that balances the need for closeness and the fear of it. By accepting the stigma and symptomatology as the "identified" patient, the borderline individual takes the onus off his or her parents and in return is able to establish some distance and keep some part of himself alive for another day. In this light, aggressive and self-destructive acting-out may represent panic attacks caused by the patient's struggle for personal survival. For example, in the case of many drug addicts who have a borderline diagnosis, the obstinacy of the symptom may be a form of self- and other-directed aggressive defiance, which is one of the few forms of self-affirmation the patient manifests in relation to the parents and the therapist.

CLINICAL ILLUSTRATIONS

Case 1

One patient was a very unhappy 30-year old man who entered treatment because of an inability to find a satisfactory sexual role. At various times, he participated in heterosexual, and bisexual relationships but acted as though he could never find more than fleeting pleasure in any of them. Some additional features of this case was the patient's addiction to a wide assortment of hard drugs, his compulsion to pluck hairs from his face, and a generally wasted life that involved clowning around, titillating friends by singing in falsetto, impersonating female entertainers, all followed by periods of deep depression.

What I remember most about this man was how quickly he developed a precipitously positive, idealized transference. Despite several previous unsuccessful experiences in treatment, in his work with me many of his original complaints rapidly cleared up and he reported feedback from his friends that indicated significant changes in the way that he carried himself. Every chance he got, he would conscientiously report advances or slippages that occurred in terms of being true to himself and behaving the way he really felt. I regarded this whole scene with some astonishment and felt I was observing somebody who was engaged in a very subtle but cruel bargain with the devil. The patient seemed to be feeding me things to cure him of, almost generating pathology that seemed so obviously gross in terms of the patient's actual capacity to curb his behavior that it was simple to reduce the early presenting symptomatology. Among other things, the patient would describe slave-like masochistic adorations for mean, exploitative men; after about two interpretations, these "chronic patterns" magically abated. The patient reported he was going to look for meaningful relationships. The patient would describe extremely child-like dependencies on both his parents (e.g., having his father get up in the middle of the night to change a tire, having them pay for his car insurance, calling them up at the slightest hint of illness). Again, these seemingly ingrained habits seemed to change after only a few interpretations, with no real working through or any kind of in-depth understanding. One last point: Despite his masochistic tendencies, this man found his most deeply satisfying relationship in homosexual arrangements. However, he was never able to go public and to really accept this part of himself. He resisted joining homosexual organzations, did not let fellow workers who were themselves homosexual know about his secret, and he always kept this part of himself from his parents. He tried very hard to disgust me, to present the raunchiest, seediest aspects of homosexuality in such a way as to try to shock my sensibilities. By providing me with these red herrings to sift through and "satisfy my need to save him from this sordid existence," it was my impression after a time that the patient was acting as though he was willing to surrender this part of his behavior as long as I did not ask him to give up his homosexuality.

Eventually in treatment the meaning of the "plucking of hairs" symptom became clear. These hairs represented "wild hairs"; that is, real, growing parts of himself that were there but were not supposed to be noticed. If the patient removed them before anybody became aware of them, then the patient had the fantasy that he might seem damaged (castrated), and perhaps even crazy, but his basic capacity for life, change, and growth would be preserved. The self-mutilation that the plucking represented and which was acted out in so many other ways by this man was ultimately seen as a ploy to distract the superego and its externalized representation from ever realizing that life was throbbing under the surface, for he feared that if this was ever discovered, he would surely vanish. This was all poignantly summarized in a fantasy he described, "You remember during World War II? The minesweeper would chase the submarines. The submarines would shoot oil slicks, garbage and pieces of debris out through the torpedo tubes and up to the surface. When the pursuers would sight this debris, they would think they sank the sub and they would leave. The submarine would wait until nightfall when it seemed safe, and then slowly slip away."

Case 2

A woman in her mid-thirties was obsessed that something terrible was going to happen to her nine-year-old son. Early in treatment she described a dream where she imagined that her son was her own "inner lining." "Everything he does I watch like a hawk. Every move, every hurt, every possible pitfall, I anticipate. I know it's nuts but I can't help it." This woman had a mother who "did everything for me. My mother told me very directly what kind of person I should be — good-natured, outgoing, and smart. She always exaggerated how much she loved me and was always telling me who I was and what I was feeling. Once in a while, I would tell her I was unhappy and she would say, "spare me your hurt; things aren't as bad as you're making them; be happy — it's the best way!" The mother's self-centered, engulfing presence created a number of significant developmental disturbances in the daughter. The patient's inability to differentiate clearly self from object can be traced to impeded processes of internalization and identity formation. The expected response reinforced a false other-oriented attitude. Any anger or despair that was aroused could rarely be expressed because even a small degree of unhappy behavior was experienced as risking object-loss. The relationship with the son was interpreted as a reenactment of an undifferentiated symbiotic tie with the mother. Manifestations of hate that took the guise of love through possessiveness, reveillance, and apprehension were then undone by sugar coatings of love, demonstrativeness, and suffocating affection. The net result was a child who was rapidly developing disturbing symptoms and a mother who was acting out another version of the very kind of mother she despised.

Very early in treatment, I pointed out some of the more obvious parallels. After a short while, the patient's response was to agree that the primary problem was herself and not the son. She kept prefacing this insight with the statement, "I'm not trying to please you—it's just that I now know that if I help myself, I'll help my son." I suggested that this was all very well except that she seemed more concerned with giving the correct response rather than voicing her own fears and concerns that persisted regarding the son. The patient then became very agitated and confused. It became apparent that if the patient was stripped of the characteriologically ingratiating attempts at fusion she was immobilized. "I don't know what to say. Anything I think of sounds like a lie. Do you mean that if I don't try to please, there's hardly anything else left for me?"

Several months later, this same woman was describing some positive changes that she had undergone. "I have a sense of relief with my son—he stopped blinking and I'm less hovering with him, I'm buying more clothes, keeping the house nice, and I cut my hair. The only thing I'm not doing well with is my weight. I eat for relief. Sometimes I think I like to be heavy. It gives me a more comfortable feeling. When I'm thinner, I feel empty; I feel something's missing."

DISCUSSION

Now what do the personality organization of these two patients have in common? The male patient came from a home where both parents were insistently loving. They actively offered tokens of unconditional, indiscriminate availability and acted very hurt and angry if their need to be needed was thwarted. The female patient's background was somewhat different. Her father was a passive, unresponsive preoccupied man. This created a vacuum whereby the valence of the mother's offerings were heightened. The mother's engagement and stimulation were seductively appealing despite the risk of suffocation. The potential for the acting out of selfishness, masked aggression, and ego destructiveness is great. The result in both instances is a character structure consisting of shallow friendliness and pseudo-submission covering an emotional detachment, which seals off an extreme amount of primitive anger. After a while, the patients were able to express some degree of anger toward their parents but the effects of splitting and dissociation were evidenced in the utter lack of emotional awareness regarding the extent of the deeply felt rage.

I believe that many borderline patients inflict pain of themselves, feel empty if they have no problems, and are thereby highly creative masochists. I suggest a twofold hypothesis to account for this: (1) Acute hurt and anger cut through numbness and reflect the only thing these patients are able to call their own. Although the borderline patient is capable of distinguishing between internal experience and external perception and his reality testing is largely preserved, this capacity is lost during emotional moments which cause regressive episodes. There is a confusion at these times between what is occurring "inside" and what is taking place "outside." The patient, by causing his own pain, can at least partially regulate and control what is taking place, thereby distinguishing between himself and outside events. This very costly resurrection of ego boundaries is worth the price if the patient believes that it defends him against going crazy. In effect, pain or depression can temporarily stabilize a lost sense of identity and halt a terrifying cycle of pathological projective and introjective processes. (2) Another affect is that the chronic generation of self-induced pain is a highly symbolic

attempt to reestablish a fantasy relationship with the idealized "loving" mother. In an overdetermined way, the patient
acts out the internalized experience of underlying hate that
the parent originally manifested, passively offering himself as
a damaged object to be "loved," transformed, and experimented with, to gratify the parents' narcissism and unconsciously demonstrates an original truth, i.e., that the
earliest need-satisfactions occurred in a climate of hidden
sadism and resulting ego injury. In a very condensed fashion,
the individual expressed his own distorted beliefs concerning
the necessary conditions for love. From this point of view,
deepening the pain experience is a triggering mechanism
designed to revive the paradisical fantasies, split off from
early experiences of harm and resulting ego injury. In effect,
the patient's myth of the idealized, loving parent, has also
become a felt need.

THE TREATMENT SITUATION

Throughout this chapter it had been emphasized that the
pathological boundary structuring that borderline patients so
commonly employ is unconsciously designed to create a
closed interpersonal system to counteract a regressive temptation to merge with the bad preoedipal mother. It has been
stressed that the predominance of negative affects and self-
destructive behavior in many of these cases seem to reflect a
desperate attempt at ego integration, where "bad" is the only
thing that is experienced as real. Aggressive negative affects
are split-off, expelled, and projected onto significant others.
Painful negative affects are not felt as part of an emotional
experience but are used instead as mentioned above, for
defensive differentiation purposes.

Kernberg (1975) and later Zane Liff (1978) have commented on the early developing ego of the borderline as being
incapable of integrating opposite contradictory emotions.
Liff has speculated that there may be a separate imprinting
for pleasure and pain in the rudimentary structuring of the

memory system:

> These affective grooves, as living interpersonal scripts fixated in the unconscious memory processes, store the cumulative traumas, i.e., of ongoing pain from emotionally unavailable, inconsistent, or toxic parenting, and become more deeply imbedded in the psyche and the contemporary boundary-structuring system. Implicit within both emotional memory tracks are buried childhood fantasies, actual events and experiences, and, of course, the adaptive defenses to survive. When these dual units do not become integrated and modified through later interpersonal experiences and are solidified by ongoing reinforcements, they become hardened intrapsychic channels that determine adult interpersonal relationships through self-perpetuation and self-fulfilling prophesies. Thus, the frozen, once adaptive script, is played out in the form of set-up operations or role-induction behavior. With the negative emotional pathways predominant, all positive communications, including the therapeutic, cannot be easily assimilated. It is as if such patients are living with one major transmission-reception channel open and the other relatively weakened. Patients within this category have been described as sadomasochistic in their attachment to the pre-oedipal "bad" mother. They are the help-rejecting complainers who, in an attempt to make the outer world consistent with the inner, hold on to the bad. Their inner world, through its boundary-structuring activities, expels and is unaffected by that which dosen't "groove," fit, or make sense. All information, emotional and cognitive, is filtered according to the precursor referent interrelationships. Interrelationship is stressed because there also may be innate deficits in such primary autonomous ego functions as regulation, stimulus barrier, perception, and memory. These biochemical or biogenetic components obviously influence the infant's activity toward the mother as well as the mother's reactions to the infant. (p.xx)

This splitting of affect succeeds in idealizing or denying inner experiences in the face of unbearable life situations where the individual feels that he can neither change the environment nor alter his own basic nature. It constitutes what Winnicott (1957) has referred to as the "false-self". From this viewpoint, diffuse identity formation which is at the heart of the borderlinne dilemma, rests on the faulty scaffolding of transformed inner experiences. This disinclination to experience what is actually experienced personally becomes the chief object of analytic investigation. The analyst's primary responsibility is to fashion his inferences from his experience of what the patient does not experience. Resistance in this light can be schematized on two levels: (1) the surface level where the patient defends his right not to experience what he would feel threatened to experience, and (2) on the deepest level where the patient defends his right to experience what he is actually experiencing.

The analyst's earliest interests should focus on alterations of the patient's attention, on his transfigurations of affect. Exploring the nature of these operations (Level 1) can provide the analyst with a key to understanding encoded experiences. Over a sufficient period of time, "never" becomes "I never was" becomes "It never was" becomes "I forgot". As memories are reclaimed, so are the feelings that accompanied the original experiences. In his investigation of the second level of defenses, the analyst's focus on the split-off vicissitudes and projected feelings helps to synthesize a fragmented ego. The following case proves this point.

> R. continuously defended against dealing with his feelings by taking a devil's advocate position. He continuously thwarted the analyst's attempts to bring feelings into the limelight by raising hypothetical questions, becoming impossibly obsessive in accepting any interpretations as totally true, and was forever raising qualifications. ("What if...") that made him appear insatiable. These defensive structures together with his extreme emotional isolation threatened to turn every session into a sterile intellectual debate.

> R.'s background consisted of a rejecting, critical father, a warm, overprotective mother, and a household where everyone was forever bickering and at odds with one another. When R. complained to his mother about his father's negative attitudes, the mother, in the interests of avoiding further confrontations, advised him not to let it bother him, that he had to

accept the way his father was, and that R. was too sensitive. Multiple exchanges of this nature in the context of a relationship that he was most dependent on, ultimately had the effect of causing R. to lose confidence in the legitimacy of his emotional demands on the mother. Instead of experiencing his wish to be taken care of as a valid expression of the role that the mother customarily invited, R. now tended to treat his needs as aggressive demands that only succeeded in alienating the mother.

In the context of this chapter, R's obsessive style and his passive aggressive behavior represent pseudo-neurotic defenses against a deeper pathology. His sometimes infuriating doubt-ridden behavior and indecision can be interpreted as primitive defenses against the anxiety of influences from the outside. In the analytic setting, with the warm, encouraging climate promoted by the analyst, R. transferentially projected a sense of seductive manipulation that only served to remind him with alarm of an earlier time when he was pressured to surrender his living reality of being disturbed. Accepting even the most conservative interpretation at face value became symbolically equivalent to capitulating, leading to a paranoid dread that he would be giving up his rights forever. The indecisive behavior, which was his chief presenting symptom ("I can never make up my mind about anything") was also R.'s structural defense against losing himself in the other.

Consequently the therapeutic strategy was to support R.'s compulsion to oppose and deny, while simultaneously exploring the boundary function of these self-defeating efforts. In the third year of treatment, the working through of varied aspects of these operations finally culminated in a different level of awareness and emotional understanding. R. came to this particular session feeling unusually depressed. He had been offered an opportunity to move to a different division of his company but was unsure whether this represented a promotion or reflected a failure. "I'm not sure whether they don't think I'm doing an adequate job with my present assignment or do they think I'm particularly suited for the new division." It turned out that R. was given the present job with all kinds of promises that he would be supported, supervised, and backed up by his boss. When things became hectic and R. needed assistance, the boss did not make himself available. R.'s inclination was to blame himself for not handling crises more effectively. As he got more into his associations, however, he began to express deep disappointment at how the supervisor had let him down. Through a transparent dream he connected "promises that were never kept" with his mother's betrayal of him vis-a-vis the father. The sadness and bitterness began to fall out of him as never before. R. now recognized that the tendency to attack himself was displaced anger that protected the boss-mother from his "unreasonable" (now viewed as perfectly sensible) demands. R. approached the boss for a discussion about the promotion. He discovered that the boss realized that R. had done a good job under the circumstances at his previous assignments. The boss felt badly that he could not devote as much time to supervision as he realized was necessary and was suggesting the promotion as a way of rewarding R. and making things easier for himself (by putting someone in the previous job who did not require so much supervision). R. now realized that his investment in staying at the present assignment was to prove to himself that he was adequate. The way he was going about this, however, was basically masochistic. In reality he needed help: instead, by frantically throwing himhimself into every crisis situation, he was vainly trying to live up to the mother's fantastic model of the idealized son, someone who can rise above his feelings and pretend he never has needs. The inner acceptance of resentment and disappointment not only enabled R. to become more assertive and decisive but through the boss's explanations, R. was able to view the boss with ambivalence. The boss's acknowledgement of his own laziness furthered R.'s acceptance of himself as a complex person who quite naturally has a mixture of feelings toward significant people in his life.

Clinical experiences with borderline patients suggest the presence of a strong latent, negative transference covered by emotionally shallow therapeutic relationships (Kernberg, 1975; Knight, 1953). It is easy for the analyst to be deceived by surface changes and reports of improvement that are more apparent than real. The key requisite for broadening the observing ego and solidifying a true therapeutic alliance is to work constantly at preventing the development of insoluble transference-countertransference binds. Borderline patients offer the therapist superficial parts of themselves to rescue, rehabilitate, and approve of, thereby perpetuating the myth of the idealized, giving-loving parent. The purpose of this maneuver is to protect the inner self against the dread of control and fusion. During the course of treatment, after first establishing an early positive supportive relationship, the therapist can reveal and interpret evidences of manifest and latent negative transference (Kernberg, 1975).[3] The rationale behind this is to repeatedly demonstrate to the patient that he is primarily engaged in gratifying the therapist's assumed need for dominance. By taking this passive-submissive role, how could the patient feel anything other than frustrated, empty, and weak? The acting out of the transference by attempting to please the analyst is highlighted as the main resistance to further change. If a patient is jealous but deals with it as though it is a problem to be worked on and conquered, and he dependently requests that I collaborate in overcoming this shortcoming, I tell him it must make him very angry if he feels that a normal emotion must be eliminated. In the case of my patient who basically preferred his homosexual orientation, I wondered out loud why he found it necessary to degrade something he enjoyed by acting obliged to emphasize the lurid details and masochistic aspects of his escapades. I believe that my siding with his underlying feelings served as a transitional executive ego function for the patient. His absorption and integration of these inputs led to internalized structure building. In the case of R., the patient

---

[3]David Schecter has pointed out that the analyst must take care in the course of frequently interpreting the patient's ingratiation, that the "growth buds" of relatedness are not discouraged.

acceptance of R.'s resistance against "giving in," helped him to gradually perceive the analytic relationship as mutual, involving two independent egos. Only under this aegis, was cooperation and autonomy feasible.

Most analysts would agree that treating patients "attracted" to failure (Racker, 1968) is extremely frustrating. Despite repeated "correct" interpretations and a good deal of energy expenditure, the persistence of the patient's illness derides controls, and dominates the analyst's best efforts. Many of these patients come for treatment after having already humbled several previous analysts. One common occurrence is for the analyst to rise to the challenge by becoming very active. A combination of the patient's passivity, frightening regressive tendencies, masochism, and despair drives many analysts to play Messiah and strive to "save" the patient from himself. This attitude is a common therapeutic error in dealing with many types of patients. In the case of more severely disturbed individuals, however, the therapist's identification with the extent of the patient's helplessness, confusion, and despair, force the frightening regressive tendencies that are counteracted by grandiosity and the need to control. It is precisely the early recognition of these traps and the analyst's grasp of the vicious cycle that could easily be reenacted which is of decisive importance to the entire future course of treatment. It is easy for the analyst who is unconsciously seeking to restitute his own narcissism, to get enmeshed in the patient's hidden resistances. The analyst begins to feel anxious over the possibility of failure and can get quite angry with a patient who makes him aware that he has been living in a fool's paradise. If this anger is repressed and translates itself into the disguised form of precipitous attempts to restructure a patient's life, an overconcern with the reduction of presenting complaints, a tendency to "give a lot to the patient," and an unconscious pacification of a patient's transference needs, then a repetition of the patient's past is set in motion. The analyst is drawn into a self-centered, omnipotent compensation for his bruised ego with the patient unconsciously encouraged to surrender his autonomy to protect the analyst's insecurity. The crucial early mother-child interaction is blurred over and acted out instead of being worked through. A precious opportunity is thus lost for cultivating more genuine object relationships. The analyst who has analyzed his own narcissistic tendencies will have a greater capacity for tolerating frustration, will be less likely to get bogged down in untenable countertransferential traps, and will be able to selectively focus, within the transference, on the borderline patients' pathological defenses.

An interesting case in point was recently encountered in a self-perpetuating treatment impasse in working with a very depressed woman. The patient's life story was one of fortitude and courage in the face of repeated overwhelming trauma. Her background consisted of an unstable, suicidal schizophrenic mother and a passive, helpless father. Since she was a young girl, the patient's response was to precociously assume a responsible, self-sacrificing, supportive role in order to stabilize a chaotic family atmosphere. The patient's presenting problem was depression in relation to an absence of a close male relationship. Throughout the duration of the therapy the patient was stuck in a bottomless pit of despair, cynicism, and hopelessness. Even when things were going well, the patient noticed her tendency to revert back to unhappy thoughts, as though something terrible would occur if she even momentarily forgot how unhappy she was. All attempts at analyzing this attraction to pain was strenuously resisted. On the one hand the patient accused the analyst of not being helpful; on the other hand, she tenaciously held on to the very thing she wished would go away. As the patient slowly began to observe, with some discomfort, her compulsion to drift toward the negative, she shared the following fantasy: "If I feel happy, I would feel that the rest of my life, everything that went on before, was meaningless." She then began to remember some of her father's attitudes: "Go out and have a good time; forget about it" (after the mother had smashed every window in the house or had a violent tantrum in front of the patient's friends). Another family saying was,

"Close the door and it will all be behind you; look to the future." The denial of what was real to her, the pain, despondency, and anger was necessary to maintain the connection with the available stable love object. This false orientation provided security at the expense of inner craziness (having to pretend what is, is not). Holding on to depression then represented a form of reality testing, a protest that took the form of "I have a right to suffer." The process of analysis, particularly the analysis of the masochistic-depressive core became threatening because it jeopardized a link to feeling alive and real. The waves of depression that seemed obsessive and onmipresent were now revealed to reflect a kind of self-preservation through rebellious self-righteousness. Beyond that it was a hostility transferentially directed at the analyst-father who wanted her to be happy and forget the rest of what she was and what she felt.

This case is illustrative of an increasing portion of the patient population that are commonly encountered, namely, intensified neurotic symptoms that serve as defenses against the fear of a deeper pathology. My clinical experience has been that once the regressive fear is aborted, the ego investment in masochistic symptomatology is lifted and patients' affective mood states are more closely linked to the actual ups and downs of reality. The analyst's role is crucial in helping such patients to arrive at this denial of objectivity. Through projective identification, the analyst is induced to feel like the hateful, depriving beast who deliberately denies relief from pain and lifelong suffering. Under the sway of this influence, there is a powerful undertow to arrange the patient's life for the better. The analyst may be tempted to make constructive suggestions, to take responsibility for decisions, and ultimately to resent the persistence of depressive symptomatology. The patient's primary narcissism is gratified and a state of helplessness is reinforced through secondary gain. The analyst's capacity to have worked through an ability to endure being temporarily assigned a hateful object role, without experiencing narcissistic insult, is vital here. Only under these optimal conditions will the borderline patient's tendency to see interpretation as attacking projections in reverse, be reduced.

REFERENCES

Berliner, R. Masochism & the ego, *11,* 450-471, International Journal of Psycho-Analysis, 1947.

Fairbairn, W.R. *Psychoanalytic studies of the personality.* New York: Basic Books, 1952.

Fenichel, O. *The psychoanalytic theory of neurosis.* New York: Norton, 1945.

Giovacchini, P. (Ed.) *Tactics and techniques in psychoanalytic therapy.* New York: Jason Aronson, 1972.

Grinker, R., Werble, B., & Drye, R. *The borderline syndrome.* New York: Basic Books, 1968.

Guntrip, H. *Schizoid phenomena, object relations, and the self.* New York: International Universities Press, 1968.

Kernberg, O. *Borderline conditions and pathological narcissism.* New York: Jason Aronson, 1975.

Kernberg, O. Ego distortion, cumulative trauma, and the role of reconstruction in the analytic situation. *International Journal of Psycho-Analysis,* 1964, 45, 272-279.

Knight, R.P. Borderline states (1953). In: (Eds.) R.P. Knight and C.R. Friedman, *Psychoanalytic psychiatry and psychology.* New York: International Universities Press, 1954.

Khan, M. Clinical aspects of the schizoid personality: Affects and technique. *International Journal of Psycho-Analysis,* 1960, *41,* 430-437.

Kohut, H. Forms and transformation of narcissism. *Journal of the American Psychoanalytical Association,* 1966, *14,* 243-272.

Liff, Z. Psychotherapy in the 1980s. *Group,* 1978, *2,* (3), 194-206.

Mahler, M.S. Non human symbiosis & the vicissitudes of individuation, Vol. I. Infantile Psychosis. New York: International Universities Press, 1968.

Mahler, M.S. (1971) A study of the separation-individuation process and its possible application to borderline phenomena in the psychoanalytic situation. The Psychoanalytic of the Child, 1071, 26:403-424.

Menaker, E. Masochism — a defense reaction of the ego. *Psychoanalytical Quarterly,* 1953, *22,* 205-220.

Pearce, J., & Newton, S. *The conditions of human growth.* New York: Citadel Press, 1963.

Racker, H. *Transference and countertransference.* New York: International Universities Press, 1968.

Reich, W. *Character analysis.* New York: Orgone Institute Press, 1933.

Reik, T. *Masochism in modern man.* New York: Farrar & Reinhart, 1941.

Reik, T. *The secret self.* New York: Grove Press, 1952.

Sullivan, H. *The interpersonal theory of psychiatry.* New York: Norton, 1953.

Winnicott, D. *The family and individual development.* London: Hogarth Press, 1965.

Winnicott, D.W. *Mother and child.* New York: Basic Books, 1957.

Chapter 3

THE RESOLUTION OF THERAPEUTIC IMPASSES IN BORDERLINE STATES*
Ted Saretsky, Ph.D.

*This material is an expanded version of an article that appeared originally in *Contemporary Psychoanalysis,* Vol. 13(4), October, 1977, 519-532, Journal of the William Alanson White Institute and the William Alanson White Psychoanalytic Society, New York. It is reprinted here with permission.

> G-d revealed His Name to Moses,
> and it was: I AM WHAT I AM

Over the past decade, there seems to be growing consensus in the literature that the major function of primitive defense systems in severely regressed individuals, is to maintain some organization in a psyche where there is a lack of integration, unity, and harmony (Guntrip, 1969). In the case of borderline patients, this adaptation has been characterized in terms of a fixation at a preoedipal level of identification of the ego with an object. Fairbairn (1954), Kernberg (1975), and Jacobsen (1954), amongst others, tend to view recurrent indications of splitting, dispersal of diffuse affects, and paralyzing emptiness that have been observed in these individuals as an outgrowth of insoluble emotional dilemmas created by panic attacks occurring within the matrix of early object attachments. These preverbal events have been conceptualized in terms of the grim choice the offspring of the not-good-enough mother faces, namely, experiencing overwhelming, threatening affects as a separate entity (which results in feelings of aloneness and isolation) versus becoming overidentified and merging with the need system and mood states of the significant other for the sake of protection against disorganizing ego experiences.

Current psychoanalytic thinking formulates this fundamental conflict as follows: The fear of loss of a unified sense of identity coupled with anticipated withdrawal of attachments by internalized and real love objects leads to a profound struggle between the wish for fusion of the ego with the object and the opposing wish for separation of the ego from object (Guntrip, 1969). To put this in somewhat different terms, the ego, rather than being an orphan, acts crazy in the name of the parent, renounces its own phenomenological world, blends into the parent's attitudes, and even accommodates, when necessary, by becoming a hate-provoking object. The resulting clinical picture is one of unpredictable upsurges of aggressive feelings; contradictory, confusing behavior; isolated, vacillatory involvement with others; and transiency in object relations. Within the analytic setting, the borderline patient is frequently regarded as a difficult person to treat because he seems spiteful, provocative, chaotic, and is often not very likeable.[1]

As treatment progresses, this manner of presentation soon lends itself to what has been described as a transferential symbiosis or fusion state (Giovacchini, 1965). Instead of the patient experiencing himself as distinct and separate, he seems to identify with the analyst as a means of maintaining his own ego. The attitude of passive surrender depends on continuous surveillance and monitoring of every mood, feeling, attitude, and piece of behavior communicated by the analyst. This psychological annihilation of the ego is slowly accomplished through the patient's loss of sustained alive

---

[1]Therapists often report feeling drained, ignorant, bored, depressed and uncertain after working with borderline patients.

participation in his own feelings. The givenness of the patient's feelings, what existentialists call his "is-ness" and his authenticity is the blackmail that the patient pays to keep a feared reality (loss of the mother bond) from becoming manifest. The abdication of moment-to-moment awareness and acting upon real feelings contributes to a sense of non-being, preservative aspects of the ego, a counterreaction is set in motion. At this time, we can observe a prevalence of intense oppositional behavior, cloudiness, and a powerful resistance against being understood. This behavior can be defined in terms of a confused, foredoomed attempt to express autonomy, individuality and separateness. The strange way that these self-boundaries are established, however, is not conducive to healthy adaptation. Others cannot decipher the meaning of such aberrant behavior. They feel and act unrelated to the patient. A vicious spiral of in and out behavior is established as a life style. During the analytic hour, these operations set the stage for such regressive mechanisms as feelings of influence, the magical expectation that one's mind can be read, a breakdown of the subjective-objective dichotomy ("Am I feeling this, or are you feeling this"), extreme isolation, megalomania, and an utter sense of helplessness. When acted out within the transference, these phenomena can be understood as maladaptive patterns of gaining a fragile sense of belonging and identity within the framework of an organic oneness with mother.

The recent development of these theoretical formulations has stirred up a great deal of interest and controversy in analytic circles and has undoubtedly succeeded to some degree in clarifying the chaotic and mysterious events surrounding patients with severe developmental arrest. In this chapter I would like to address myself primarily to ways of applying this knowledge therapeutically so that the analyst will be in a better position to plan ego-building strategies to restore the internal integrity of these patients.

THE ANALYTIC SITUATION AS A PARATAXIC FIELD

One dimension of treatment that rarely gets much attention in the literature is the contractual arrangement between patient and analyst whereby a merged system of basic, unexplored assumptions are rapidly established and perpetuated and then selectively ignored. The literature on family dynamics can be informative in this regard (Bowen, 1966; Haley, 1959; Lidz, 1958). It is generally agreed that families are ruled-governed systems. Members behave among themselves in an organized, repetitive manner and this patterning of behavior can be abstracted as guiding principles that determine the quality of family life. Each and every family has its own unique set of homeostatic mechanisms by means of which tribal norms are delimited and enforced. These values represent a sort of private code that excludes certain areas from dispute and encourages agreement on how things are to be disputed (Haley, 1959). Clinical experience suggests that the therapy dyad functions in much the same way, so that after the first few contacts, each patient-analyst pairing develops its own unique, pattern and anxiety-reducing mechanisms. One common danger of this folie-a-deux arrangement is that both parties can get caught up in subtle, double-binding traps. Patients are tempted to play out the role of the good patient (or rebel against it) in order to protect the analyst from having to deal with narcissistic injuries resulting from a failure to live up to the ideal of the good analyst.

This reciprocal induction field is a potential pitfall in any authority-dependency relationship, but the special nature of the emergent symbiotic transferences within the regressive climate of the analytic situation with borderlines deserves particular attention. The importance I assign to this phenomena stems from its striking resemblance to the original basis for severe ego disturbances, mainly, the infant yielding to the parental need for centrality and significance by denying and subjugating his own subjective awarenesses.[2] I am reminded here of the story, "The Emperor's New Clothes." The emperor wore no clothes but only a child saw the truth and dared to say it. The other subjects did not trust their perceptions because quite obviously the king did not want to hear what he did not want to know. But I wonder what happened to the child after he embarrassed the king? Would he truly be rewarded for puncturing a deeply ingrained belief system in anything but a fairy tale? And what about the little boy who cried wolf; nobody ever asks about why he had to cry wolf so often. If he was not properly attended to the first few times, we might interpret his alarmist, worry-wart behavior as a way of scapegoating himself to spare the parents any awareness of their own uncaring attitudes.

There is a good deal of evidence to suggest that even such basic mechanisms as sensation and perception, to say nothing of attitudes, beliefs, and opinions, can be altered in the face of early parental influences (Jacobsen, 1964; Mahler, 1968). If the earliest available emotional support system is the prototypical grid that shapes the young child's sense of confidence and trust in himself, then if this environment works instead to reinforce a constriction of those emotions that arouse tension and anxiety in those around us, a gradual process of relinquishment and denial of feelings occurs.

To return to the analytic setting, a situation was brought to my attention recently whereby an analyst with a crippling disability had many patients attempt suicide. The analyst was described as warm and mothering and tended to divert attention from his handicap by becoming impatient and discouraging references to it. If the analyst, through his denial, conveys the impression that his feelings of despair and helplessness are too painful to deal with, we might presume that certain of his patients are being encouraged to surrender their own

---

[2]Subliminal recognition of this possibility may account for a bit of humor that is making the rounds these days: "The analyst is someone who expands to fill up the room that he occupies."

despair and resentment toward him, so that he would not have to be confronted. This seductive mothering attitude then, not only cripples the patient but also makes it far less likely for the patient to learn to accept and work through his own anger. The analyst's compensatory need to feel "good" (whole, intact) and generous must be appeased at all costs. The price the patient must pay is to give up his complaints (autonomy) before he might be personally ready to take such a step. The patient is now in a "no-win" position. The suicidal decision is a self-destructive but affirmative statement that says, in effect, "You'll never get all of me. Your offer is tempting but I won't pay that price. I hate you and I'll hurt you. I'll sacrifice my life defiantly and in that grand gesture I'll finally do what I want with it."

In another instance, an analyst was feeling very provoked over a period of months by a patient's physical assaults on his furniture and his body (kicking his foot). Finally, the analyst could restrain himself no longer: "If this continues, I will no longer see you." Soon after this, the patient terminated treatment. If we examine this process from the perspective of the collusive denial system, it would seem that the analyst was implicitly inviting the patient to (1) Protect the analyst from any awareness that he had difficulty in handling his own anger; and (2) Perpetuating the fantasy that he was superunderstanding and tolerant. The patient's "impossible" behavior can be viewed as a disguised attempt to get the analyst to provide a role model for being appropriately resentful and "intolerant" (setting realistic limits). When the analyst's threshold was finally reached, he overreacted to the situation by employing emotional blackmail (behave or leave), thereby confirming the patient's worst fears and teaching him a sad lesson that he already knows. Unfortunately, both parties are skirting the central issue. What kinds of fears and reasonable demands is the patient repressing so that he is impelled to act out in such an infantile way?

I cannot answer these questions specifically because this was not my patient but in working on a similar case with a highly provocative patient, an interesting hidden agenda emerged. The patient wanted to change his analytic hours because he had gotten a job (growthful step). I had no other open hours but instead of conveying this clearly, I became somewhat defensive and pressured the patient into speaking up to his boss to get off early. The patient interpreted this to mean that I saw his request as somewhat of an annoyance and a burden. Instead of feeling encouraged toward healthy self-assertion, the patient was left with the impression that I felt I was doing him a favor by putting up with his irritating demands and that we would get along much better if he acted dependent and compliant. We could mistakenly dismiss the patient's perceptions as simply reflecting projections and distortions, and of his subsequent outrage as transference. This reading, however, neglects the analyst's participation. To go back to the analyst who allowed his foot to be kicked, if his ego-ideal was to see himself as implacable and transcendently accepting, then the patient is being unwittingly trained not to cause any slippage from this role. When the patient submits or rebels against this control, the result is often the so-called "treatment impasse." One wonders what would have happened if the analyst took responsibility for his own feelings early on and simply said, "I can't listen to you while you're hurting my leg."

What I have been describing is not simply an artifact of the treatment situation. Instead, I would submit that the narcissistic struggle between the two existing egos (analyst and patient) provides us with a rich therapeutic opportunity. I see it as a reactivation through transferential fusion, of the earliest mother-child interactions. Can the mother (analyst) respect and accept the separateness and individuality of the child (patient) while simultaneously gratifying his realistic dependency needs or will the mother's unresolved needs have to be continuously identified with before the child can participate in his own?[3]

[3]One patient described the conflict as follows, "If the analyst greets me at the door with a warm smile and a hearty welcome and asks me how things are going, he's acting as though he needs to feel that things are

CLINICAL AND THEORETICAL OBSERVATIONS

There is a substantial body of evidence which suggests that if an infant suffers an intensified, terrifying sense of object loss, then his reality testing and secondary process thinking can be seriously impaired (Mahler, 1968). The particular relevance of these findings for the psychoanalyst treating borderline patients is that in these instances, there is a furthering of the projective identification process. When confusion arises between what is inside and what is outside, the boundary distinction between self and object dissolves into a semipermeable membrane. With the further occurrence of internalization, a highly unrealistic primitive interaction begins between aspects of the individual and fantastically distorted inner objects. The therapeutic task in these instances is to keep focusing on "who is saying or doing what to whom now or why" (Heiman, 1950). Kernberg gives a somewhat similar emphasis when he states, "It is only after such primitive relationships have been diagnosed, clarified, and spelled out repeatedly while their self and object aspects are exchanged, as it were between patient and analyst, that the defensive quality of the mutual dissociation of these primitive transferences can be diagnosed and interpreted and integration of self and object components occur" (1975, p. 167).

With the growing acceptance of the significant contributions of ego psychology and object relations theory, there has been an abundance of books and articles written on the subject designed to sharpen and elaborate upon the theory (Fairbairn, 1954; Guntrip, 1969). Many of these contributions have drawn major implications from the theory and have attempted to formulate techniques that will facilitate differentiation and self-identity. I would like to share certain concepts with the reader that can be useful in understanding the borderline state and then go on to describe how I had attempted to apply these insights into a coherent treatment design.

better. What do I do when I feel bad inside? Should I sound better to make him feel better, should I sound worse than I feel to rebel; it's so hard to stay with what I actually feel."

The Experience of Feeling Oneself

If we can imagine a dyadic interaction as constituting a tension system that must retain a relative homeostasis in order to remain stable, then in pathological relationships the more dependent partner increasingly assumes the major responsibility for reducing the tension. For example, if an infant cries for some unknown reason, let us suppose that the mother becomes anxious, insecure, and helpless. If the mother's nervous reaction is to withdraw or to become hostile, the infant will ultimately experience himself in a number of different ways. At first, perhaps the urge to cry is felt as a human response to a felt need. If he gets frequent "bad-me" reactions from the mother in this and other areas, he will gradually dissociate the need and the accompanying emotion from his repertoire ("not-me"). After this last stage is reached, the threatening inner promptings are disregarded and treated as a foreign body. The child no longer views the anxiety as his own but something that has to be detoxified, something that "shouldn't be." This lack of entitlement to what is real and actual evolves into internal structures and regulatory mechanisms that are consistent with the maintenance of the good-me image, thereby reducing the mother's apprehension. This trend can lead to a repression of anxiety feelings or an exacerbation of anxiety leading to panic. As I see it, the exaggeration of anxiety is an attempt to repossess the right to feel anxious. Thus when somebody reports *feeling* terribly anxious, I view this as an attempt to feel anxious, and to establish and argue for the legitimacy of being anxious without being embarrassed, threatened or rejected. What I am saying about the feeling of anxiety holds true for every emotion (excitement, pleasure, depression, repulsion, anger, pain, etc.). This concept is not an easy thing to describe. Perhaps some case examples would point out exactly what I mean.

A patient in group the week after President Kennedy was assassinated wondered how soon after getting the sad news, did Lyndon Johnson feel good about finally attaining a position he had so long sought. She followed this up with another thought, "I wonder who the next person will be that Jackie Kennedy will have sex with." Most of the group responded to the surface cynicism of these statements and in the case of Johnson, understood her comments in keeping with his public way of being a self-serving, uncaring individual. The latent issue, however, is relevant to the position that I have been taking. One week after the patient's father died when she was 10 years old, she innocently asked her mother if she could wear a new dress to school. The mother gave her a weary look and said some other things as if to suggest that the patient should not be thinking of such frivolous things during a time of such grief and mourning. Thereafter the patient remembers carrying around the lifelong burden that she did not care enough about her father. Among the effects of this and similar interchanges from infancy on was an almost total amnesia with regard to the father, a radical denial of her femininity, intense irrational hostility toward her husband, and an unbelievable complainer. It would seem that the indictment of selfishness meant that her own way of feeling sad was bad. I would not interpret this in terms of guilt or its internalization as a form of self-punishment. Rather, in the case of borderline individuals, I understand it to mean that the patient was not allowed to suffer in the first place.[4] Her continued suffering represented a compulsive need to justify the suffering. The mother had staked a claim for exclusive rights to be the family sufferer and the patient had collaborated with this by being a different kind of sufferer, the kind that annoyed everybody including herself, and never got sympathy as the mother did. Another issue worthy of exploration is: What is the effect of regarding the wish for self-preservation in the face of terrible loss as incompatible with deep sorrow?

I could cite many more examples to make my point but one more will suffice. A patient recollects walking nude into

---

[4]Proust once said, "To heal a suffering, one must experience it to the full."

the midst of her mother's Mah-jongg group at age four. The mother screamed at her. The patient's emphasis was on the mother's look of shame, embarrassment, and humiliation in front of the company. The patient could not easily get in touch with these same feelings within herself. Her lifelong orientation has been to play Red Cross nurse, soothing the bruised feelings of others. This social sensitivity and supreme empathy can be viewed as a projective transformation design-ed to treat the disowned parts of herself.

When borderline patients project part of themselves onto others (projective identification) and the significant other accepts it (introjective identification), a situation is created whereby the patient is split in two. The polarization that is established is an external representation of conflicts between internal objects. In effect, the alienated, fragmen-tary parts of an individual compartmentalized him. By draw-ing the analyst into a complementary role, the patient is dialoguing with himself, trying to integrate his separate selves. Only to the extent that the analyst can help to revive this primitive process during the analytic hour can the inter-nal integrity of the patient be restored.

TREATMENT APPROACHES

In the following section, I would like to describe some approaches that I have employed which contribute to the capacity for improved relatedness and reintegration.

1. I encourage participation in the here and now, in the immediate moment, in the content and structure of present experience. In order to promote "now" awareness, I avoid intellectualized "aboutisms," tendencies to dwell on future fears and fantasies and past hurts.[5] I try to discipline myself

---

[5]Buddha's condition for the wise man includes:
Do not hark back to things that past,
And for the future cherish no fond hopes:
The past was left behind by thee,
The future state has not yet come.
But who with vision clear can see
The present which is here and now
Such wise one should aspire to win
What never can be lost nor shaken.

against laborious genetic reconstructions since the initial history and the early transference dispositions bear little resemblance to what really happened anyway. Since the patient is expressing himself largely through primary process thinking, what we hear are fantastic versions of internal relations of dissociated aspects of the self with part objects. Only in the later stages of treatment with the borderline patient does personal history become germane to present personality structure.

2. I work at validating the patient's perception when they are accurate. This means that I try to take responsibility for my own mistakes, moods, and countertransferences. This does not imply that the therapist should go into a neurotic confessional; rather, I try to continuously tease out and verbally discriminate between what is the patient's and what is mine.

3. I have come to realize that a deep understanding of another person within their own frame of reference requires an enormous amount of effort and concentration and is very difficult at best. The patient's suffering combined with our own professional and personal needs, impels us to change them or to explain their feelings away. Despite our ostensible neutrality and formidable theoretical foundations, there exists the strong temptation to pacify our own need for twinship and connection. If a patient seems unreasonable in a relationship, wants to get a divorce, or is not getting along well on the job, analysts often try to ameliorate situations, to maintain the union, to explain the other person's point of view. At these times, we are falling victim to the patient's transference and misidentify the patient. The inclinations reflect poor judgement in any case; in work with borderline cases, it is disastrous.

Efforts to persuade or cajole, appeals to the patient's sense of justice and fair play, attempts to undermine his stubbornness and give up what looks self-destructive are strenuously resisted and rightfully so. The intransigency of symptoms can be interpreted as a disguised but heroic attempt to maintain self-respect and ego integrity, even if this has to be done by foolish means.

Along the same lines, one should stick with the patient's metaphors, and his terms of phrase as much as possible. Unnecessary paraphrasing, comments such as "What you said reminds me of what I was just thinking," are often felt as controlling and disrespectful. They do not properly acknowledge the patient's input sufficiently and suggest that there's a better way of looking at things. If the patient temporarily seems to yield his position and the credit he has earned, soon thereafter we may expect to see disorganization, rebelliousness, or regression. In effect, we must try to model and assist patients to identify with Winnicott's conception of the healthy, separate person: Someone who is able to be alone in the presence of others. (1958)

4. Borderline patients have a special need to affirm themselves as "doers" in contrast to acceptance of the role of the "done to" object. The acceptance of one's own feelings of tragedy and joy, of love and of hate is the basis for motivation and is a spur to action. From this standpoint, the inner emptiness of these patients is seen primarily as a function of passivity. An active orientation does not necessitate motoric, aggressive behavior. Rather it involves mastery and competence over what has been learned and felt. The denial of these aborted potentials is what renders life into death, and whole people into cardboard figures. What I am leading up to is for the analyst to be alert, curious and interested in every evidence of positive qualities and interests that the patient manifests. When a patient frequently mentions an affinity for pets, growing plants, and enjoyment of a T.V. program or a hobby, this should not be passed over lightly. Wherever the heart beats, that's where the analyst has to go. This "extraneous" material which is often discarded as irrelevant interludes to the meat of the treatment session, deserves cultivation and support. An acceptance and deeper appreciation of one segment of the self influences all parts of the system.

5. The classical assumption that countertransference is a reflection of unresolved neurotic residues in the analyst has given way in the past 20 years to the possibility of making

positive use of countertransference in the course of analysis (Little, 1957; Sandler, 1976; Tauber, 1954). Paula Heimann (1980), for example, has indicated that a judicious appraisal of one's countertransference may be the first clue to what is really going on in the patient. If the analyst is willing to be honest with himself in trying to connect his inner reaction to the existing analytic process, then an important lever to break the treatment impasse may be at his disposal. The identification of these countertransferential trends is not an easy assignment. Particularly in work with severely disturbed patients, it is quite natural to attribute many of the analyst's reactions to objective factors. Personal analysis, supervision, and peer group supervision provide an opportunity for greater understanding. Other sources of insight are the analyst's dreams and fantasies regarding certain patients, capturing the way that certain patients disturb him, the patients that he compulsively talks about to his colleagues, the ones he gives bills too late or chooses to change their appointment times as opposed to other patients, etc. The interested analyst should be aware of his general countertransferential potential. What I mean by this is that we all have certain core areas of special sensitivity and predisposition. Through past experience, we hope to identify the typical issues (e.g., money, control, dependency, perfection) that bring out overpersonalized reactions. The extent to which we can sort out and neutralize these blind spots will determine our ability to stop misidentifying our patients.

Borderline patients are frequently successful in making the analyst fall victim to their profound primitive transferences. This often results in a frozen bilateral stalemate. If the analyst is not induced to act precipitously to reduce his tension, something new and creative will inevitably begin to happen. The analogy would be that just as a dream arises from current frustrations in the patient's life, so the countertransference response can be viewed as a hinting, telltale reaction to the dyadic frustration.

Over a period of months, an analyst had drawn out, supported, and ultimately joined the patient's characterization of her mother as a mean, selfish, and jealous person. During one session the patient described how the mother was different on holidays when the father was around. "She enjoys him. She used to wait on the front steps, waiting for him to come home. I feel very sad thinking of this. You shouldn't have to wait for someone coming home to feel alive. Why couldn't my mother and I have a good time without father? My mother can be a barrel of laughs." The analyst acknowledged the need that both of them had for external stimulation and then made a now-familiar interpretation regarding the mother's need being so great that she must have felt jealous of the daughter. The patient fell silent and withdrawn. The analyst thought this behavior strange considering the fact that both of them had agreed many times in the past that the mother was indeed a very jealous woman.

At this moment of confusion, the patient spotted a spider on the ceiling, made a move to kill it and then stopped. The analyst was prompted to kill it himself but sensed that the patient wanted it to live. The analyst asked the patient whether she wanted him to help her and for her to help him to protect the alive, "good" mother. She relaxed at this point. "I was thinking my mother and I were both sad together. It makes me sad to think that but it helps me to understand my mother and me more. It makes me feel closer to her." The analyst said, "You were afraid that you would have to give in to my condemning attitude toward your mother and give up that warm, close feeling." She said, "Yes, that's why after I told about my mother and me sitting alone and waiting, I stopped. I felt you getting restless. Like you were getting ready to attack."

Here we see how the analyst acted out a grasping, greedy role in competition between the girl and her mother. By overlooking the growth buds (tender identification with the mother), the analyst gave vivid testimony to the threat he experienced when the patient was no longer faithful to him and his interpretations. In the past, the patient had quickly anticipated this and sided with the analyst's need to destroy the mother. The good spider episode alerted the analyst to his countertransferential proclivities and he was able to enrich the dialogue by making a maturational intervention.

A male patient of twenty-three wanted to go into group therapy but his analyst kept putting him off. Inwardly, the analyst felt that the patient was too young and not solid enough to carry himself in the group. The analyst was deliberately vague with the patient under the illusion that he was protecting him from hurt and disappointment. As the patient in a very mature, direct way confronted the analyst with his "put-off" attitude, the analyst became aware of the real basis for his discouragement. The patient had a complex, double-binding, powerful mother and a less intelligent, more understanding, passive father. The patient's previous protection of the analyst that was carried out by not confronting was a transferential reaction to a wishy-washy but loving father. The patient did not want to identify with the contempt and impatience that his mother constantly felt toward the father. The analyst's part of the collusion was in projecting onto the group members a composite critical mother. The result was two men who liked and respected one another with considerable strength and resources between them, acting and feeling helpless in deference to some higher power. By sharing this contemporary paralysis with the patient, the analyst freed the patient to see the potentials for a strength and decisiveness in both his father and himself in a new light. Another door that was opened was the patient's apparent guilt and hesitancy in allowing himself to know better than the analyst. This information was used subsequently to demonstrate to the patient (1) his fear that if he took care of the analyst (father), who would take care of him; (2) his concern that the analyst (mother) would be hurt or threatened if his role as the know-it-all expert were taken away from him; and (3) anxiety regarding the assumption of a more peerish role concomitant with a greater acceptance of his own opinions and intuition. On his behalf, the analyst gained a sharper understanding of how he indeed did have a certain stake in remaining on top and fostering an unnecessary dependency.

SUMMARY

Separation-fusion issues have been focused on here as being of central importance in understanding early developmental arrest in general and developing appropriate treatment interventions for borderline patients in particular. Transferential fusion states and the corresponding countertransference reactions evoked are suggested as prime sources of information for exploring the struggle between the wish for fusion of ego with object and the opposing wish for separation of ego from object. The task of analysis in these cases is defining in terms of assisting in the revival of the real self. The emphasis throughout is that being real and feeling intact is more a process of letting go than it is the effort of changing and becoming something else.

REFERENCES

Bowen, M. (1966). The use of family theory in clinical practice. Comprehensive Psychiatry, 7: 345-374.

Fairbairn, W.R.D. (1954). A synopsis of the development of the author's view regarding the structure of personality in An Object-Relations Theory of Personality. New York: Basic Books, pp. 162-182.

Feiner, A. (1977). Countertransference and the anxiety of influence. Contemporary Psychoanalysis, 13, 1: 1-16.

Feiner, A. and Levenson E. (1968). The compassionate sacrifice. Psychoanalytic Review, 55, 4: 552-573.

Giovacchini, P., "Transference, incorporation and synthesis." Int. J. of Psychoanalysis. 46: 287-296, 1965.

Guntrip, H. (1969). Schizoid Phenomena, Object Relations and the Self. New York: International Universities Press, pp. 17-48.

Haley, J. (1959). The family of the schizophrenic: A model system. Journal of Psycho-Analysis. 30: p. 199.

Heimann, P. (1950). On countertransference. International Journal of Psycho-Analysis, 31: 81-84.

Jacobson, E. (1954). "Contribution to the metapsychology of psychotic identifications." Journal of the American Psychoanalytic Association, 2: 239-262.

Jacobson, E. (1964). The Self and the Object World. New York: International Universities Press, 1964.

Kernberg, O. (1975). Technical considerations in the treatment of border-line patients. Paper presented at meeting of the Washington Psychiatric and Psychoanalytic Societies.

Kernberg, O. (1975). Borderline Conditions and Pathological Narcissism. New York: Jason Aronson, Inc.

Lidz, T. (1958). Intrafamilial environment of the schizophrenic patient: The transmission of irrationality. Archives of Neurology and Psychiatry, 79, 305-16.

Little, M. (1957). "R"-The analyst's total response to his patient's needs. International Journal of Psycho-Analysis. 38, 32-40.

Mahler, M.S. (1968). On human symbiosis and the vicissitudes of indivi-duation, in Infantile Psychosis. New York: International Universities Press.

Sandler, J. (1976). "Countertransference and role-responsiveness." Inter-national Review of Psycho-Analysis, 3, 38-51.

Tauber, E.S. (1954). "Exploring the therapeutic use of countertransference data." Psychiatry, 17, 317-331.

Winnicott, D.W. (1958). Collected Papers: Through Pediatrics to Psycho-analysis. New York: Basic Books.

Chapter 4

THE IMPERFECT CONTAINER — THE ANALYST AS A MATURATIONAL AGENT
Ted Saretsky, Ph.D.

> All living phenomena can be viewed as content occurring in the framework of a container which circumscribes and describes the content, and, reciprocally, the content has great influence in transforming the nature of its container.
>
> James Grotstein

In connection with his discussion of the problem of working through Freud introduced the terms "compulsion to repetition," "adhesiveness of the libido," and "physical inertia" (1914, p. 150; 1937a, pp. 241-242). These concepts were devised by Freud to account for the so-called "intractable" clinical situations that "could not be immediately resolved by mere interpretations." Freud described these manifestations as being "resistances of the id," possibly as expressions of the death instinct (1937, p. 242). Over the years, numerous formulations have been offered to account for the seemingly inevitable phenomena of recurring pathological fixations that stubbornly defy any and all efforts towards resolution. The paradoxical intensification of symptoms as a result of accurate interpretations has been variously attributed to a disbelief in an alternate way of life (Singer, 1965); a struggle against awareness that life has no predetermined meaning and therefore demands a personal self-definition (Bugental, 1964, 1965); a generalized expression of hostility toward the analyst (Horney, 1936); as evidence of unconscious guilt, the need for suffering, and the masochistic ego (Asch, 1976); as defenses against symbiotic fusion with an ambivalent preoedipal love object (Olinick, 1964); and as deriving from the need to reinstate narcissistic omnipotent control as protection against an emerging sense of dependent vulnerability and helplessness (Rosenfeld, 1975). It should be noted that each of these interpretations defines the treatment impasse in terms of a negative therapeutic reaction based on the patient's intrapsychic disturbances. This frame of reference is consistent with Freud's initial model of the psychoanalyst as a blank mirror with the accompanying illusion of therapeutic neutrality. Within such an orientation material presented by the patient is explained as occurring in an isolated organism, a closed entity, according to deterministic cause and effect mechanisms.

The construct of the participant observer, introduced by Sullivan (1953) greatly expanded the classical patient-analyst contract so that the new object of study became the transactional, relational processes linking patient and analyst into an indivisible unit. The observer and the observed both now became part of the same therapeutic field. Despite the general acceptance of this contribution, its actual relevance to constructive clinical practice did not assume the proportions of a fundamental treatment breakthrough until very recently. Only when analysts began to encounter an increasing number of developmentally arrested patients who employed very primitive defenses, were they compelled to alter the nature of the therapeutic alliance. Instead of the interpretive model, which relies heavily on metapsychology, insight, and free association, more confrontational approaches were given consideration. Analysts became more concerned with the sharing of experiences, giving feedback, and injecting their own selves in the therapeutic process. This ongoing interchange minimizes the authoritarian position of the analyst. More importantly, it focuses attention on the analyst's awareness of his own actions, reactions, and feelings, as an intuitive guide to further inquiry. Within the swirl of projective and introjective identifications, regressive tendencies and primitive splitting processes, both patient and analyst must involve themselves in complex transactions which require that they each define themselves in terms of their respective roles and their reciprocal relationships.

In keeping with the classical tradition, it should not be surprising that even the concept of transference, which Freud considered to be his greatest accomplishment, is exclusively established within a framework of involuntary participation by the analyst. The general trend in the psychoanalytic literature has been to see transference simply as a continuation of the status quo of a fixed world image. Through a regressive, anachronistic reliving of the past, the patient restructures current reality to make life safe and predictable. Whether the process was defined as an inappropriate means of achieving belated mastery over a traumatic psychic event (Fenichel, 1945a) or as a new edition of an old object relationship (Freud, 1905c, p. 116), transference has traditionally been regarded as a projection whose primary function was to reduce anxiety and avoid threat.

An illustration might be helpful here. Greenson (1967), in describing transference feelings that are acted out as attempts at wish fulfillment, stated: "Patients will experience feelings toward the analyst that can be construed as a sexual seduction by the father, which are later revealed to be a repetition of a wish that occurred originally as a childhood fantasy" (p. 153). The problem with understanding this vignette in such a restricted way is that it ignores other possibilities that might be fruitfully investigated. For example, if the original feeling in the child was innocent curiosity and joy in discovering the pleasurable sensations of her own body, and this developmental line was contaminated by inappropriate responses on the part of the father (e.g., seductiveness), the adult patient's current behavior can be parsimoniously interpreted as the wish for a nonseductive father who will not interfere with the emergence of sexual feelings. According to the theory represented by this viewpoint analytic transactions should be studied from the frame of reference of an interactional bipersonal field (Langs, 1976a, 1976b). This expanded conception of the analytic situation requires that we modify our understanding of the working alliance as a vertical structure. Instead, the new paradigm construes the complex flow of a session as a pervasive choreography, structurally delineating the influence of each participant on the other. From this perspective, it becomes increasingly clear that the patient and analyst are enmeshed in a dialectic that is highly idiosyncratic both in a personal and interpersonal sense. The patient's style of involvement and his verbal communications can be best understood as one half of a more inclusive mutually adaptive process. This outlook is consistent with recent advances in ego psychology and object relations theory which hypothesize that the dual unity existing in the symbiotic relationship between mother and child is the prototypical grid that significantly patterns all future intimate relationships (Giovacchini, 1972; Little, 1960; 1972). The symbiotic context of mutual dependency for vital narcissistic supplies lays the groundwork for the arousal of powerful feelings, the introduction of primitive defenses to cope with threatening feelings, the establishment of a body of rules and tension-reduction purposes, and fantasies of interpenetration of boundaries, omnipotent and omniscient attachments, and identification between self and object. Introjective processes may lead to the shadow of the object hiding the self, the self being perceived as having the characteristics of the object. Splitting and projective identification may lead to attributing to the object those elements which are experienced as undesirable, as alien to the self-representation. The object is

[1]In this regard, Gorney (1979) quotes a recent observation by Andre Green: It is now beginning to be recognized that often " . . . the patient's aim is directed to the effect of his communication rather than to the transmission of its content," just as it can no longer be denied that "the analyst even influences the communication of the patient's material" (Green, 1975, p. 3).

then perceived as being dominated and controlled by the self, while at the same time there is a vague awareness that the object is like the self. What was projected can be reintrojected. Within this twinship matrix of dynamically interacting components, identifications form the glue which hold the system totality together.

The reverberations of this reconstruction of early models of relatedness has significantly influenced psychoanalytic thinking in the fields of marital therapy, in the treatment of disturbed families, and in group psychotherapy. Both Obendorf (1938) and Mittelman (1944) have commented that the neuroses of husbands and wives complement each other and that there is a dovetailing of conflictual and defensive patterns. Giovacchini (1965) was impressed by the fact that his patients often complain or describe their spouses in terms similar to their own self-descriptions. What was also striking in marital partners when they projected elements of the spouse onto the analyst, was the fact that what was projected was also a self-representation. Another observation made by Giovacchini was that significant changes in the marital equilibrium constitute changes in an important object relationship, for both husband and wife. In a similar vein, family therapists have noted that improvements in the family scapegoat causes a shift in the status of the entire system, accompanied by symptomatic outbreaks in the "healthier members" (Haley, 1963). An examination of group phenomena also suggests patterns of complementarity, the meshing of characterological structures between members, and the evocation of proxies who act out feelings that the members themselves would deny and find ego alien.

From the burgeoning literature in the traditional one-to-one psychoanalytic setting, it would also appear that an increasing cross fertilization process involving an incorporation, blending, and integration of these new concepts, has caused a ferment in a sizeable portion of the psychoanalytic community. This has been accompanied by an increased focus on the very earliest phases of development, closer scrutiny of preoedipal dynamics, and a reevaluation of previous formulations pertaining to identity formation—all in the framework of studying the ego's attempt to preserve and maintain viable relations with its libidinal object. This recasting of developmental theory has been accompanied by a fresh impetus for questioning some fundamental assumptions underlying the analytic situation.

More specifically some of the new pathways that have been adopted include:

1. *The analyst's active participation in shared behavioral experiences as the central guiding principle for successful treatment outcome.* This is in keeping with Guntrip's (1971) discussion of "personal relationship therapy":

> I cannot think of psychotherapy as a technique but only as the provision of the possibility of a genuine, reliable, understanding, and respecting, caring personal relationship in which a human being whose true self has been crushed by the manipulative techniques of those who only wanted to make him "not be a nuisance to them," can begin at least to feel his own true feelings, and think his own spontaneous thoughts, and find himself to be real. (p.11)

This emphasis is reminiscent of Harry Stack Sullivan's belief that the analyst is essentially human as is his patient, and thus his contribution to the analytic field is not simply his observing methodology and his techniques of inquiry. Instead, the analyst's total participation as a whole person is a valuable resource.

2. *Without the firm establishment of trust and feeling understood, any interpretive attempts will be experienced as premature, persecutory assaults.*[2]

Some historical antecedents for this viewpoint include Margaret Mahler (1968) who has done considerable research

---

[2]An eight-year old child put this concept into the clearest possible terms. She was given a reading assignment and then asked by the teacher if she understood. Her answer was a very wise one. "I couldn't understand it because the book didn't understand me."

on the optimal human symbiosis necessary for the vicissitudes of individuation and for the establishment of a cathectically stable sense of identity. Mahler convincingly illustrates the extreme vulnerability of the young child to failures in the hatching process, interferences with the achievement of object constancy, distortions in the formation of a stable body image, and the absence of sufficient narcissistic mirroring. Conceptualizations such as the "good-enough-mother" (Winnicott, 1960) the "holding environment" (Winnicott, 1965) and the maternal object as a container of split off feelings (Bion, 1955, 1962, 1963) further highlight the pivotal importance of structure-building participation on the part of the caretaker. The maternal object's capacity to be empathic, resilient, protective, supportive, and responsive are increasingly recognized as being decisive in determining the future course of ego synthesis.

Winnicott believes that the management of experience through maternal provision is basic to the completion of developmental tasks. "Living with" others which is an extension of the growing capacity for developing object relationships, is dependent on "the infant changing from being merged with the mother to being separated from her" (p. 45). 1965. Winnicott stresses the holding environment as an essential parameter that enables a continuity of being. Unsatisfactory maternal support during this phase exposes the infant to stimulations and impingements that are experienced as overwhelming primitive anxiety. Winnicott suggests the infant's need to compensate for faulty environmental provision is the principal factor behind gross disturbances of ego functioning.

In this regard, Winnicott (1965) believes that a child needs his mother to perform two functions:

> The object mother becomes the target for exciting experiences that satisfy crude instinct tensions. The other mother has to be found to survive the instinct-driven episodes, which have now acquired the full force of fantasies of oral sadism and other results of fusion. (p. 75)

It is the environment mother who "wards off the unpredictable and who actively provides care in handling and in general management." (p. 75) Furthermore the environment mother has a special function, which is to continue to be herself, to be empathic toward her infant, to be there to receive the spontaneous gesture and to be pleased" (pp. 75-76). Bion's (1955-1956) description of the maternal object as a potential "container" of jealous and angry feelings supports the important role that Winnicott's "object-mother" plays in the psychic life of the infant.

Melanie Klein has described an aspect of projective identification concerned with the modification of infantile fears; the infant projects a part of its psyche, namely its bad feelings, into a good breast. Then, in due course, they are removed and reintrojected. During their presence in the good breast they are modified in such a way that the reintrojected object has become tolerable to the infant's psyche. From the above theory, Bion has abstracted the model of a container into which an object is projected and the object that can be projected into the container. Container and contained when permeated with emotion, provide a framework for growthful experiences. When the container does not permit or is not accessible to projections, the "contained" is denuded of emotion and vitality. Bion suggests that under these circumstances, both container and contained become as inanimate objects to one another.

Kohut (1977) epitomizes the prevailing sentiments regarding how the analyst can provide a framework for working through these traumatic interruptions in self-object experiences. He indicates that the beneficial transformations occurring in successful analysis do not take place as a result of insights. Instead, the analyst making himself available as a compensatory precursory substitute for a not-yet existing psychological structure is essential. Giovacchini concurs with the view that a therapeutic regression occurs within the comfortable safe analytic setting. This seems to be accomplished as a result of the constant reliability of the setting (Winnicott, 1960a, 1960b), its intrinsic supportive elements (Boyer & Giovacchini, 1967) and the structuralizing potential of interpretations (Giovacchini, 1975). As the patient's superstructure slowly dissolves and reveals the precarious and defensive unity and cohesion of the ego state, the patient begins to organize himself and adapt to the new anxiety-provoking circumstances by invoking certain primitive mechanisms. In keeping with this viewpoint, splitting, projective identification, denial, and finally transference all involve attempts to establish a stable equilibrium by constructing a familiar environment based on the private reality of early infantile experiences. In this way, the patient tries to support his defenses and perfect his character structure by reproducing an ambience corresponding to infantile stages of development, on the basis of fortuitous elements in analytic setting. Giovacchini (1975) put the matter very succinctly:

> It is the analyst's response that permits the patient to continue projecting introjects, rather than successfully constructing the disappointing environment that is consistent with such a deep regression. If the analyst consistently functions as an analyst, that is, non-judgementally observing and not anxiously responding, the patient will continue projecting, but will not be able to fixedly reproduce his world. He can maintain such a world only when the analyst is willing to participate in it (p. 43-44).

The nature and quality of the external object (the analyst), his suitability for being the recipient of ego-alien, split off inner psychic contents, has come increasingly into focus. Rosenfeld (1975) and Bion (1956) have applied the concept of projective identification to the analyst's capacity to endure constant accusations that he is the persecutor. Searles (1963) makes a similar point regarding the impropriety of interrupting the schizophrenic's need to project a part of himself into the analyst. "Moreover it is my experience that the chronic schizophrenic patient actually needs a degree of symbiotic relatedness in the transference, which would be interfered with were the analyst to try, recurrently, to establish with him the validity of transference interpretations." Searles suggests a receptiveness without an encouragement of these projections, and an attempt at understanding their meaning without the fear that these projections will destroy the analyst. Searles (1975) visualizes treatment progress in three steps:

a. A highly pathological transference symbiosis.

b. The nuclei of reality within this distorted symbiosis can become sufficiently evident to both patient and analyst that this symbiosis can evolve into a "therapeutic symbiosis."

c. The creation of this mutually growth-enhancing structure, like that of normal infancy, offers multiple opportunities (working through) for both participants to deal with the mutual gratification and growth-facilitating aspects of this mode of relatedness. Only within this context of symbiotic worth and of having made a valuable contribution, can the patient feel free to move to healthier levels of deep, full individuation.

Winnicott (1951), in *Hate in the countertransference* indicates that in order to retain relative objectivity, the analyst must be prepared for being placed in a position where he must store intolerable feelings. "Above all he must not deny hate that really exists in himself. Hate that is justified in the present situation has to be sorted out . . . and available for eventual interpretation." Spotnitz (1976), while acknowledging the general need for analysts to remain free of emotional involvement with patients, suggests that certain patients may have a need to experience feelings and reactions from the analyst. Even under these circumstances, Spotnitz recommends careful timing and graduated reactions. He warns that subjective elements have to be purged out of the objective countertransference before they contaminate the transference reaction.

A major stumbling block to the analyst's ability to provide maturational experience is his own narcissistically invested infantile ideals. Historically, the analytic model has always been associated with neutrality, objectivity, detachment, and impulse control. Deviations from this "emotional code of ethics" has been regarded as dangerous revisionism

bordering on wild analysis. If, as a result of projective bom-
bardments, the analyst feels himself slipping from this set of
identifications, there is the strong possibility that he will have
difficulty in sustaining the patient's need for environmental
constancy. Epstein (1977) has dealt with this issue by indicating that by neutralizing and detoxifying himself of intense feelings that are induced in him by the patient, the
analyst is in a position to provide feedback in the service of
satisfying maturational needs. Similarly, Malin & Grotstein
(1966) have indicated "that it is only by perceiving how the
external object receives our projections and deals with it, that
we can now introject back into our psychic apparatus the
original projections but now modified on a newer level" (p.
28). By confirming those constructive and "good" aspects of
the patient and absorbing the destructive "bad" parts, the
analyst facilitates a higher order of ego integration. This
siphoning of intense emotions prevents the accumulation of
overwhelming anxiety and contributes to incremental
strengthening of the ego.

3. *Many treatment impasses stem from unexplored
transference-countertransference issues.* By silent agreement,
both parties to the therapeutic contract conspire to ignore
and deny feelings that jeopardize this pseudo-working
alliance. This level of coexistence mandates that issues that
are very germane to the presenting problems must be
dissociated from here-and-now exploration if they pose a
threat to either partner.[3]

In many of these cases, the analyst establishes himself
with the patient as a kind of unwilling collaborator. Through
masochistic submission, he deflects aggression from himself
to external objects, identifies himself with the patient's
aggression, paranoid projections and depressive guilt, and

[3]Since anxiety is a threat to the essential security of a person, Sullivan
described it as a "cosmic" experience. Freud believed that in anxiety the
object is ignored. May (1950, p. 196) suggests that "anxiety is objectless
because it strikes at that basis of psychological structure on which the
perception of oneself as distinct from the world of objects occur."

altogether engages in a complementary relationship that is cemented by the mutual influence of projective identification in patient and analyst. This fixed countertransferential position duplicates the patient's emotional position, effectively undermines the stability and neutrality of the analyst and threatens to dramatically revive the original vicious cycle of the patient's interaction with the parent image.

These manifestations of countertransference reflect a perversion of transient trial identifications with the patient (Fleiss, 1953; Spitz, 1956). The very quality that enables the analyst to empathize with the patient (regression in the service of the ego) makes him susceptible to excessive and more permanent identifications with the patient. These counter-identifications come about as

a. A result of reactivation within the analyst of anxiety connected with early conflicts of an aggressive nature, which are now directed toward the patient;

b. A loss of ego boundaries in the interaction with this particular patient, and a compensatory stress on more advanced ego functions.

c. The compulsion to control the patient in connection with an identification of the patient with lost objects from the analyst's own past (Kernberg, 1965). If this matching and meshing of character structures goes unnoticed and becomes a continuous part of the analytic process, it is harmful, of course, to both participants. Such a folie-a-deux compatibility, if sufficiently reinforced by a reciprocal arrangement of narcissistic gratifications and secondary gains can perpetuate itself for many years.[4]

d. These intense countertransference reactions are often

---

[4]A patient cut down on treatment because of ostensible financial problems that were never challenged as resistance. The analyst felt the time pressure to simplify issues and wrap up each session in a neat package. The patient got the impression in the meantime that the analyst did not want to see her more often. This collusion to avoid dealing with underlying resentments lasted over a six-month period. Interestingly enough, the manifest content of the sessions revolved around the patient's feeling incomplete, insecure, and dependent as she attempted to assume greater control of her life.

objectively induced by patients with more primitively organized personalities (Epstein, 1977) and are not simply a function of the analyst's pathology.

Considering the pernicious and pervasive sense of confusion, frustration, and despondency that the vicissitudes of working together with disturbed patients can force upon us, psychoanalysts have increasingly turned in the direction of constructively utilizing these negative components. The "totalistic" approach believes that the analyst's conscious and unconscious reactions to the patient can be useful in gaining more understanding of the patient. Adherents of this school of thought, Cohen (1952), Fromm-Reichmann (1958), Heimann (1950), Racker (1957), Weigert (1952), and Winnicott (1960) feel that:

1. The patient's influence on the analyst gives much important information about the nonverbal communication between patient and analyst which tend to be overlooked when efforts center on eliminating the analyst's emotional reactions.

2. When the analyst feels that his induced emotions are important resonances for understanding and helping the patient, the analyst can be freer to face his positive and negative emotions in the transference situation.

3. Patients with severe character disorders and those with borderline and psychotic levels of organization tend to evoke the most intense countertransference reactions. Many times the analyst's inner awareness and identification of these currents provides the most meaningful understanding of what is central in the patient's chaotic transference expressions.

4. The emotional experience of the analyst may provide valuable diagnostic and genetic information. Helene Deutsch refers to the identification of the analyst with transference objects of the past (complementary identifications). "In that position, the analyst experiences the emotion that the patient is putting into his transference object while the patient himself is experiencing the emotion which he experienced in the past in his interaction with that particular parental

image." (Kernberg, 1977, p. 7). A remarkably vivid reproduction of the texture of the early childhood environment is now available for examination. For instance, the analyst may identify with the superego function connected with a stern, prohibitive father image, feeling critical and tempted to control the patient, whereas the patient may be experiencing fear, submission, or rebelliousness connected with his relationship to his father. Another useful concept here is what Racker (1957) has classified as "concordant identifications" whereby the analyst, by identifying with corresponding parts of the psychic apparatus (e.g., ego with ego; superego with superego), can experience within himself the primary emotion that the patient is experiencing at the same time.

According to this viewpoint, transference and countertransference represent dynamisms in an experiential field that are a natural outgrowth of flux and interaction. The ability and willingness to grasp this and to deal with it by modifying our therapeutic procedures may bring about a breaking of deadlocks and what Zaphiropoulous (1961) has termed, "a most illuminating experience for both analyst and patient." In a very courageous early paper on this topic, Tauber (1954), although acknowledging the possible pitfalls of countertransferential acting out, emphasized the reestablishment of hope and the possibility of improved contact. The element of surprise, of strategically but spontaneously sharing feelings and fantasies for mutual exploration, becomes the basis for stimulating stagnant analytic situations.

5. Transference reactions, instead of merely repeating the past reflect persevering efforts by the patient to prompt the analyst into maturationally corrective interactions.

This particular trend leads away from the attitude that all subsequent experience simply recapitulates earlier patterns. It moves more in the direction of Sullivan's concept of parataxic distortion, Fromm's idea of discovering a new experience in the process of attempting to reconstruct a past atmosphere and Schachtel's observation about being able to see what is actually in a situation instead of being limited by looking for something that's supposed to be there. One is also reminded of Edgar Levenson's (1972) view that the need for closure leads to premature conclusions based on previous beliefs. The more successfully the concept "transference" and its application have become established, the more its precision becomes an obstructive rigidity; the very clarification that it provides becomes a stumbling block for a deeper level of comprehension. In a highly provocative paper, "The patient as therapist to his analyst," Harold Searles (1975), with his characteristic courage and brutal honesty, urges that we must redefine our conceptualization of the nature of the curative process. Only by exploding comfortable formulations can we arrive at any new ideas with which to approach impasse. Despite surface awareness of the nature of reciprocal interaction, the "analytic field," and the analytic framework as a two-party interpenetrating system, the existing literature has always emphasized the improvement of the analyst's skills and understanding so as to assist in the treatment of a patient. There is a conspicuous absence in classical psychoanalytic accounts on what the patient is trying to do to (and for) the analyst. The crucial issue here is whether or not there is an alliance for a mutual growth encompassing both participants in the treatment situation.[5] Searles' hypothesis is:

a. that the patient unconsciously needs to stimulate countertransference reactions in the analyst that will integrate within the analyst (parent) that which the original parents had to dissociate.

b. that this will succeed in eliciting nurturant or optimally frustrating responses that will be metabolized or synthesized by the patient, eventuating in further growth.

Searles makes a strong argument for the possibility that much of what has been regarded as psychotic transferences, primitive operations, and altogether scattered, bewildering behavior, should be recognized as the patient's therapeutic effort to enable the mother (in the analytic context, the analyst) to become a whole and effective mother (analyst) to

[5]Freud frequently stressed that he was constantly learning from his patients.

him. As an example, Searles cites the case of a patient whose transference reaction to the analyst is that of a harsh dominating father. At some point, the transference evolves so that the analyst is now perceived as a much gentler but still threatening, devouring mother. If this wish succeeds in modifying the analyst's real harsh father identifications, the patient has succeeded in reality, in sculpting the kind of responses that would be more therapeutic to him at this time. Essentially Searles urges us to permit the patient to educate us.

The thrust of Searles' argument, that the patient's communications should be taken as unconscious messages as to the most beneficial form of treatment, is a radical departure from conventional wisdom. Very few psychoanalytic authorities have worked along similar lines (Singer, 1965; Langs, 1976a; and Fromm, 1978).

However, this view, which Searles (1975) refers to as "the patient's psychotherapeutic strivings" has been supported by research findings in other disciplines. Animal studies by Harry Harlow (1978) showed that monkey mothers who had been traumatized as infants grow up to be neglectful and abusive toward their own babies. If, however, one of the abused infant monkeys persists in intense efforts to make contact with the maternal body, some of the wish for contact, warmth, and softness seem to "rub off on the hard heart and head of the unmaternal mother." These mothers tended to undergo a gradual but progressive rehabilitation. They were, says Harlow, "impressively more normal in the teatment of subsequent infants." Benedek's (1978) statements to the effect that mother and infant influence each other reciprocally, and Winnicott's view that healthy babies create a family, further support this contention. In detailed tests of hundreds of newborns, Bridger (1963), Chess (1977), and Segal and Yahraes (1978) have found a remarkable constancy in the extent to which the infant's mood, temperament, responsiveness to people, attention span, persistence, and adaptability to new situations significantly influences how the mother will treat him now and in the future. Numerous illustrations are provided for how children behaviorally shape their parents' attitudes and behavior. Evidence is also accumulating that older children as well can train their parents as to how to raise them. Bell and Harper (1977) concluded that for many years psychologists have led themselves to mistakenly believe that restrictive parents cause dependent children. But what if instead of acting restrictively, the parents are reacting in a controlling way because the child's very dependency makes it more likely that the parents will organize and manage their children's lives to an excessive degree.

FURTHER THEORETICAL CONSIDERATIONS

Otto Kernberg (1977) in outlining a general theory of the origin of the basic units (self-image—object-image—affect disposition) of internalized object relationships, suggests that the nucleus of the ego gels under the influence of pleasurable vs. distressing experiences involving the infant and his mother:

> Simultaneous with the development of this good self-object representation, another primary undifferentiated self-object representation, is built up integrating experiences of a frustrating painful nature; the bad self-object representation, centering around a primitive, painful affective tone. It needs to be stressed that the organization of these two good and bad primary intrapsychic situations occur separately because they are organized under different affective circumstances, determining two separate constellations of affective memory (p. 9).

Kernberg goes on to say that experiences which activate the gratifying and constructively frustrating self-object representations contribute to the gradual differentiation of self-from-object components. "In contrast, excessive activation of 'bad' self-object representations under the influence of frustration or deprivation brings about the development of severe generalized anxiety." This panic disorganizes the ego and interferes with early attempts toward self and object distinctions.

Kernberg's findings are consistent with the contributions of other object-relations theorists (Diatkine, 1973; Rosenfeld, 1971; Sandler, 1978) in suggesting that pathogenic experiences in early childhood create an excessive dependence on splitting and projective identification mechanisms as a means of maintaining a functioning ego. These adaptive devices fragment the ego, causing primary structural defects in the self, which later manifests itself in the form of severe psychopathology. For purposes of this discussion, however, I would like to focus on two important implications of Kernberg's work. First it reaffirms the developmental model discussed earlier which indicated the close connection between investment in the self and investment in objects because self and object representations stem from a common, undifferentiated self-object representation out of which narcissistic and object investment develop simultaneously. Kernberg stresses "the ever-present dyadic, polar quality of human experience, although it may be played out temporarily in primarily intra-psychic terms" (p. 65). Secondly, there is the suggestion that "the earliest intra-psychic experiences integrate affect and cognition in the context of the earliest units of internalized object relationship" (p. 60). These internalized object relationships (organized around primitive affects) serve as the earliest guiding principles which direct and channel inborn behavior patterns into drive systems centering around self and object representations.

In simple terms, Kernberg sees the nucleus of the ego as being organized under the influence of gratifying or frustrating experiences involving the infant and the mother. Because the earliest subjective experience of self is conceived in terms of primitive affects (pleasure or unpleasure), two separate constellations of "affective memory" are established. As minute internalizations occur and gradually consolidate into self-object-affective disposition units, an increasingly discriminating grid takes hold. New libidinous objects revive memory traces of analogous genetic self-object-primitive affect representations. In this way, the ego's perception of reality is structured by emotional processes that appraise each new situation as desirable or harmful. Current experiences, symbolically equivalent to unempathic mothering behavior (the less than average expectable environment), activate anxious, defensive responses that have become stylized over the years. In effect, character patterns are compromise formations designed to reconcile inner needs and environmental possibilities, with a minimum of anxiety. Homeostatic disturbances, expressed by pathological symptom formation, and the outbreak of primitive painful affects signify an inability to complete this equation. Devices of the ego that have thus far been mentioned, such as splitting and projective identification, seem to be unconsciously designed to preserve the security and survival of the ego. Silverberg (1952) is alluding to similar considerations when he distinguishes between autoplastic and alloplastic mechanisms. Autoplastic refers to a form of self-molding, an attempt to adapt to environmental dangers by producing alterations in the organism's own impulses. Aggression, for example, can be disowned, dissociated, and "split-off" from the rest of the personality. Alloplastic devices are "other-molding." In the main, they are oriented toward altering the environment from a dangerous place to a safe one. Where the ego is primarily concerned with inner modifications of the basic self, through our manipulation of the environment, some kind of self-balancing cycle, determined by a basic need for constancy and homeostasis, takes place.

Within this conceptual framework, if the internalization of the experienced traumatic interpersonal relationship extends over a significant period of time with a predominance of splitting and projective identification, then the smooth developmental continuity of ego identity is interfered with. The self-representation will be pathologically modified by regressive introjections, global (all good or all bad) primitive identifications, magical and persecutory thinking, and intense, disruptive affects. Since character pathology constitutes the final outcome of pathological identification processes, within the regressive context of analytic transference relationships, character patterns become "unfrozen," and past pathogenic, internalized object relationships (representing particular core conflicts) come pouring out. It is Kernberg's (1977) belief that active transference consistently reveals the activation of units of self and object representations linked by a particular affect.

> While projecting a parental object representation onto the analyst, the patient reactivates a self-representation in the interaction with that transference figure; or at other times, the self-representation is projected onto the analyst, while the patient identifies himself with the corresponding parental representation. In addition, the psychoanalytic exploration of character pathology frequently reveals that the internalized object relationship is expressed not so much in the relationship of the patient with the analyst, but in the intrapsychic relationship that becomes activated between the patient's ego and his superego (p. 59).

For example, a hysterical patient struggling with a conflictual identification with the powerful, domineering, threatening mother "introject" (a superego identification), is forced to repeat the same controlling and domineering attitude she hates in her mother in her own interactions with her husband and children. Under these circumstances, character traits of a domineering, controlling, sadistic quality may become activated in the transference, and the patient then appears to identify with her mother while treating the analyst as she felt mother had treated her; at the same time, in behaving like her mother, she also actualizes a submission on the part of her ego to her mother image internalized in the superego. In this regard, it is the patient's superego introject which now treats the patient's self as mother had treated her; and the establishment of character traits which are an imitation of this aspect of mother represents an internalized submission to the superego, one aspect of the classical identification with the aggressor (A. Freud, 1936).

In attempting over the years to integrate and synthesize the various contributions from psychoanalytic instinct theory, contemporary ego psychology, and object relations theory, and developing a means for making these data clinically useful, several major working hypotheses have come to the fore.

1. The analyst's major task is to serve as a maturationally facilitating object.

2. If feelings represent a context wherein self and object representations are linked, then the most economic way of reversing pathological processes (e.g., splitting, projective identification) that break down the boundaries between self and object, is by making an investigation of feelings the primary treatment issue.

3. If the exploration of emergent feelings are proposed as the most crucial analytic lever, the analyst must be prepared to employ his own feelings, personality, and inner experiences in new experimental ways that stretch the bounds of tradition.

4. The personal "limitations" of the analyst, his very defectiveness as a perfect object, can help put him deeply in touch with what the patient is unconsciously seeking. It is only through the crystallization and clarification of the patient's unmet needs that the analyst is in a position to gauge what will be most valuable to provide.

5. Finally, I propose that cure does not take place primarily as a result of interpretation but instead is a natural outgrowth of the rich tapestry of healthy interchange between patient and analyst. Detoxified introjects are slowly incorporated and become the basis for the gradual growth of strong, autonomous ego structures. Through this process of transmuting internalizations, the self becomes solidified and develops a greater capacity for feeling alive, real, and worthwhile. Each of these points is elaborated with numerous clinical examples below. Before, however, I shall discuss synchronous relations, namely, how the analyst can let the patient experience being known and related to.

Maturation is the development from environmental support to self-support. This progression is a natural sequence that depends on the quality of maternal care that is available in helping the child meet development tasks. Under optimal circumstances, this successful partnership forms the basis in the child for a sense of identity, sameness, continuity, and hopefulness. Under favorable circumstances, the child has a tendency to regress or fixate at a stage where he felt deprived, abandoned, or imcomplete. Apropos of this, in the beginning, the analysis of transference was still subservient to retrospective analysis, to the reconstruction through anachronistic fixations, of childhood events. Today, there seems to be an increasing awareness that transference is a tool for understanding present dynamics. Indeed, I would contend that transference can be meaningfully interpreted as an unconscious attempt to mobilize the present environment to do something corrective. Instead of making use of his own resources, the patient attempts to manipulate the analyst to meet an unfulfilled need. Analysis gets stuck to the point of impasse when the patient cannot produce his own support and when the analyst's response is less than satisfying. A major reason for stalemate in working with preoedipal problems is that intellectual interpretations have the effect of explaining away feelings, reify the process, perpetuate the myth that "I know more than you," and only succeed in motivating the patient to rebelliously await for a reaction that is not yet forthcoming. My thesis is that this blockage is a consequence of unfinished business incomplete need cycles, a high level of tension that has not been reduced, and intense affects that are not being expressed. The flow of behavior is clogged with interferences because the patient is depending on the analyst to supply something that is missing. Transference seems to include the patient's expectations of certain forms of relating on the analyst's part. The analyst's task is to carefully monitor this information and construct maturational paradigms relevant to the patient's highest level of ego adaptation. By flexibly accommodating to the patient's frustrated infantile needs for firmness, stability, nurturance, support, protection, and limit-setting, the patient's ego boundaries are strengthened and he can develop a separate sense of himself.

ILLUSTRATIONS

Case 1

D. was preoccupied with her great neediness. This voracious dependency on others was coupled with a compulsion to ingratiate, constantly seek approval by niceness and an obsessional empathic identification with the feelings of others. Her presenting problem was a marked fixation on her eight-year-old son, whom she vigilantly protected against rejection by peers.

After a year of combined group and individual sessions, D. called to inform the analyst that she could not come for a while because her car broke down and it would take several weeks to purchase a new car. Although the analyst had no special reason for doubting the veracity of the patient's explanation, he began feeling strangely indifferent about D.'s absence. After 6 weeks, he still had not heard from the patient but on the other hand, he never thought about her nor did it ever occur to him to call her and find out what was going on. The group members became increasingly annoyed at the analyst for his secretiveness surrounding D.'s absence and for his not seeming to be interested in following up on D. This attitude alternated with attacks on D. in her absence, for not being more involved and her seeming indifference to group participation.

Upon D.'s reentry into treatment (after 7 weeks), the analyst, despite some anxiety about hurting the patient, decided to share his unexpected indifference toward her. Over the ensuing weeks, other group members expressed similar feelings. Some of the group issues that emerged at this time included:

1. A questioning of whether the anger and urgency directed at the analyst for not being more caring might not be a projection about their own uneasiness about not caring sufficiently; and

2. Whether these emergent ambivalent responses were simply a reaction to D.'s procrastination about returning or whether they might not reveal more basic hostilities and

begrudging attitudes that were defended against by a group code which mandated that we must all care a great deal for one another and be deeply committed and involved in the group.

Oddly enough, D. seemed to be relieved by this turn of events. During subsequent sessions, D. began to examine her past history in a very new light. She had always presented her mother as a cold, rejecting person which then became the basis for explanations of her own feelings of inadequacy, insecurity, and neediness. She now began to remember that the basic uncaring mother was concealed by constant protestations of love and adoration. In the face of this hypocritical onslaught, D. felt compelled to be loving in return. Her actual feelings were anger turned into deadness, but she forced herself to respond caringly to protect the mother's need to maintain a personal mythology of herself as a loving mother. "I want a period of indifference, where I wouldn't have to give a damn and people wouldn't make me feel guilty by being nice to me. When people in the group get angry it seemed to free me from having to work for them. I want to be here, but not under false colors." The analyst recollected a gentlemen's agreement not to press her for late payments. Her pleas of poverty had caused him to back off from legitimately pursuing this resistance. His "kindness" and "understanding" combined with D.'s obvious admiration and appreciation of his warmth and compassion. The total effect was a cozy indifference to the therapeutic misalliance that had taken hold.

To recapitulate, it would appear that the mother had projected her own feelings of deprivation poisoned by anger onto D. who accepted this projection and identified with it by acting as though she was the depriving one. Her compliance and sugar-coated niceness represents the "good" half of the split that is employed to further dissociate the "bad" half (e.g., a feeling of being cheated with resultant rage). D's reports of a sense of "inner emptiness" with the accompanying symptom of obesity may very well be an outgrowth of this dynamic. The obsessive loving protection of the son against outside rejection seems to be both an identification with his vulnerability and a compensatory denial of basically selfish, periodically indifferent attitudes toward him. In fact, despite her chronic anxiety about his welfare, her intrusive need to arrange his life to spare him hurt, actually reflected relative disregard for his own capacity to deal with his own feelings. With all of this as a backdrop, how do we account for the analyst's successful impact in communicating neutral, less-than-enthusiastic feelings? We can begin to understand this phenomena if we realize that the indifferent reaction created a feeling of shame in the analyst. This counter-transference reaction (the indifference), despite its seeming irrationality (after all, the patient's car was destroyed and her excuse was perfectly legitimate) cut through the surface amiability and made the analyst sharply aware of many other points of potential friction that he had conveniently cir-cumvented. By permitting himself to unashamedly confess to the same feelings that heretofore the patient had trouble ac-cepting (e.g., I don't care as much as I pretend to), the analyst and the patient had been more successful than ever before in letting each other know where they actually stood in their relationship.

To return to one of my earlier statements, the patient in this instance by her prolonged absence had finally succeeded in evoking the appropriate maturational response. The revelation that "you're not so good" makes the inner ex-perience of "I'm not so bad" that much more palatable. The fear of being discovered as being corrupt and shallow in her love can be progressively reduced and worked through now that feelings of ambivalence, holding back, and changing at-titudes are universalized. The analyst's de-idealization as the paragon of virtue minutely begins to eat at the pathogenic in-ternalized self-object representations by attacking the primitive affective linkage. The affect in this case is hate turned into indifference. By implicitly accepting the patient's indifference and employing himself as an introjective model, the patient's "selfish," "greedy," and "demanding" com-ponents are in this way identified as perfectly understandable bits of behavior.

Case 2

L. came to treatment because of a great emptiness and dissatisfaction with her life. She had graduated from college with honors but could not find a career that caught her interest, her relationship with her husband was amiable but boring, she was involved in a series of short-lived affairs, and she was overweight. She described herself as a child as pleasant, placid, easy to get along with on the outside but in a continuous state of near panic on the inside. "Nobody ever knew what I felt. I never tried to let anybody know what was really going on inside of me." During a year of treatment, L. neutralized all attempts to investigate the marital situation by suggesting that something terrible would happen if she tried to change anything. The following excerpt is taken from a sequence that occurred during the 14th month of treatment.

L. arrived at the session in an acute state of agitation and just "fit-to-be-tied." She came directly from her house where an electrician, a plumber, and a carpenter "had not done their work the way they were supposed to." The analyst, picking up on the fact that the mistakes were only "little mistakes," had focused in on L.'s perfectionism and impatience with anything going wrong. L. recollected critical, perfectionistic attitudes of her mother. "When I was eight, I made a couple of wrong stitches on a sweater I was making. She made me rip the whole thing out and do it all over again." Despite the fact that she had volunteered this information, L. strenuously resisted the notion that there was anything wrong with her mother's standards or that her distress with the workmen had anything to do with expecting the world to run smoothly, "without any hitches." She left the session quite irritated and annoyed at the analyst for not understanding her at all.

She began the following session by asking about her sister's three-year-old daughter who, in the act of kissing people, ends up biting them. She described how at first she was very disturbed by what transpired during the previous session but "then a strange, uncomfortable joy came over me. I realized that I was showing you for the first time how I really feel most of the time. It felt good to get it out and persist even though you kept sidetracking me with your interpretations." The analyst conveyed this understanding that she simply wanted to get her feelings out without having to examine them or categorize them. At this point, L. asked in an apologetic way, "Do other people tell you how to do things?" The analyst answered, "Most other people aren't so helpful." L. explained, "I don't think you understand me most of the time. You're inconsistent. One time you tell me I don't share my feelings with you; other times when I come in upset, you seem to get upset by my upset and try to stop me from being upset." The patient then described fantasies she had about the nature of the therapeutic process. "It should be formal, aloof, impersonal, non-involved; the analyst should never reveal anything about himself, he should be non-demanding, and let the patient go at their own pace. I feel you're unprofessional. You react to me, you let me know how I'm making you feel, you seem interested in how I'm feeling, you expect things of me. I walk in here because I care because it's my life; but you care too and it scares me. That extra quality is frightening. It's different than with my mother; I always cared; I didn't feel she cared even though she acted like she did."

The erratic quality of the analytic process here can be conceptualized as follows: the analyst, responding to the overwrought, terribly anxious disposition of the patient, attempted to relax her by appealing to her observing ego. By putting things in perspective, he hoped to get her to see that the events that she was "overreacting" to were a normal part of living. After all, part of being human is having to deal with change, mistakes, and continual demands. The patient's response to this approach was to come to quick intellectual agreement on the basis of mature, pseudo-adult recognition of the wisdom of the analyst's advice. This compliance was followed, however, by infantile outburts wherein the analyst was accused of curbing L.'s feelings. The analyst felt caught in a position of having to thread a needle in order to placate the patient's wrath and began to feel resentful about being controlled and bullied in this way.

If we begin to examine the self-object-affective state, the confusing patterns in this case become increasingly clear. L.'s mother's narcissistic tendencies made her a poor container for anxiety and upset. The mother's intolerance for the developmentally appropriate fumblings and distress of early childhood pressured L. to bind her anxiety in order to spare the mother from feeling unduly put upon. For example, accepting an imperfect sweater instead of insisting on a perfect product was more than the mother was capable of. From this perspective, L.'s transference was intended to unconsciously inform the analyst to let her continue to be anxious and disturbed (imperfect). The freedom to explore the parameters of this kinds of behavior was apparently more meaningful than misguided attempts to curb her anxiety by getting her to see a better way of handling things (once again imposing a kind of perfection on her). Instead of regarding L.'s behavior as controlling and ultimately defeating his therapeutic interests, the analyst can make use of the feelings that are evoked in him, in a constructive fashion. Through the mechanism of projective identification, the patient is asking the analyst to understand how difficult it is to continue to be anxious and to allow oneself to be upset, in the face of another person who will not permit you to make them tense.

Case 3

R. was a 31-year-old woman who had entered treatment four years earlier in a severe depression. Her mood was cynical and pessimistic, she was rebounding from a bad romantic experience, and she was bitter and furious about her terrible childhood. R.'s background consisted of a schizophrenic mother who suffered a breakdown when R. was 10 years old and a relatively weak and ineffectual father who could not bring himself to commit the mother, thereby dooming the family to a permanent state of chaos, tension, and despondency. R. became father's confidant and consoler and adopted a motherly role in relation to the two younger siblings (brother nine years younger and sister five years younger). During the four years of treatment, R.'s core depression lifted considerably. She became more youthful, warmer, more outgoing, and prettier. Nevertheless, her unsuccessful social life continued to be a sore spot that gave rise to periodic outbursts of rage, impotence, and despair. This negative phase reached such proportions during her fourth year in therapy that at times the therapist found himself hoping that she would get angry enough to break off treatment. In anticipation of each session, the therapist braced himself for yet another onslaught of accusations that he was trying to control her, that she was tired of analyzing the same old things, that he was not helping her as much as her sister's analyst was helping her sister, and why should she examine herself when the people outside were not looking at themselves. Most of all, R. resented having "to work," namely to be forced to alter herself to get along with others considering that she felt that she had been taking responsibility for others (mother, father, siblings) all of her life.

The manifest content of the session during the fourth year revolved around R.'s jealousy toward her pretty, bubbly, popular younger sister. Intellectually, R. acknowledged that despite her ostensible envy, she felt guilty if she excluded her sister from her activities, suppressed her own positive experiences when sister was around, and played a passive, remote role when together with sister and father. During one session, R. recollected an early childhood memory of watching her sister run into the gutter and thinking for a moment, "I hope she gets run over," but then running after the sister and rescuing her. The therapist suggested that whatever nasty thoughts she had were simply a fantasy but that indeed she was protective. The following session R. shared the wish that she could let her father know how much she appreciated his efforts in the last few years, to understand her feelings. Something having to do with her sister, however, stood in the way of showing these warm sentiments. R. then had a fantasy about M., a patient who had been in the same group as R. but who had left treatment two years earlier. R. had developed a very intense symbiotic attachment to M. wherein she acted out many of the ambivalences she felt toward her sister. On the one hand, she felt resentful of M.'s manipulative dependency and exploitative and self-centered nature. And yet, R., for the most part, did whatever M. wanted, neglected her own needs in the relationship, and altogether behaved very guilty. Although this relationship had been discussed many times before, on this occasion, the therapist forced himself to say something that was embarrassing him and made him feel unprofessional. "Many of the things that disturb you about M. bothered me also. I don't think that your feelings were without realistic justification. I have to admit though that your constant complaining and negativity gets to be too much; you begin to feel like a pain in the ass."[6]

These "shameful" confidences, which the therapist had been controlling for over two years, proved to be a significant turning point in R.'s treatment progress. Many crucial issues which had been supposedly explored and interpreted could now be examined for fresh inquiry on a level of much deeper feelings. (1) R.'s jealousy and resentment did not seem nearly so reprehensible once the therapist acknowledged similar feelings. (2) This identificatory validation provided the support and encouragement that R. needed to accept her jealousy and resentment instead of simply talking about such feelings. An important principle here is that when patients talk about feelings, therapists frequently incorrectly assume that patients own and accept such feelings. My sense is that feelings are repeatedly brought up as an attempt to work them through and accommodate them within the self-representation. (3) I believe that we can safely make the assumption that the self-

---

[6]There is, to be sure, a danger that if the analyst remains consistently patient and understanding under a continued barrage of abusiveness session after session, that the implication may arise that the analyst is absolutely inhuman. It therefore is sometimes therapeutically desirable that under extreme circumstances the analyst be free to give vent to his feelings (Nydes, 1963).

object-affective unit operative at age 8 is a symbolic extension of much earlier self-object-affective constellations. The mother's premorbid personality was at best infantile, pathologically possessive, and very fragile. In effect R. had to restore the mother to a maternal role by supporting her first and then hoped that the mother was strong enough to take care of R. At first in therapy, R. masked the crucial issue of her own deprivations by imagining the siblings' competitiveness and envy of her for her close relationship with her father. This at best partial interpretation seems to represent the split-off aspects of her own jealousy and resentment. (4) The therapist's confession freed R. to identify the father as possibly having similar thoughts but being ashamed of even letting R. know that he was such a small person. "I bet my father felt like leaving my mother many times but he probably couldn't face the social embarrassment. There must have been times when he wished none of us were born so he could run away." By identifying in this way with the father, R. not only succeeded in relieving her guilt about these ego-alien feelings but she also helped herself to see the decent elements in both her father and herself. "I could have been rotten to my sister and brother. My father could have been cruel to my mother and abandoned us all. He didn't. I didn't." This deidealization of the father and the analyst served to temper the patient's own harsh superego, thus rendering her self-image less reprehensible. (5) Epstein (1978), Searles (1965), and Spotnitz (1976) all have commented on the potentially damaging effects of benign understanding as a fixed analytic stance. Among the advantages of strategically conveying back to the patient objective or justified anger, Epstein cites (a) the establishment of a trustworthy emotional matrix (e.g., if one is acting hatefully, reactive anger is an expected and valid emotional response); (b) the patient gains reassurance that he is capable of affecting and influencing the significant other; (c) the patient is discouraged from viewing himself as the all-bad person who is being burdensome to a paragon of virtue; and (d) the patient is protected from nihilistic fantasies of his own destructive nature by being reassured that the libidinal object will survive and has a separate identity.

Case 4

M. was an effete, ingratiating individual who used haughtiness and condescension to conceal a serious inability to directly confront conflictual situations. During a group therapy session, the analyst commented on the superior tone M. employed in addressing another member. M. acted rather annoyed and, by his general demeanor, made it quite evident that he was not inclined to pursue the matter further. M. had adeptly neutralized the analyst's inquiries many times in the past with similar expressions of disdain. More often than not, the analyst would feel pressured and responsible for making something happen. M. would sit back with an air of compliant ingratiation and wait patiently for the analyst to think of something new to try out. The analyst suddenly realized that he had always assumed this burden without ever responding to M.'s subtle, ever-so-polite way of declining invitations to discuss certain pertinent issues. On reflection, the analyst realized that if he persisted, M.'s irritated withdrawal tended to arouse considerable anxiety in him. On the other hand, not to comment on these disengaging patterns frequently aroused a feeling of frustration, disinterest, and underlying resentment. In this instance, the analyst chose to override his trepidations and repeated his earlier statements. Predictably, M. detached himself from the potentially conflictual interchange only to criticize the analyst 30 minutes later for being such a nag. Several days after this incident, during a private session, the analyst shared a dream he had about M. with M. "Impotence is caused by rearranging the furniture." In the dream M. then went on to say that he had once been in a Japanese concentration camp. M. was asked to associate to the analyst's dream. "Rearranging the furniture makes me think of a study in apparent motion with no real movement. It reminds me of shifting things around with no actual changes taking place. Maybe the impotence means not dealing with things." The analyst indicated that for some reason M. did not want to enter into a dialogue with the analyst in the group when confronted. What feelings were being experienced then? "Anger for being picked. I felt unmasked and naked. I felt that you were pushing too hard to get me to see something that was embarrassing to me. You were really on my back and I wanted to shrug you off. But I didn't know how to get rid of you except by ignoring you." Patient and analyst proceeded to explore the consequences of not dealing more directly with M.'s feelings of being overwhelmed and intruded upon. M. still could not get deeply in touch with why he was afraid to get more angry. The analyst then shared a fantasy he had about the concentration camp comment. "When I was a young boy I saw a newspaper caption, *The Rape of Nanking*" (the Japanese had conquered the Chinese city). The accompanying picture showed a Japanese soldier with a bayonet. For years, I mistakenly thought that rape had to do with cutting off women's breasts. Do you have any associations to what I'm saying?"

During the next few months, M. shared a dream that transparently indicated an infantile fantasy that castration and impotence was somehow related to the fear of losing the breasts. Twice during one session, he confused vasectomy with mastectomy. As we begin to unravel the phenomenology of the critical incident in the group, M. related the following association: "I felt paralyzed and dead inside (impotent) after you criticized me (abandonment equals cutting off the breasts). So long as I remain passive and compliant by not letting you know that I felt dumped on, I remain numb. There's something about eliminating part of my reactions that makes me feel bad and not whole." These admissions were particularly striking considering M.'s typical superior attitude. M's contempt for raw emotions as petty and dirty ("I've been in analysis too long to behave like an infant."), enabled him to successfully avoid dealing with aggressive, threatening emotions. This pseudo-maturity, defensively employed by someone who is bright, articulate, and intellectually perceptive was heretofore a formidable obstacle that interfered with a deepened sense of enfeeblement and fragmented masculine identifications.

I have presented this case to illustrate the fact that under certain circumstances, the sharing of selected counter-transference reactions including dream material, for mutual exploration, opens the way for an expansion of the analytic frame. The analyst, in suggesting that the arousal within himself of specified tensions inhibits his functioning, and precludes the possibility of discussing charged areas, is encouraging the patient to see if there is anything familiar within his own experience, relating to similar attitudes. In raising the possibility that more tension and complexity exists in the relationship than is generally acknowledged, the analyst is attempting to circumvent avoidance mechanisms such as ingratiation and superiority, and encouraging the patient to be more interested in the silent anxieties that prevailed during the course of this most "amiable" relationship.

DISCUSSION

As we contemplate the rich harvest of clinical material, one thing becomes clear — that every pre-oedipal patient that we treat is unconsciously searching for the impossible disappearance of the limits which separate him from the object. The fantasy of a primary narcissistic state is not conceivable without the establishment of an ambivalent object (Diatkine, 1973). The appearance of anxiety connected to ambivalence introduces the nostalgia for a former state in which the object could be fully satisfying. The ego ideal is then formed as a projection of the necessary conditions for the regaining of paradise lost. It has been suggested that it is precisely the corresponding attempts on the analyst's part to find paradise by providing a perfect union between himself and the ideal object (the improved patient) that ultimately leads to many treatment impasses. I have attempted to discuss how the unpleasurable affects (with their accompanying ideational representations) that are provoked in the analyst, provide important clues as to the way the patient uses the analyst.

Patients who utilize primitive defenses based on splitting and projective identification, will unconsciously try to use us to project anxiety into, to collude with them to deny anxiety, and to otherwise carry and contain various parts of their internal world. If the analyst is able to control his own countertransferential dispositions toward these pathological introjective identifications and successfully monitor his own affective responses, then in the course of the working through process, he can continuously differentiate between himself and the patient. By clarifying this distinction, while at the same time explaining the feelings which seem to underlie the patient's resistance against taking responsibility for himself, the analyst is striving to strengthen the therapeutic alliance while simultaneously dissolving the transference neurosis.

At times, this approach may falter and create a dilemma especially if the analyst is premature in making explicit to the patient the analyst's own ultimate inability to accept responsibility for someone else's inner experiences. Winnicott's concept of the environmental mother comes to mind at this point. The analyst's understanding, patience, and empathy in the broad context of his relationship with the patient, has a great calming influence. The anxiety and aggression that the patient might ordinarily experience when forced to confront a split-off feeling, is considerably reduced by the at least partial realization that the analyst has not really abandoned him. I remember once seeing a woman whose family situation was saturated with seductive, "disgusting," and guilt-ridden sexual overtones. The patient constantly asked me to reassure her that I would not try to make her have sex before she was married and during the early part of treatment was preoccupied with the suspicion that I was trying to reverse the moral values of her upbringing. She was 28 years old at the time, but had never had any close contact with a man. Two years into treatment, she shared an experience that had occurred 10 years earlier: "I was at Shea Stadium and Paul McCartney (a famous rock star) looked at me. When our eyes met, I almost fell off my seat with excitement." It soon became apparent that this woman's vitality, enthusiasm, sensuality, and potential interest in men were condensed in this wish-fulfilling fantasy. Within this safe encapsulated memory, hidden from the intrusive influence of her environment, for 10 years this woman had kept alive her secret vital core. During the ensuing five years of treatment the patient made it abundantly clear that Paul McCartney was a real person to her. She had listened to all of his records, read every bit of material pertaining to him that was available and had conducted a fantasy relationship with him for years. She wondered aloud many times whether she would ever meet him, how he would react to her, and whether he would think she was crazy. This obsession seemed to serve two significant mother stayed home, but that I expected the patient to keep frightening social relationships, and it maintained a positive link, if only on a fantasy level, between herself and a man.

When I finally felt prepared to use this relationship as a bridge to promoting real life contact, I never directly challenged the sensibleness of being in love with someone whom one has never met. Instead, I expressed an understanding for the qualities that drew her to Paul McCartney—his earthiness, his animal vitality, the raw emotions that he conveyed, the masculinity that he projected. I suggested that I could see why she chose him as a soul mate since the two of them shared so much in common except that he had found a vehicle for expressing his sense of being alive, but that she had kept her joy buried under craziness for so many years. My point here is that the gradual extinction of this fantasy relationship was only possible because of the cumulative effect of our previous relationship together. This patient's inner organization was such that she required me to maintain an attitude of unintrusive nonattached availability. I tried to offer myself as an absorbent container of her infantile tirades, her self-centered demandingness, and her intolerance for differences between us. I tried to capitalize on her good sense of humor, and her observing ego's capacity to respect limits and boundaries when they were not enforced in a primitive way. Once the patient called me during a light snowstorm and said that she would have to miss the session because her mother said it was snowing and the bus would not be running. I told her that it was alright with me if her mother stayed home, but that I expected the patient to keep her usual appointment time. In the course of relating to an object who is strong enough to be independent and limiting while simultaneously caring and supportive, the patient can synthesize and introject these experiences in such a way as to strengthen her own ego.

The analyst's capacity to wait without any preconceptions, that is to selectively hold back from a predictable stereotyped response, is a crucial factor in the curative process. Patients apply great pressures on the analyst to behave like significant adults in the patient's earlier life. In the case cited above, for example, if I would have quickly moved to confront the patient with the unrealistic aspects of her fantasy, I would have been identified with the anti-libidinous maternal introject. The analytic literature typically stresses the advantages of a conscious use of one's observations as to how one fits in with the patient's archaic needs. In the course of digesting these articles, however, I would hope that the reader can now see that by taking note of his own discomfort and anxiety, the analyst can also empathically grasp unverbalized conflictual patterns in the patient. The patient's influence on the analyst, his effect on the analyst's tension level, is a remarkable directional signal for sorting out content areas that warrant further investigation. Cohen (1956) has defined countertransference as follows: "When anxiety is aroused in the analyst with the effect that communication between patient and analyst is interfered with by some attitudes in the analyst's behavior (P. 38)." I would say that in the course of the analyst's difficult struggle to maintain his identity and separateness in the face of the temptation to conform to the patient's wishes or defensively avoid them, something new and illuminating comes forth. The resonance of this subjective inner experience can be fruitfully applied to isomorphic patterns in the patient. It is no coincidence that analysts, being only human, report on good days and bad days. Sometimes, everything seems to go right. Just about every session is productive, meaningful, and progressive. At other times, the patients seem to be resistive, negativistic, and incomprehensible. To the best of my knowledge, no research has been done on the effect of the analyst's mood in their work with patients. Fortunately, these broad-based cause-and-effect relationships take place infrequently. Except for the most extreme examples of personal stress, the well-analyzed analyst tends not to be preoccupied. The feelings and fantasies that develop occur as a result of interactions in the now, with this particular individual.

Returning to Kernberg's conceptualization that self and object representations are forged in the context of specific affective dispositions, I would like to quote Bion on this subject. Bion begins by citing Freud's statement in *The Ego and the Id* to the effect that things become conscious by their connection with the verbal images that correspond to them (Freud, 1923). Fortified by this statement, Bion (1955a) goes on to state:

> The development of projective identification would be particularly severe against the thought of whatever kind that concerned itself with the relations between object impressions, for if this link could be severed, or better still never forged, then at least consciousness of reality would be destroyed even though reality itself could not be . . . . in fact, not only is primitive to thought attacked because it links sense-impressions of reality with consciousness, but thanks to the psychotic's overendowment with destructiveness, the splitting processes are extended to links within the thought processes themselves . . . all these are now attacked until finally two objects cannot be brought together in a way which leaves each object with its intrinsic qualities intact and yet able, by their conjunction, to produce a new mental object. Consequently, the formation of symbols, which depend for its therapeutic effect on the ability to bring together two objects so that their resemblance is made manifest, yet their differences left unimpaired, now becomes difficult (p. 269).

In this description of fragmentation of the ego, Bion concludes that the interference of the linkage between object impressions and sense impression are central to differentiating between psychotic and nonpsychotic parts of the personality. Bion's views on this matter are closely related to Kernberg's observations in one fundamental respect. Both believe that splitting and projective identification are used by regressed patients as a substitute for repression. When the patient tries to reintegrate any of the expelled feelings, he feels invaded, intruded upon, and assaulted. The most important focus then for purposes of effective analysis is intensive investigation of that which is split, projected, expelled, and whose reincorporation is resisted. The acceptance, ownership, and ultimate taking of responsibility for these ego-alien feelings becomes the sine qua non of effective psychoanalysis.

To summarize the framework that I have found helpful in clearly communicating to patients these affective operations:

1. The small child perceives the parents "bad" actions as unpredictable and irrational.

2. The primitive anxiety that is aroused reaches catastrophic proportions because the child feels that he exercises no control over these threatening outside forces.

3. Projective and introjective identifications are rudimentary precursors of later forms of identifying one's needs as causing the negative response.

4(a). The child alters his own needs (self) to avert the "bad" response and/or (b): The child manipulates the environment to further reduce the possibility of having to contend with negative reactions.

5. Ego-alien feelings, that is impulses that jeopardize the status quo, must ultimately be repossessed, otherwise the ego will forever feel incomplete. On the other hand, attempts to incorporate these projected "impure" aggressive impulses is a source of severe anxiety. A fairly integrated self-concept can only come about if the ego can accept and synthesize formerly split-off feelings.

6. In order for patients to overcome this threat and mend their polarized, segmented egos, the analyst's feedback and self-representation plays a vital role. The analyst comes to

represent for the patient, through the split-transference, the patient's "all good" or "all bad" self and/or object images. By detoxifying the patient's projections and metabolizing them, the analyst provides the patient with a fresh opportunity to coalesce differentiated and separated representations into integrated ones. He can now identify with the total person of the analyst and gradually absorb the concept of good and bad possibilities within a unitary structure. In this way, not only are healthy boundaries and distinctions established between the self and the object, but also a more peaceful coexistence is attained between discrete aspects of the self (e.g., ego ideal and superego).

7. A theme that I have tried to emphasize repeatedly in this chapter is the analyst's optimal role in breaking pathological introjective-projective cycles. I have suggested that the analyst's presence and participation as a whole, real person, fully capable of not only identifying and experiencing but sometimes even judiciously expressing some of the very same feeling that the patient is undergoing, is the key ingredient in changing the patient's psychic structure.

REFERENCES

Asch, S. Varieties of negative therapeutic reaction and problems of technique. *Journal of the American Psychoanalytic Association,* (1976), *24,* 383-407.

Bell, R., & Harper, L. *Child effects on adults.* New York: Halsted Press, 1977.

Benedek, T., quoted in The baby as therapist. Psychology Today. 1978, *12,* 94.

Bion, W.R. Language and the schizophrenic. In: M. Klein, P. Heinmann, and R. Money-Kryle. (Eds.), *New directions in psycho-analysis.* London: Tavistock; New York: Basic Books, 1955a.

Bion, W.R. *Differentiation of the psychotic from the non-psychotic personalities.* Paper presented to the British Psychoanalytic Society, characterological and Schizophrenic Disorders. New York: Jason

Bion, W.R. *Learning from Experience.* London: W. Heinemann, 1962.

Bion, W.R. *Elements of Psychoanalysis.* London: W. Heinemann, 1962.

Boyer, L.B. and Giovacchini, P.L., Psychoanalytic Treatment of characterological and Schizophrenic Disorders. New York: Jason Aronson, Inc., 1967.

Bridger, W. The baby as an individualist. *J. Albert Einstein College of Medicine,* 1963, *7,* 63-69.

Bugental, J. The person who is the psychotherapist. *Journal of Consulting Psychology,* 1964, *28,* 272-77.

Bugental, J. *The search for authenticity.* New York: Holt, Rinehart, & Winston, 1965.

Chess, C. *Temperament and development.* New York: Brunner-Mazel, 1977.

Cohen, M.B. Countertransference and anxiety. *Psychiatry,* 1952, *15,* 231-243.

Diatkine, R., The development of object relationships and affects, *International Journal of Psycho-Analysis,* 1978, *59,* 277-296.

Epstein, L. The therapeutic function of hate in the countertransference. *Contemporary Psychoanalysist,* 1977, *13,* (4), 442-461.

Epstein, L. *On the therapeutic use of countertransference data and the problem of interventions in the psychoanalytic therapy of borderline patients.* Unpublished manuscript, 1978.

Fenichel, O. *The psychoanalytic theory of neuroses.* New York: Norton, 1945.

Fleiss, R. Countertransferences and counteridentification. *International Journal of Psychoanalysis,* 1953, *1,* 268-284.

Freud, A. *The Ego and the Mechanisms of Defense.* New York: International Universities Press, 1936.

Freud, S. Three essays on the theory of sexuality (1905). *Standard Edition, 7,* 123-243. London: Hogarth Press, 1953.

Freud, S. On the history of the psychoanalytic movement (1914). *Standard Edition, 14,* 7-66. London: Hogarth Press, 1953.

Freud, S. The ego and the id (1923). *Standard Edition, 12.* London: Hogarth Press, 1953.

Freud, S. Analysis terminable and interminable (1937). *Standard Edition, 23,* London: Hogarth Press, 1953.

transference. *Contemporary Psychoanalysis, 14,* (2), 279-290.

International Journal of Psycho-Analysis, 1975, *56,* 1-22.

Fromm-Reichman, F. Some aspects of psychoanalytic psychotherapy with schizophrenics. In: F.B. Brody and F.C. Redlich (Eds.), *Psychotherapy with schizophrenics.* 1958.

Fromm-Reichmann, F. Chicago: University of Chicago Press (1959), Basic problems in the psychotherapy of schizophrenia. *Psychiatry, 21,* 1-6.

Fromm, M.G. (1978) The Patient's Role in Modulation of Countertransference. *Contemporary Psychoanalysis, 14* (2), 279-290.

Giovacchini, P. Treatment of marital disharmonies: The classic approach. In: B. Greene (Ed.), *The psychotherapy of marital disharmony.*

New York: The Free Press, 1965.

Giovacchini, P. The symbiotic phase. In: *Tactics and techniques in psychoanalytic psychotherapy.* New York: Science House, 1972, pp. 137-169.

Giovacchini, P.L. (1975) Tactics and Techniques in Psychoanalytic Therapy; Countertransference. New York: Jason Aronson, Inc.

Gorney, J. *The negative therapeutic interaction.* Unpublished manuscript, 1979.

Green, A. The analyst, Symbolization and absence in the analytic setting. *International Journal of Psycho-Analysis,* 1975, *56,* 1-22.

Greenson, R. *The technique and practice of psychoanalysis.* Vol. I. New York: International Universities Press, 1967.

Guntrip, H. *Psychoanalytic theory, therapy and the self.* New York: Basic Books, 1971.

Haley, J. *Strategies of Psychotherapy.* New York: Grune & Stratton, 1963.

Harlow, H. quoted in The baby as therapist. *Psychology Today,* 1978, *12,* 94.

Heimann, P. On countertransference. *International Journal of Psycho-Analysis,* 1950, *31,* 81-84.

Horney, K. *The Neurotic Personality of our Time.* New York: Norton, 1936.

Kernberg, O. *Object relations theory and clinical psychoanalysis.* New York: Jason Aronson, 1977.

Kernberg, O. Notes on countertransference. *Journal of American Psychoanalytic Association,* 1965, *13,* 38-56.

Kohut, H. The restoration of the self. New York: International Universities Press, 1977.

Langs, R. *The Bipersonal Field.* New York: Jason Aronson, 1976(a).

Langs, R. *The Therapeutic Interaction.* Vols. I and II, New York: Jason Aronson, 1976(b).

Levenson, E. *The fallacy of understanding,* New York: Basic Books, 1972.

Little, M. On basic unity. *International Journal of Psycho-Analysis,* 1960, *41,* 377-384.

Little, M. Early mothering care. In: *Tactics and techniques in psychoanalytic psychotherapy.* New York: Science House, 1972, pp. 310-336.

Mahler, M. *On human symbiosis and the vicissitudes of individuation.* Vol. I. *Infantile psychosis.* New York: International Universities Press, 1968.

Malin, A., & Grotstein, J. Projective identification in the therapeutic process, *International Journal of Psycho-Analysis,* 1966, *47,* 171-180.

May, R. *The Meaning of Anxiety.* New York: Ronald Press, 1950.

Mittleman, B. Complementary neurotic reactions in intimate relationships. *Psychoanalytic Quarterly,* 1944, *13,* 479-494.

Nydes, J. The Paranoid character. *Psychoanalytic Review,* 1963, *50,* 2-17.

Obendorf, C. Psychoanalysis of married couples. *Psychoanalytic Review,*

1938, *25*, 453-471.

Olinick, S. Question and pain; truth and negation. *Journal of American Psychoanalytic Associations,* 1964, *5*, 302-324.

Racker, H. The meaning and uses of countertransference. *Psychoanalytic Quarterly,* 1957, *26*, 303-357.

Rosenfeld, H. (1971) A clinical approach to the psychoanalytic theory of the life and death instincts: An investigation into the aggressive aspects of narcissism. *International Journal of Psycho-Analysis,* 1971, *52*, 169-178.

Rosenfeld, H. Negative Therapeutic reaction. In Giovacchini, P. (ed.) *Tactics and Techniques in Psychoanalytic Psychotherapy,* Vol. 2. New York: Jason Aronson, 1975.

Sandler, J., Counter-transference and role-responsiveness. *International Review of Psycho-Analysis,* 1976(b), *3*, 43-47.

Searles, H. Transference psychosis in the psychotherapy of chronic schizophrenia. *International Journal of Psycho-Analysis,* 1963, *44*, 249-291.

Searles, H. *Collected papers on schizophrenia and related subjects.* New York: International Universities Press, 1965.

Searles, H. The patient as therapist to his analyst. In: P. Giovacchini (Ed.), *Tactics and techniques in psychoanalytic therapy.* Vol. II. New York: Jason Aronson, 1975.

Segal, J., & Yahraes, H. Bringing up mother. *Psychology Today,* 1978, *12*, 90-96.

Silverberg, W. *Childhood experience and personal destiny.* New York: Springer, (1952).

Singer, I. *Key concepts in psychotherapy.* New York: Random House, 1965.

Spitz, R. Countertransference: Comments on its varying role in the analytic situation. *International Journal of Psycho-Analysis,* 1956, *4*, 256-265.

Spotnitz, H. *Psychotherapy of pre-oedipal conditions.* New York: Jason Aronson, 1976.

Sullivan, H.S. *The interpersonal theory of psychiatry.* New York: Norton, 1953.

Tauber, E. Exploring the therapeutic use of countertransference data. *Psychiatry,* 1954, *17*, 331-336.

Weigart, E. Contribution to the problem of terminating psychoanalysis. *Psychoanalytical Quarterly,* 1952, *21*, 465-480.

Winnicott, D.W. Hate in the countertransference. *International Journal of Psycho-Analysis,* 1951, *30*, 69-76.

Winnicott, D.W. Parent-infant relationship. *International Journal of Psychoanalysis,* 1960a, *41*, 583-595.

Winnicott, D.W. Ego distortions in terms of the true and false self.

International Journal of Psycho-Analysis, 1960, *41,* 486-497.

Winnicott, D.W. Countertransference. *British Journal of Medical Psychology,* 1960c, *33,* 17-21.

Winnicott, D.W. (1965) The Maturational Processes and the Facilitating Environment (London: Hogarth; New York: Int. Univ. Press).

Zaphivopoulos, M.L. Tender Hearts and Martinets: Some Varieties of Countertransference. Presidential address delivered at the William Alanson White Psychoanalytic Society on March 16, 1961.

Chapter 5

THE ANALYST'S NARCISSISTIC VULNERABILITY AND ITS EFFECT ON THE TREATMENT SITUATION*
Ted Saretsky, Ph.D.

*This material is an expanded version of an article that appeared originally in *Contemporary Psychoanalysis,* Vol. 16 (I), January, 1980m 82-89, Journal of the William Alanson White Institute and the William Alanson White Psychoanalytic Society, New York. It is reprinted here with permission.

I said to my soul, be still, and wait without hope
For hope would be hope for the wrong thing; wait without love
For love would be love for the wrong thing; there is yet faith
But the faith and the love and the hope are all in the waiting.
Wait without thought, for you are not ready for thought.
So the darkness shall be the light, and the stillness the dancing.
— East Coker by T.S. Eliot

Recent formulations on the nature of the therapeutic process in the treatment of patients with borderline and narcissistic personality organizations, has focused increased attention on the psychoanalytic setting as a maturationally facilitating interpersonal matrix (Winnicott, 1965; Langs, 1976; Giovacchini, 1975; Epstein, 1977). Within this framework, the analyst's capacity to successfully address himself to the patient's ego-splitting and projective tendencies and make corrective interventions, are generally regarded as central to the strengthening of ego boundaries and the development of a sense of separateness and significance (Guntrip, 1971; Kernberg, 1975; Saretsky, 1977). From an adaptive point of view, there is a growing tendency to define transference as reflecting something more than simply the patient's repeated attempts to force the analyst to assume the role and function of some part of himself or of some internalized other. This departure from the classical conceptualization of transference takes into account the possibility that the analyst-parent is being offered a fresh opportunity to react in such a way that would have a positive, mutative effect on the patient's ego (Epstein, ibid.; Searles, 1975). Greenson (1967), Racker, 1968; and Feiner, 1977 have suggested that the analyst's ability to meet this challenge—to contain, treat, and transcend his raw countertransferential responses—is crucial in the determination of whether the patient can be helped to break away from familiar pathological self-object relationships.

This chapter is an attempt to investigate those narcissistic tendencies in the analyst that interfere with the maintenance of an optimal degree of objective interest and relatedness, so as to overcome induced reactions which invariably lead to treatment misalliances. I propose to draw certain correspondences between the analytic interaction and certain aspects of the mother-child situation both in regard to normal and pathological development, with a view toward clarifying the bilateral nature of both types of relationships (Winnicott, 1947). More specifically my hypothesis is (1) that the cohesiveness and integration of the self in parent and analyst are continuously tested by the very assumption of a caretaking role; (2) the insufficient dissolution of the idealization of these roles can lead to strong unconscious anxiety and guilt feelings (Racker, 1968) and (3) the extent to which these persecutory bad self-images take over in parent or analyst significantly influence whether or not a maturational response is forthcoming.

There seems to be considerable evidence in the recent literature which suggests that the vicissitudes of individuation that exists within the symbiotic dual unity operating between mother and child during the very earliest stages of life are essential for the establishment of a stable sense of ego identity (Benjamin, 1961; Mahler, 1968). Among the essential ingredients necessary in furthering this process, the mother figure's capacity to be a need-satisfying object and provide homeostatic equilibrium is considered to be of primary importance. Winnicott's concept of the "good enough mother" is relevant in this regard. His formulations suggest that neither perfection nor omniscience is a prerequisite for healthy parenting (1954). Rather, the mother's relative ability to provide interest, accessibility, protectiveness, and recognition of her child as a unique and separate individual seems to be significant in determining whether ego distortion or ego integration occurs.

The analytic literature further indicates that the mothering figure's sensitivity, caring, and understanding of the child's needs, tensions, and pleasures are closely linked to the nature of internalized object relationships (Kernberg, 1975; Winnicott, 1965).[1] In this light, the precious balance between internalized self-object representations in the parent is significantly related to the influence that the child has on the parent's self-concept (Zetzel, 1949). A parent possessing unstable, pathological self-structures will tend to have an exaggerated investment in the child organized around her own narcissistic interests (Little, 1972; Searles, 1965; Sullivan, 1953). The prevailing affective state that a child arouses in a parent has important implications for the present and future attitudes of the parent toward the child. Kernberg (1975) has theorized that "each bipolar unit of self and object image is

---

[1]Erikson (1959, p. 87) has approached the same issue from more of an interpersonal point of view when he suggests that the mother projects her own needs and feelings into the infant and responds to the child's perception of these needs.

established in the context of a particular affective connotation." If the predominant self-object affect unit evoked by the child is negative (aggressive or guilt ridden), then a likely consequence for the parent is diminished self-esteem accompanied by a sense of narcissistic injury. From a classical psychoanalytic standpoint, mood states that impair the mother's capacity to experience herself as a good and loving person (e.g., anger, repulsion, ambivalence, guilt, feeling burdened) unleash critical superego attitudes that can be seriously disruptive to idealized internal standards. Up to this point, I have stressed what the mother brings to the parenting role by way of her own history of unresolved maturational needs, internalized self-object relationships, and projective trends. What I would like to concentrate on, however, is the fundamental issue of whether the mother can consistently deal with the child as a real and separate object with actual properties of its own versus being preoccupied with restoring her own devalued self by reconciling disturbing self-object representations with the ego ideal.

Winnicott (1965) gives the following illustration.

> "Usually the mother of an infant has live internal objects, and the infant fits into the mother's preconception of a live child. Normally the mother is not depressed or depressive. In certain cases, however, the mother's central internal object is dead at the critical time in her child's early infancy, and her mood is one of depression. Here the infant has to fit in with a role of dead object, or else has to be lively to counteract the mother's preconception with the idea of the child's deadness. Here the opposite for the liveliness of the infant is an antilife factor derived from the mother's depression. The task of the infant in such a case is to be alive and to look alive and to communicate being alive (p. 191).

If the mother is unable to elicit this reassuring communication from her child, she feels depressed and perceives the child as depriving her of enjoyment. In an earlier article written in 1947, entitled "Hate in the countertransference," Winnicott discusses the pathological environment provided by parents who are very intolerant of the hateful aspects of their ambivalence toward their children. In order to reconcile ambivalences and create harmony between conflictual internal objects, the child is viewed as a part object whose function is to protect or supplement that which is lacking in the parent. In effect, the child is misidentified, encouraged, and manipulated so as to perpetuate the parental self-image of adequacy, love, and decency. "If only you could be different (sex, intelligence, temperament, achievement, interests, appearance), then it would be so much easier to care for you (which would make me feel like a better person)." Child rearing is a torture test for the parent with low self-regard. Even the best equipped adult is, at times, overwhelmed, perplexed, and disgusted with the responsibilities of being a parent. The likelihood of repeated narcissistic anxiety is ever present and the child is seen as a threat to personal preoccupation.

If we shift our focus now to the analytic setting, we recognize that a primary function of the therapeutic environment is to provide an atmosphere that can help to reverse deeply embedded disturbances in the relationship between the patient's self and his internal objects (Giovacchini, 1977). The analyst's capacity to permit the patient to continue projecting introjects through the transference without contamination by the analyst's personal anxiety or value judgements is essential if reinternalization of a higher level of ego organization is to occur (Zetzel, 1970). Many workers (Boyer, 1967; Winnicott, 1954) have referred to this issue in terms of the protective climate of the analytic hour; constant reliability, intrinsic support, and the structuralizing potential of interpretation seem to lend themselves to therapeutic regression. By participating in the patient's system without getting caught up in it, the analyst helps to reconstruct the traumatic past by not repeating it.

All of us know, however, that the classical model of analytic neutrality and "evenly hovering attention" is easier said than done. McLaughlin (1978) has touched upon some of the realistic problems and personal sacrifices in being an analyst that are not often considered in the literature.

"Not much is written about occupational hazards of analytic
work, but they are real, nevertheless, and are an additional
burden. First of all, there is the necessity to work essentially in
isolation. The demands of privacy and confidentiality are
powerful ones and challenge the personal and professional integrity of each of us; though the group superego and ego
ideal offer support as well as some fear of censure, it is the individual analyst who is ultimately responsible for his own conduct and his care of his analvsands. That so few fail to meet
these responsibilities is remarkable (p. 15).

The cumulative effect of working alone, the inevitable
postponement of results, having to constantly live with uncertainty and critically question one's intuition, and the draining
continuous exposure to stormy emotions and great emotional
pain frequently leads to temporary periods of emotional
numbness and periodic bouts with depressions. In the face of
these massive assaults on his self-esteem and extended ego
identity, there is a seductive appeal to illusions of gratification of grandiose narcissistic fantasies. Either through identification with powerful charismatic leaders or becoming
enamored of faddist movements (e.g., Gestalt, primal
therapy, encounter groups), individual analysts are tempted
to unite the ego and the ego ideal by seeking the comfort of a
group (Chasseguet-Smirgel, 1976). The constant and intense
interaction with patients employing primitive defense
systems, insatiable infantile demands, and archaic
transference projections has the potential for creating uncomfortable tension states, which can then become a
breeding ground for countertransference reactions. It is suggested that the interface between the ego ideal of the
psychoanalyst and the patient's unmet infantile needs and
consequent projective identifications are the most crucial
arena for therapeutic misalliances.

Since analysts, like most individuals, measure the fulfillment of their ego ideals through their successes or failures in
their work, it is imperative that the analyst clarify for himself
his personal definition and expectations in facing therapeutic
tasks, and crystallize the nature of his ego-ideal system so as

to anticipate its intrusion within the analytic field. In Freud's early work on the origins of the ego ideal, he saw it principally as a return to a state of primary union with the mother, a narcissistic phase where he was his own ideal (1914). In his *New Introductory Lectures* Freud (1933) revised his thinking and described the ego ideal as "the precipitant of the old picture of the parents, the expression of admiration for the perfection which the child then attributed to them." This oedipal level compensates for preoedipal disappointments in the parents and drives man toward a completed genitality. Through identification with the genital father, a powerful, admired, and loved individual, a reunion with the primal mother can be reestablished, and a state of primary narcissism can be achieved. Peter Blos (1975), Hartmann and Lowenstein (1962), and Esman (1971) have similarly emphasized the developmental vicissitudes of the ego ideal and the natural thrust toward a maturational ideal. The reorganization, growth and solidification of the ego ideal takes from infancy to adulthood. "We can trace a continuous adaptation of its basic function to the increasingly complex system by which the self measures itself, as it progresses along the developmental lines" (Blos, 1975). This developmental shift is from a preoedipal ideal reflecting drive-gratifying wishes of aggrandizement, in the direction of a more phallic-oedipal support of sublimatory efforts encompassing progressively mature standards. Jacobsen (1964) states that this transition is "in fact, the final stages in the development of the ego ideal that demonstrates beautifully the hierarchical reorganization and final integration of different earlier and later value concepts, arising from both systems (ego and superego) in a new and coherent structure and functional unit." Joseph (1978), in summarizing this developmental point of view, brings us closer to the unique pitfalls of the analytic role. In describing the ego ideal as a regulator of self-esteem, Joseph indicates that it has taught perfection, reflecting its earliest origins, as well as striving constantly toward unattainable achievements which betray its later origins. "Its structuralization and formation are much affected by the various developmental vicissitudes that beset psychic development over the course of time from birth to maturity, and often its form and content are determined by the outcomes of conflicts, relationships, vicissitudes of instinctual forces and object relationships, interacting together" (Joseph, 1978, p. 382).

The primitive unconscious acting-out of the analyst's ego ideal expresses itself through the wish for fast cure, a surrendering of resistances, perfect understanding, Messianic identifications, and a recreation of the idealized couple (e.g., a positive transference-positive countertransference pairing). The mature ego ideal modifies these unattainable standards and substitutes more realistic goals. Value concepts such as truthfulness, integrity, commitment, interest, and hard work make the achievement of therapeutic goals feasible. Nunburg (1932) and Kohut (1966) have further suggested that the qualities that are necessary to continue persisting in the face of frustration involves a labor of love, caring, concern, and involvement drawing their energies from the lost omnipotent parents who were so loved and admired in early childhood, and who aroused remembered feelings of gratitude and appreciation. The mature structuralized independent ego ideal manifests itself then as a striving for excellence as opposed to perfection, and an interest in growth and improvement rather than grandiose self-fulfillment. It has been suggested that the responsible analyst must be particularly alert for those characteristic conflicts narcissistic fantasies, and identifications that are activated by imposed transferential roles and treatment impasses.

Let us now turn to those impingements on the mature structure of the analyst that threaten his stability and raise a great likelihood of countertransference reactions.

1. The patient attempts to place the analyst into a state of dependence upon the patient (Widlocher, 1978). The analyst's independent existence is reinforced by the very presence of the ego ideal. The more the analyst is his own judge and regulates his own self-esteem, the more his narcissism is protected against the patient's criticisms. Certain

patients see the analyst's ego ideal as a rival for who is loved the most, the patient (child) or the analytic (parental) narcissistic ideal. Many negative therapeutic reactions can be conceptualized as examples of the patient attempting to control the analyst by undermining his confidence, thereby making him susceptible to the patient's influence. Conversely, patients can defensively idealize the analyst to satisfy their own ego ideals. If these positive resistances are not analyzed because the analyst's narcissism needs this stroking, the fiction of a good analytic hour (which revives memories of the happy family) interferes with diligent attending to relevant phenomena.

2. It has already been noted that it is important for the analyst to be able to accept in a transitory way the bad roles ascribed to him by the patient's projective identifications. This empathic tolerance of anxiety, without a countertendency to apply pathological defenses and iatrogenic defenses is a cornerstone for finding a correct perspective for interpretation. The analyst's response to being a repository for the patient's superego demands can pertain to the prevailing treatment dynamics and the patient's readiness to understand the intervention. It is only possible however for the analyst's choice of response possibilities to be dictated by an unconscious need to repair his own self-image. The need to reconcile intrasystemic value conflicts is particularly evident when transference attitudes of the patient evoke categorical imperative superego conflicts in the analyst. I should always understand what is taking place; I should not be angry, greedy, jealous, upset, selfish; I should always care and always feel hopeful; I should not be bored or look frustrated; I should never reveal despair or a sense of hopelessness; I should always be in control.

3. Patients with defective egos usually require years of treatment, often with no obvious gains for a long time and with very little gratitude. The analyst who has an over-cathected need for goal direction and an achievement orientation will find it very difficult to be content with laying back and allow for the slow and subtle development of complex

processes. The jaded analyst can be inclined to introduce reflexive formulas that are carry-overs from work with previous patients and which do not directly bear on the unfolding processes in the here and now. Pressure on the patient to perform and make progress can often be traced back to the analyst's narcissistic need to feel giving and experience his inner contents as good and substantial.

4. There is a significant (and exasperating) time lag between the analyst's intellectual grasp of patient dynamics and emotional insights on the part of the patient. The anxiety tolerance required in many such cases is more than the analyst can bear. Some analysts tend to identify with patients' resistance and introject a sense of passivity. To counteract a feeling of paralysis and deadness, these analysts become overactive and interpretive and unconsciously set the pace of each session. Instead of understanding these inner reactions as possibly representing projections of roles forced in the patient earlier in their lives, the analyst may feel compelled to fortify his own narcissistic need for potency and aliveness.

5. Many patients with borderline, schizoid, and narcissistic disorders behave as if the analyst does not exist. If in the face of this denial of significance, the analyst finds it necessary to frequently affirm his own significance and importance in the patient's life, a dependent role is fashioned for the patient. Such operations only serve to fulfill these patients' worst separation fears, leading to an exacerbation of symptoms and further acting out.

6. The analyst's interpretive activity, which is his stock and trade, is frequently viewed by patients as though it is interrupting their experiencing of affects. At the same time, patients complain of feeling deprived and suffering and demand that we do more for them. Analytic impotence, a resultant of anger and reaction formations against anger, is a frequent occurrence. If the analyst remains confused about what is expected of him and through this field dependence is ripe for manipulation by the patient, then the patient can be misidentified as a depressing, accusatory internal object.

CLINICAL VIGNETTES

Case 1

Martha came to treatment for an obsessive insecurity and agitated depression regarding her nine-year-old son. Whenever the boy seemed the slightest bit unhappy or was temporarily left out of his play group, Martha became ruminative, alarmed, and felt compelled to intervene. This ever-hovering, engulfing attitude preoccupied the patient, culminating in a near phobic response concerning the child's welfare. After about 15 sessions the analyst's interpretations regarding Martha's overidentification with her son in terms of her own experiences with an intrusive mother, seemed to provide considerable relief. When the analyst attempted to draw Martha into a deeper exploration of herself as an individual, however, the patient construed this to mean that her original concern was no longer considered important. Her attempts to cooperate with the analyst's interests were soon revealed to be shallow, half-hearted, and ultimately, to be passive resistive. When this was pointed out, the patient for a time became very confused and disorganized. She could not longer return to her previous position of concern over her son's problems nor could she actively involve herself in a sharpened examination of herself as an individual (aside from her relationship with the son).

Martha's paralysis can be explained on the basis of the fundamental conflict between loss of self (minimizing continued anxiety regarding the son to please the analyst) versus loss of the love object (reaffirming the persistence of her phobic concern regarding her son and disagreeing with analyst's priorities). Within the context of this chapter, however, I would like to return to a very basic issue. What is transpiring within the analyst that threatens Martha to the extent that she is almost willing to surrender her alarm at the continued presence of her phobic attachment to the son? If Martha is misperceiving the analyst's heightened interest in herself as an individual as reflecting a negation of the significance of her anxious concern regarding her son, this opens the way for a transference interpretation. But what if, as is so often the case, the analyst's focus is determined by an intolerance for being besieged by Martha's suffering? What if the analyst's endurance for being in the presence of severe identificatory pain ignites his own identification sensitivities? Under these circumstances, can the attempt at cognitive anchoring (with the focus on Martha), represent a blessed escape from the fearful impotence at not being able to provide relief for a person in agony?

Case 2

Mrs. H. was a harried, disorganized and rather martyrish woman whose life seemed to consist exclusively of mini-crises. She characterized her husband as a distant, unsympathetic man who subjected her to his terrible temper if he did not get his way. Her interpersonal problems were acted out in the analytic situation by her frequently making the analyst feel as though he was not as caring and loving as he should be. Early in treatment, Mrs. H. invited the analyst to a party and was turned down. She brought in cookies that she had baked and was politely refused. She often tried to change the appointment time on the basis of difficulty in getting babysitters, conflicts with her work schedule, and general inconvenience. After showing considerable flexibility early on, the analyst refused to accommodate her any further. Interpretations suggesting that her husband might be reacting negatively because she could be disregarding his feeling, were met by such demonstrations of hurt and defensiveness ("I love him — I'd never do anything like that to him") that the analyst was made to seem like a heel for even suggesting that the patient was capable of an unkind act.

Giovacchini (1977) has indicated that patients who threaten the analyst's identity by making functional aspects of the analyst's identity sense inoperative, evoke powerful countertransferential reactions. In this case, frustration of the patient's wish for gratification through compliance and pity met with strong reactions designed to induce guilt. The success of these maneuvers can be measured by the fact that the analyst became gun shy at confronting the patient regarding her own selfishness, was reluctant to make reasonable demands on the patient, and often felt as though he was humoring her. The anger and resulting compensatory guilt soon made each session an unpleasant experience. The analyst terminated this misalliance by suspending treatment, leaving the patient with the illusion that she was alright. This fiasco was complicated when the husband came for treatment and a coalition quickly developed between the analyst and the husband regarding Mrs. H.'s castrating, manipulative, and immature manner.

Complications in this case arose when the analyst surrendered his analytic stance in the service of being reciprocally loving and giving. If the patient, despite all the hardships in her life and everything she had to put up with, could still manage to be thoughtful and considerate, and motivated enough to come for therapy that she could ill afford and look so sincere and conscientious in this endeavor, the analyst in his role of setting limits, trying to understand and not taking sides, slowly came to regard himself as cold, heartless, and petty. The analyst's incapacity to deal with the transference projections had the predictable effect of causing him to dissolve a relationship that damaged essential aspects of his self-esteem.

SUMMARY AND CONCLUSION

If we take into consideration the unspoken needs that most analysts share in common, it is not difficult to comprehend why severely disturbed patients frequently upend our sense of well being. Among the implicit assumptions that most analysts work with is (1) that he is engaged in a meaningful encounter, (2) that he is making an impact, that he has some influence, (3) that his interpretations make sense, (4) that he can be helpful, and (5) that there is hope and that his efforts will be rewarded by change. Taken as a whole, these propositions normally sustain us in our work and enable us to be involved and interested despite painfully slow progress and seemingly endless resistance. But (1) what if the patient fears being understood out of concern that his individuality will be taken away, (2) what if the patient tends to deny and minimize the importance of the analyst and to reject his influence, (3) what if the patient never or rarely acknowledges that anything transpiring is in the mainstream of what he is experiencing, (4) what if change involving taking of responsibility and initiative, is resented by the patient, even if it would benefit him, and (5) finally, what if many forms that resistance takes in the new types of patients that are being seen today (e.g., borderline, schizoid, narcissistic character) go unrecognized and lead to frustrating transference-countertransference stalemates?

Ralph Greenson quite aptly calls psychoanalysis "That impossible profession." The theme of this chapter, however, is that despite their personal doubts, frustration, despair, and disillusionments, individual clinicians are capable of reaching a relatively mature and realistic hopefulness about the therapeutic endeavor. As the analytic literature continues to indicate that the real relationship existing between patient and analyst is at the heart of the truly therapeutic encounter, analysts are beginning to more courageously examine their own personal experiences, attitudes, and involvements. Erwin Singer, for example, writes of the analyst's anxiety in exposing his inner nature to his patients' judgements. In a later chapter on the need for supervision, it is stressed that it is important for the analyst not only to keep abreast of his countertransference potentials, but also to honestly consider those values and expectations that can seriously warp the treatment process. This ingredient, the full human availability of the analyst's self, is a missing resource that goes far beyond technical expertise and theoretical constructs.

REFERENCES

Benjamin, J.B. The innate and the experiential in child development. In: H. Brosin (Ed.), *Lectures on experimental psychiatry.* Pittsburgh: University of Pittsburgh Press, 1961, pp. 19-42.

Blos, P. Geneaology of the ego ideal. *Psychoanalytical Studies of the Child,* 1975, *29,* 116-139.

Boyer, L.B. Psychoanalytic treatment of characterological and schizophrenic disorders. In: L.B. Boyer and P.L. Giovacchini (Eds.), New York: Aronson, 1967.

Chassegeut-Smirgel, J. Some thoughts on the ego ideal. *Psychoanalytical Quarterly,* (1976), *45,* 345-373.

Epstein, L. (1977). The Therapeutic Function of Hate in the Countertransference. Contemporary Psychoanalysis, *13,* 442-469.

Erikson, E. (1959) Identity and the Life Cycle. Psychology Issues I.

Esman, A.H. (1971). Consolidation of the Ego Ideal in Contemporary Adolescent Psychosocial Processes *2,* 47-54.

Feiner, A. (1977). Countertransference and the Anxiety of Influence. Contemporary Psychoanalysis, *13,* 1-16.

Freud, S. On narcissism: An introduction (1914). *Standard Edition, 14.* London: Hogarth Press, 1953.

Freud, S. New Introductory Lectures in Psychoanalysis (1933). *Standard Edition, 20,* 179-258. London: Hogarth Press, 1953.

Giovacchini, P. Various aspects of the analytic process. In: *Tactics and techniques in psychoanalytic therapy—Countertransference.* Vol. II. New York: Jason Aronson, 1978.

Greenson, R. (1967). The Technique and Practice of Psychoanalysis. New York: International Universities Press.

Guntrip, H. (1971). Psychoanalytic Theory, Therapy and the Self. New York: International Universities Press.

Hartmann, H. and Lowenstein, R.M. (1967). Notes in the Superego. Psychoanalytic Study of the Child, 17.

Jacobson, E. (1964). The Self and the Object World. New York: International Universities Press.

Joseph. E. The ego ideal of the psychoanalyst. *International Journal of Psycho-Analysis,* 1978, *59,* 377-385.

Kernberg, O. (1975). Borderline Conditions and Pathological Narcissism. New York: Jason Aronson.

Kohut, H. Forms and transformations of narcissism. *Journal of the American Psychoanalytical Association,* 1966, *14,* 243-272.

Langs, R. (1976). The Bipersonal Field. New York: Jason Aronson.

Little, M., & Florsheim, A. Early mothering care and borderline psychotic states. In: P. Giovacchini (Ed.), *Tactics and techniques in psychoanalytic psychotherapy.* New York: Science House, 1972, pp. 310-336.

McLaughlin, F. (1978). Some perspectives on psychoanalysis today.

Journal of the American Psychoanalytical Association, 1978, *26,* 3-20.

Mahler, M. *On human symbiosis and the vicissitudes of individuation.* New York: International Universities Press, 1968.

May, R. *The meaning of anxiety.* New York: Norton, 1951.

Miller, D. The study of social relationships: Situation, identity, and social interaction. In: *Psychology: A study of science.* Vol. 31. New York: McGraw-Hill, 1959, pp. 639-737.

Nunburg, H. *Principles of psychoanalysis.* New York: International University Press, 1932.

Racher, H. (1968) Transference and Countertransference. New York: International Universities Press.

Searles, H. *Collected papers on schizophrenic and related subjects.* New York: International University Press, 1965.

Searles, H. (1975) The Patient as Therapist in Tactics and Techniques in Psychoanalytic Treatment-Countertransference Aspects, ed. by Giovacchini. New York: Jason Aronson Press.

Singer, E. (1971) The Patient Aids the Analyst: Some Clinical and Theoretical Observations, pp. 56-68 in In the Name of Life— Essays in Honor of Eric Fromm, ed. by Landis, B. and Tauber, E.S. New York, Holt, Rinehart, Winston.

Sullivan, H.S. *Interpersonal theory of psychiatry.* New York: Norton, 1953.

Widlocher, D. The ego ideal of the psychoanalyst. *International Journal of Psycho-Analysis,* 1978, *59,* 387-390.

Winnicott, D.W. Metapsychological and clinical aspects of regression within the psychoanalytical set-up (1954). In: *Collected Papers.* New York: Basic Books, 1968.

Winnicott, D.W. (1947) Hate in the Countertransference. International Journal of Psychoanalysis, *30,* 69-75.

Winnicott, D.W. The theory of the parent-infant relationship. In: *The maturational processes and the facilitating environment.* New York: International Universities Press, 1965.

Zetzel, E. Anxiety and the capacity to bear it. *International Journal of Psychoanalysis,* 1949, *30,* 1-12.

Zetzel, E. The concept of transference. In: *The capacity for emotional growth.* New York: International Universities Press, 1970.

Chapter 6

MENDING AFFECTIVE SPLITS
THROUGH THE USE OF PROJECTIVE
AND COUNTERPROJECTIVE
IDENTIFICATION PROCESSES
Ted Saretsky, Ph.D.

In 1946, Melanie Klein described the mechanism of projective identification in her paper "Some notes on schizoid mechanisms." With the introduction of this concept, psychoanalysts were offered a unique opportunity to explore heretofore hidden aspects of the therapeutic interchange, particularly with regard to psychotic transference phenomena. According to Klein, projective identification consists of an omnipotent fantasy that unwanted parts of the personality can be split, projected and controlled in the external object into which they have been projected. As a result of this process, the patient is able to induce different roles, affects and fantasies in the analyst who unconsciously feels himself "carried along" to play and experience them (Grinberg, 1957).

Grinberg (1979) distinguishes two contrasting consequences of this arousal in the analyst:

[a] In one, the analyst is the active subject of the patient's introjective and projective mechanisms. The analyst selectively

introjects the different aspects of the patient's verbal and non-verbal material. The analyst works through and assimilates the identifications resulting from the identification of the patient's inner world. The analyst reprojects the results of this assimilation by means of interpretations. [b] on the other hand, the analyst can also be the "passive object" of the patient's projections and introjections. Two further situations may develop: [1] the analyst's emotional response may be due to his own conflicts, reactivated by the patient's conflicting material [2] the emotional response can be a reaction to the patient's projections.

Grinberg suggests that the particular intensity of patients' projective identifications are usually related to traumatic infantile experiences. If the analyst fails to meet such violent projections in a normal way (e.g., properly integrating the projected material), the stage is set for the interruption of communicative flow. The analyst, by assimilating and acting as if he had actually acquired parts of what was projected onto him, no longer feels like his own self and finds himself being transformed into the object which the patient unconsciously wanted him to be. The patient's contribution to these strange manifestations in the analyst is of central significance to this chapter. It is proposed that the analyst's specific response to projective identifications, what Grinberg (1962) has termed "projective counteridentification," is a potentially disruptive influence but that it can also be turned to therapeutic advantage.

Racker (1960), in a detailed analysis of different types of identifications of the analyst with parts of the patient, spoke about "complementary identifications." As a result of the identification of the analyst with internal objects of the patient, the analyst begins to experience them as his own. If this activation is as a result of the analyst's own anxieties in relation to conflict with his internal objects, we can classify this response as representative of countertransference. If on the other hand, the analyst is primarily provoked into passively experiencing a predetermined emotional response as a result of feelings coming from the patient, this process falls under the heading of "projective counteridentification." The specific reaction of the analyst is significantly colored by the way the patient forces into the analyst his projective identifications. In a sense, the analyst is influenced to act or feel in accordance with an introjected superego that commands him to experience the role functions and associated affects unconsciously desired from him by the patient.

The analyst's conscious awareness of his usual disposition is of utmost significance here. When the analyst becomes uncomfortably aware that the therapeutic field is being contaminated by the recurrence and intensity of unfamiliar attitudes and affects emerging from within, he can be alerted to pay careful attention to particular projective-counter-projective processes operating in the immediate adaptive context. In most instances, an examination of the manifest and latent issues and conflicts being presented by the patient will be functionally related to the unconscious and preconscious arousals that the analyst can monitor as being operative within himself. In some case, the analyst's preoccupation is due to an emphatic identification with corresponding psychological parts of the patient (his id with the patient's id; his ego with the patient's ego). On reflection, the analyst may recognize this tendency as sometimes reflecting a positive countertransference. This awareness in itself is helpful in clarifying temporary treatment impasses due to the analyst's blind spots as a function of oversympathetic identifications. In other instances, the analyst either comes to be identified with how the patient felt in relation to significant authority figures of the past or assumed the feeling state of authority figures in the past, or of dealing in the present with the patient. If and when these unconscious fantasies, role inductions, and affective states are illuminated and formulated within the framework of the adaptive context that stimulates the patient's projective identification processes, the analyst will have access to a whole new dimension of understanding of subtle dynamics operative in the patient's past life. The analyst's full investigation and understanding of these complicated mechanics will enable him to shed important light on symbolic aspects of the shifting regressive transference reactions. The creative use of this tool, through reflection on identificatory and counteridentificatory processes, can assist the analyst in advantageously tapping in to his own inner experiencing for clues to the many obscure seemingly inexplicable treatment difficulties.

For the remainder of this chapter, I will provide some clinical vignettes that will illustrate how the analyst can frame mutative interventions by capitalizing on this phenomenon. Before we turn to the case material, however, I would like to draw the reader's attention to some interesting developmental aspects of projective identification.

Melanie Klein understood projective instinctual identification as a function of normal development whereby early representations are projected into the object and then the object is introjected on the basis of the earlier projections (not so much on the basis of the actual environmental properties of the object). In the handling of this topic, Klein never raises the possibility that projective identification tendencies in the parent are functionally related to self-esteem regulation. From this latter standpoint, the parent attempts to reconcile opposing, contradictory self-representations by projecting onto the child, archaic, ego-alien aspects of the self. If the response that is forthcoming from the child is congruent with what the parent needs to fuse the ego-ideal with the superego and create a pleasant inner state, then the child will be perceived and related to as representing a good object. In a similar fashion, if parental feedback is optimal, the child can more harmoniously accommodate the parent's ongoing attitudes and rest relatively secure in the knowledge that what he needs and how he is, is pleasing and consistent with how he is viewed. The inextricable emotional interdependency that exists, each party finding themselves in achieving a stable sense of ego identity through the other, is an extremely important concept to understand, if we are going to fruitfully conceptualize the latter-day complexities of the analytic situation. In my opinion, Klein leads us astray by her primary interest in intrapsychic events, and her almost exclusive preoccupation with unfolding developmental processes, instinctually determined and relatively unaffected by the actual properties of the object. By emphasizing what is essentially a one-person model, I believe that Klein makes it extremely difficult for the clinician to understand the interpersonal basis for symptom development and exacerbation, the intensification of resistances, unpredictable regressive phenomena, and the emergence of primitive transference. Only by translating the encounter between mother and child as a dialectic within a temporarily closed, categorically imperative, life-or-death system of narcissistic interchange, can we even begin to set the stage for gaining perspective on certain enduring treatment mysteries (e.g., masochism, phobic reactions to autonomy; the fear of success and happiness; the inability to feel deeply).

In addressing themselves to this topic, Giovacchini (1975) and Searles (1976) have contended that the containing capacity of the object in detoxifying the bad inner contents that are projected upon them, are of major importance in improving on the ability of the projector to deal with these alien feelings. Implicit in this viewpoint is that both quantity and pathology of the projections are functionally related to their experiences in optimal neutralization by the receiving object. The life space between subject and object is most vulnerable to confusion, instability, and faulty communication when both participants are trapped in a delusional system whereby they are reacting to the induced results of their own projections rather than to the other.

Take the case of a mother with faulty feminine identifications who gives birth to a baby daughter. If the child is seen with loathing and disgust as a narcissistic extension of the mother's negative identity, then the daughter becomes a persecutory object. This could be as a result of unconscious guilt concerning the mother's own destructiveness now embodied in the "bad" child or that an ego extension has been endowed with all the bad qualities of the mother and is now seen as a source of threatening denigration ("What have I wrought.") If the child identifies with the mother by introjecting her as a persecutory object, the child may be filled with oral-sadistic rage at the mother's derisive attacks. In order for the mother to be retained as the good object, the child must experience her reactive rage as reflecting its own essential badness and the mother can be idealized. If the child goes on to develop behavior problems, the mother's disappointment in her daughter can be rationalized ("I would love you if only you weren't . . .") and the child's righteous outrage can be denied ("My mother is good to me despite the fact that I'm such a problem"). Since introjection and projection interact from the beginning of life, it should not surprise us to see the same problems develop in the treatment situation. In both early development and analytic work, the defensive denial of the real qualities of the self and the object creates a perceptual arrest whereby significant aspects of the "representational world" (Sandler & Rosenblatt, 1962) are altered and important distinctions between self-object configurations are blurred and distorted.

It is important to make distinct diagnostic judgements in these instances where pathological introjective and projective identification tendencies are rampant. Defensive "ridding" of bad psychic contents across self-object boundaries requires that a minimum of self-object differentiation has already been achieved (Stolorow & Lachmann, 1977). This process stands in contrast to other instances where self-object confusion is rooted in a regression to an early symbiotic stage characterized by an inability to adequately distinguish between self and object images. As we shall see in the case material that follows, our technical approach should rest on a clear determination of whether there are developmental deficiencies in self-object boundary maintenance. "As with projection and incorporation, it should be stressed that splitting, as a defense actively employed by the ego to ward off instinctual conflict, comes into play only after a minimum of integration of oppositely cathected object (and self-) images has been accomplished through ego development. A defensive split into parts requires a prior integration of a whole" (Pruyser, 1975, p. 24). Again, our therapeutic approach to unintegrated representations will depend upon "whether they are regarded as resulting from defensive splitting or as reflecting an arrest in ego development at an early prestage of splitting characterized by an inability to integrate contrasting images." (Stolorow & Lachmann, 1977, p. 97).

Two alternative treatment intervention models emerge based on the accumulated clinical evidence:

1. Those instances in which contradictory all-good and all-bad object images are adhesively attached to two separate external objects (e.g., split transference) and are likely to come from defensive splitting which seems to ward off ambivalent conflicts. The cost of the ego being protected from experiencing primitive diffuse anxiety is an impairment in the ability to synthesize. Psychoanalytic treatment goals progress toward repairing what has been separated by this split. Through the working-through process, the patient is helped to tolerate the coexistence of aggressive and libidinal feelings toward the same object. This accomplishment goes hand-in-hand with a gradual reduction in the denial of the emotional connection between different ego states.

2. On the other hand, fluid, stormy, chaotic alternations of contradictory emotions in connection with the same external object are more likely to reflect an arrest in ego development at a prestage of splitting characterized by an impaired ability to bring together aggressively and libidinally determined self- and object-images. This chronic tendency to eruptions of primitive affective states, when occurring within the therapeutic setting, interferes with the proper blending of intellectual and emotional aspects of emerging material. Bibring (1941) has discussed emotionality in the service of the defensive function of preventing an understanding of mental conflict. "Affectualization" was characterized by Bibring as the overemphasis and excessive use of the emotional aspects of issues in order to avoid a rational examination and appreciation of them. "Feeling is unconsciously intensified for purposes of defense" (p. 64). Healthy abreaction occurs when the ego is not overwhelmed by emotions but retains an observational and integrative function. If the patient himself can form a sustained connection between the emotions and idea-

tional association, then we may assume that his ego is sufficiently differentiated to sustain readily available secondary process thinking (Volkan, 1976). If the patient lacks this capacity, then the resulting "emotional flooding" can only be viewed as a screen, a sort of counterphobic acting-out, to cut down on the threat of loss of control when the patient cannot successfully externalize "all-bad" self- and object-representation (Spitz, 1961). What is observed clinically is a sort of symbolic replay of primal affects. Spitz (1966) has stated, "affect colors perception, it makes perception important or unimportant . . . . Ultimately affects determine the relation between perception and cognition" (p. 85).

In these cases, the analyst must resort to tactics and strategies that enable the ego to control emotions by in some way helping the patient to better utilize the signal qualities of his affects (Spitz, 1961). That is, instead of dramatizing his feelings in an uncontrollable fashion, the patient must be assisted to identify his feelings, give a name to them, ask himself what the feeling is trying to tell him, question himself about what is causing the feeling, reflect awhile on what he wants to accomplish with the discharge of the feeling, and think in terms of what best serves his own needs and purposes, action or restraint. This focus is designed to continuously reemphasize the distinctions between self and object. The locus of the patient's feelings is placed squarely within himself. The weakening of boundaries by the revival of the transference of early ego states, is challenged by the analyst. The analyst, by resisting the patient's attempts to mirror his own impulses in the person of the analyst and thereby lose himself in a narcissistic merger, focuses attention on the patient's developmentally determined self-object confusion. The analyst's major thrust here is to repeatedly meet the patient's phase-appropriate need to achieve a more adequate self-object differentiation by systematically interpreting defensive projections. By subjecting fantasies to systematic interpretation, the analyst serves as a pregenital parent, an auxiliary ego. He offers his own unified perceptions as models for organization and internalization, in an attempt to assist the patient's arrested ego in the task of integration. The most important treatment approach in these cases is to avoid getting caught up in the quagmire of idealized or rageful content. Rather the analyst should attempt to convey to the patient an empathic understanding of the intense, alternating, contradictory feelings that the patient is subject to and to help him to understand this as an explanation for why he suffers from such a frightening loss of continuity and imminent disintegration. Hopefully over a period of time, the articulation and compassionate translation of these disruptive inner experiences, can provide the patient with a model for understanding and synthesizing various self- and object-representations and their associated affects.

The case illustrations that follow are intended to highlight certain components of the analytic situation as well as certain aspects of the analyst's approach, that can be especially useful in facilitating growth and maturation in patients suffering from structural conflict and arrests in ego development.

CASE 1

Working Through Emotional Numbness

A 28-year-old woman had come to the analyst three years earlier, never having gone on a date, completely lacking in sexual experience, and generally regarding men as dirty and disgusting. Paul McCartney of the Beatles singing group was the one exception. M. idolized him, followed his career with great interest, identified closely with the various romances in his life, found him sexy and exciting, and was forever lamenting the breakup of the Beatles and nostalgically prayed that they would someday get together again. Melanie Klein (1946) describes the individual's efforts to escape from persecutors by fleeing to internal idealized objects. "As a result, the ego may be felt to be entirely subservient to and dependent on the internal object—only a shell feeling that the ego has no life and no value of its own" (p. 9). When the ego serves it's good internal objects excessively, they are felt as a source of danger to the self and come close to exerting a persecutory influence. This is particularly true if the ego is compulsively subordinated to the preservation of the good internal object. Identification with the unassimilated idealized object requires splitting processes in the ego so that part of the ego can simultaneously deal with internal persecutors. Klein describes how pervasive aplitting results in the feeling that the ego is in bits.

M. had obsessed about Paul McCartney throughout the course of treatment but also returned to issues surrounding an experience that she had at a concert that she attended when she was a teenager. "I was screaming hysterically like everyone else around me. Suddenly, he walked toward my end of the arena and looked my way. I climbed up on a seat. My wig fell off. Do you think he saw me? Do you think I'll ever meet him?" The deep significance of these questions only came into focus very slowly, and gained special meaning during the session to be described below. In the course of repeatedly recounting this incident, M. was struggling to convey to the analyst a horrible realization. Her hysterical carrying on at the concert for her idol, was a sham. She was acting out a feeling similar to everyone around her but she was actually feeling nothing. The wig falling off symbolically represented the unmasking of her disguise—emotional/ability concealing a terrible void. On another level, it also seemed to be an unconscious recognition of the fragility of her ego structure, reflected in the feeling that she was falling apart if her idealization could not be supported by the appropriate accompanying affect. In normal development, this state of depersonalization is overcome by gratifications from the external good object. The patient's comments to the effect of, "Do you think he noticed me?" reflect a breakdown in the splitting defense and a crushing disillusionment of the straining idealizations. With no reality feedback or genuine enthusiasm to support her alleged blissful fantasy, the patient's ego stability is severely jeopardized. Ironically, this potentially catastrophic happening is the result of a number of growthful forces operating in M. Her pathological ego balance is disturbed principally because there is a more realistic awareness of the presence or absence of affects appropriate to the reality valence of objects. Accompanying the deidealization of Paul McCartney, M. starts to get in touch with and begins to acknowledge the hostilities and dangers of the external world. This more objective decoding of the distorted mythology of a pathological family environment that was formerly regarded as exclusively loving and desirable, paves the way for ambivalence. If the world can be seen in a mixed light (loving and hating, often from the same object), then there can be a greater acceptance and stabilization of ambivalent inner states. The interplay between projection and introjection is tamed by the fact that sadistic projections are reduced and what is reintrojected no longer seems quite as dangerous. In its place, the patient is placed in a new situation which is still very difficult, namely, coping with infantilizing, destructive, double-binding parents. As the analysis helps the patient to finally come to grips with and assimilate internal objects, the patient no longer feels so controlled by internal objects. M. begins to function on a very different developmental level when she takes on the final tasks of treatment—learning how to cope with truly controlling people, coming to respect the value and advantages of autonomy, and spotting characteristic tendencies on her part to sabotage efforts of the ego in the interests of sustaining pathological dependency gratifications.

The session to be described begins with a familiar theme. M. pressures the analyst to write a book about Paul McCartney. This insistent plea had been repeated many times in the preceding months. In this particular session, the analyst stated, "I have very little interest in Paul McCartney except as he has to do with you. You're the one who has the real interest. Why choose me to express your feelings? Why not do it yourself if you really feel so strongly about it?" In making this comment, the analyst refused to accept the notion that there was something wrong with him for lacking interest in this topic. The responsibility and basis for whatever feelings existed was placed within the patient. What follows is a verbatim transcript of the patient's attempts to come to terms with this confrontation.

1. M: "I can't feel at great depth. I try to dig deep, I even invent stories to evoke feelings. To feel I'm real, I feel I'm a shallow person. I feel other people care more. Are concerned more. Most of the time I'm not capable of deep emotions. About Paul McCartney I feel I should be feeling even more; it's not enough. That there's something underneath. I wish I could tell Paul McCartney "I like you but please forgive me if it isn't enough. Don't feel bad about it. I really do love you but it's blocked off.""

1. Analyst: "You have guilt feelings toward him."

2. M: "Too superficial. It's like an insult; you're not being true, honest, real."

2. Analyst: "But what makes you feel it's not enough?"
[M.'s disturbance here is on two levels: The admission and upset that she does not have access to certain feelings, and the resultant guilt that she feels that she's not experiencing more in regard to a love object.]

3. M: "The people in my family . . . my grandmother's always crying; bursting into tears, but then shuts it off like a faucet. Is she really feeling something? She could win the Academy Award. At the slightest provocation, the tears flow and it's all false. The people in my family, I don't know what they feel or whether they're doing it for themselves."

3. Analyst: "What's your feelings in reaction?"
[Here the patient begins to recognize that her emotional shallowness mirrors significant objects in her environment. She questions the authenticity and sincerity of what she has been exposed to and expected to live up to. The self-serving

aspect of the object is brought into view.]

4. M: "I expect myself to be so self-sacrificing. It's not even normal. I feel it in depth for every single person. Such a peak of emotion for every human being. St. Bernadette. I'm not G-d! My mother thinks she's so good, she's so good."

4. Analyst: "If your mother sees herself as so good, you seem to feel bad if you can't be so good to her."

[The patient sees that her empathic response, her oversensitivity to the needs of others is predicated on a model of unrealistic self-sacrifice that may even have a selfish basis to it. In the past, the image of the mother has been well insulated and only the father had been subject to criticism. Interventions 2, 3, and 4 are designed to get M. to attend more to her own feelings as distinct from others. In the process I am attempting to get her to reject the projective identification of other members of the family that induce her to feel unloving and ungrateful. At the same time, the goal is to softly dissolve over-romanticized notions of the happy family.]

5. M: "I am not her. I'm a different person. So nice (sarcastically); nobody's that nice."

5. Analyst: "Maybe they're not so nice, as genuine as they represent."

6. M: "They're very selfish. A lot of the reason why she has to be this good is that she wants to be the best. She wants to get the goodies back. She wants people to like her—she's no saint."

6. Analyst: "When she makes it seem that she never does a thing for herself you must feel you have to be as good as that. If you fall short, you feel that your feelings don't run as deep."

[This comment was intended to make M. aware that in part, her feelings seemed shallow only when compared with a

false standard. In addition, I am leading up to a consideration of the possibility that M.'s reactive anger blocks off a
deepening of affect. My hypothesis is that the anxiety that
has previously interfered with the anger and the unconscious
anger that had short-circuited the flow of positive affect
culminates in a sense of emotional emptiness.]

7. M: "There's a great deal of positive feelings that are
blocked off. I feel very empty most of the time. I want to express myself to get those feelings out."

7. Analyst: "If you keep talking about it, maybe it will
happen."

8. M: "It's like having a lump in your throat; like something in
your eye. I feel sick."

8. Analyst: "If you're trying to be as good as your mother
the saint but you can't be, part of you is going to be squeez-
ing to be like her; part resenting it. The false effort together
with the resentment blocks off the real feelings. I can understand why you feel so bad."

9. M.: "Do you think I have resentment against the
Beatles?"

9. Analyst: "For what?" (Analyst sneezes.)
[In fact, the Beatles represented an oasis in the desert for
M. They were the one most prominent phenomenon during
her adolescence that made her feel most normal. Her interest
in them was similar to that of many of the girls that she
looked up to and admired. The only drawback, and this was
an important one, was the absence of something inside of her
that she imagined should accompany such an interest. (Plus
the absence of real nurturing figures in her environment.) The
patient's question ("Do you think I have resentment against
the Beatles?") possibly signifies her dawning awareness and
frustration at being cut off from deeper emotions by the in-

ternal pressure to fictionalize and exaggerate what she actually felt. (Symbolic idealized parent figures).]

10. M: "Oy vay. (Analyst sneezes several times more.)

11. M: "Oy oy oy. (Patient is screaming hysterically.) You got a cold?" (False excitement.)

11. Analyst: "Resentment for what?"
[M.'s overdramatic display of excitement in concern for my sneeze is in keeping with the prevailing theme of the session thus far. Her hysterical carrying on is a caricature of maternal suffering. M.'s strained effort only succeeds in revealing the difficulty she has in connecting the degree and appropriateness of feelings with the external event.]

12. M: "They wouldn't consider me much of a person. You're not cool enough. They'd want me to have a more mature attitude, to be more liberated."
[A continuation of the dissolution of idealizing attitudes. There is an accentuation here of previous beliefs that in order to be part of a loving partnership M. must live according to the other person's expectations.]

12. M: "I wouldn't be up to par and then I would resent them. And I would resent them if I can't be part of their lives. If I met Paul McCartney, I wouldn't be the kind of person that he'd be interested in anyway; when I was fifteen, I had acne and everything, he would never have wanted to have anything to do with me."

12. Analyst: "After you've made them so important to you, you'd be so unaccepted by them."

13. M: "It makes me feel what the hell am I. What kind of fool am I to love somebody who has no concern for me. Am I crazy; I love somebody who hates me? I'm so alien to everything they believe in. I put so much energy into other

people who don't reciprocate."

13. Analyst: "A person like yourself could pursue an impossible dream and wonder whether you'd ever be good enough to approach their standards. You don't even think about what you'd expect from them.

[Her growing resentment helps her to recognize the self-exploitative aspects of living for the object. The issue of separation begins to get raised.]

14. M: "I always have to mold to everyone else. I can't say 'You can respect me for being different from you; still being a separate person.' I just don't think I'm good enough. I wonder whether I could ever get married and maintain a relationship. I also have resentment toward the Beatles' cause they broke up. They haven't got concern for their fans: so many people have asked them to please get together. Compose a few songs. Make an album. And they refuse repeatedly. You wonder where the great concern ever was. They couldn't give a shit. I used to think there was some concern and they did care."

14. Analyst: "You've devoted a lot to your family. You've been a good daughter. You've tried hard to help your family, and yet you need certain things from them and the family is so inconsiderate. They nudge you, they pick on you—it's not fair."

[Perhaps too hastily, I tried to link the metaphor of the Beatles to the family turmoil in M.'s life. Mother and father never got along. The father's identity as a man—sexual, a substantial wage earner, a person to be respected and depended upon—was never validated by the mother. Mother was depressed by her lack of satisfaction in the marriage. She saw herself trapped in an insufferable situation with an infantile, weak husband for whom she felt only contempt and repugnance. M.'s role was to attempt to bring cohesion into this chaotic structure by entering into a seductive alliance with the father (permitting herself to be the receptacle for the father's immature sexual displacements) and by offering solace and companionship to the mother. Her contributions in the form of allowing herself to be designated as the family scapegoat ("The crazy one.") was to lend strength and support to the parents' lack of maturity by bringing them together in common concern over her.]

15. M: "I was thinking of something you said, and I was very annoyed at you. I was talking about moving out and you were saying, 'You think you really want to do it, do you think you can really handle it? You know if you engage a lawyer to fight a case for you and the lawyer asks you to get up on the stand in your own defense and make a case against yourself . . . ' if my own analyst tells me I can't move out. I need my privacy."

15. Analyst: "I disappointed you."
[M. raises an interesting point here. In the previous session I had cautioned her against making any precipitous move for fear that she might not be ready for such a decision. This overprotective attitude was triggered, however, by the anxiety the patient had expressed in anticipating such a momentous decision. In effect, the patient had reenacted in the transference a typical family scenario. The parents' controlling, possessive attitude (e.g., "You should never leave us—no man is good enough for you.") is successfully masked by the patient's previous object dependency (e.g., they do her shopping, choose her clothes, pay her bills, decide on her friends). The hidden agenda here is that M. was fearful that she was disappointing the analyst by not separating from the parents more rapidly. By drawing the analyst into a fight where he assumed the role of being the controlling object, M. tries to circumvent her own anxiety about being independent from the analyst (e.g., the pace that she's moving at) and from the parents. At this point it begins to dawn on the analyst that some of the issues revolving around Paul McCartney might pertain to M.'s evolving transferential response to the analyst. As M. uses her identification with the

analyst's values to separate from the parents, she begins to realize that she can lose herself in the good object (the analyst, Paul McCartney). The fear that she will have to be something other than what she actually is with the analyst (or Paul McCartney) creates a new, potentially more easily identifiable source of anxiety.]

16. M: "I feel like I'm spinning my wheels. I'm trying to call group tours to England; they just don't have them for 7 days. Only for 21 days. Can you believe it? [manifests a good deal of anxiety and disturbance] I can't get out of the house, I can't get out of this prison. And now, of course, I will not go anywhere—and Barbara will not go anywhere. Her mother. She's nuts. She goes everywhere with her mother. A woman of that age. I want to be self-reliant but I'm not being allowed to. I'm getting older and I don't see how I'm going to handle relationships with men. Even if someone approached me, I wouldn't be able to handle it. When the hell will I be able to move out!

16. Analyst: "When you talk about the reasons for why you doubt that you'd be able to get along with men I wonder whether you have the same notion about men as you mentioned regarding your mother and the Beatles? That you have some fanciful notion about how good you have to be and it makes you very, very nervous. You don't think anybody can be that good. I wonder why you think you have to be that good."

Barbara is a person whom the patient spoke about going on a trip with. After years of being terrified about doing virtually nothing independent, the patient plans a trip to England. The overambitious nature of the trip foredooms its fruition. In reality, the patient was motivated to experiment with taking the first vacation in life away from her parents. By going over her head, she masochistically sabotages her plans and also ensures an inability to separate. Thus Barbara's dependent attachment to her mother is a symbolic derivative of the patient's symbiotic entrapment. The patient cannot take responsibility for her inability to break away and so she externalizes the blame by acting as though she were controlled ("I'm not being allowed to be self-reliant."). Once again, I get the impression that the patient is introjecting disappointments that she fears the analyst holds toward her because of her slow progress, procrastination in moving out, and not being more independent. The options she narrows herself down to are:

1. To live up to impossible standards (reflecting her conception of what the analyst-parent desires) that would make her acceptable.

2. To become an aggressively demanding object, someone who is helplessly dependent and must be catered to like a baby.

The latter ploy projects the impossible to achieve role onto the analyst and is intended to coerce him to assume a fantastic, unwelcomed responsibility (predicting into the future, making grandiose promises, taking charge of the patient's life). The ongoing unconscious process that seems to underly much of the patient's productions in this session reflect her continued hopeful but frustrated attempts to be a member of an idealized family. The vulnerable-child part of them, having experienced the significant adults as being incapable of sustaining the idyllic wish, has compensated by adopting what may be called a messianic role. In order to rescue the fantasy and deny the crushing reality of the failure of infantile omnipotence in the face of pathological environmental circumstances, M. has taken on the sacrificial god-like burden of being responsible for her family's welfare and emotional pain. If love is absent, she assumes there is something missing in her; if anger is felt, she has a conviction that this unappealing emotion is coming from within; if disappointment is felt, then she must be the source of disappointment. This magical role is depressing and masochistic at best; when dissociated affects come to the fore and must be reconciled, M. is driven into magic. The beginning of a breakthrough in this session can be attributed to numerous factors in the working-through process. Most relevant to the present purposes, however, is the patient's transferential attempts to projectively place the analyst into two roles that are actually located within the patient:

1. The grandiose responsibility of preserving harmony by being perfect to compensate for the shortcomings of others (e.g., the analyst should write the Beatle book if the patient cannot; the analyst should promise the patient a rosy future if she is unwilling or unable to take the necessary steps herself; the analyst should not sneeze if it makes the patient too upset).

2. Identifying the analyst as the punitive superego. The catastrophic anticipation that M. will lose her place in an idealized coupling if she falls short of omnipotent standards causes her to denigrate herself in a very primitive way (see comment 12). This criticality is externalized so that the analyst is identified as the source of impossible demands.

It is through the continued monitoring of the projective-introjective cycle that clear, strong boundaries are established and structuralization is achieved. The analyst's handling of what is projected onto him in the transference, his careful attention to whether the patient is introjecting what the analyst is actually feeling and intending, and connecting all of this with intra-psychic events, constitutes the heart of treatment progress with developmentally arrested individuals.

CASE 2

Forgiveness

A patient originally came to treatment for her teenage daughter who was acting out against a symbiotic possessiveness. When the mother became the identified patient, her affective reactions to object relations in her own life were revealed to be filled with great neediness and powerful resentments. The patient's mother had abandoned the father to run away with a nephew 15 years her junior when the patient was 16. The patient was unsuccessful in her attempt to adjust to living with mother and her new love. Despite the fact that the lover was provocative and seductive, the mother took the position that the patient should be able to get along without causing trouble. The patient returned to live with the father, who resented her because she was a reminder of the humiliation that he had suffered. Through the years, the patient's older siblings whose suffering was considerably less because they were already grown up and out of the house, gave her little support if she complained about her mother or father. If the patient expressed anger toward the father to the mother, the mother, who had herself hurt the father enormously through the acting-out of her own anger, told the patient that "Your father loves you very much. You have to be understanding."

This dynamic of guilt-induced understanding succeeded by exaggerated rageful reactions, recurred in the contemporary setting after a year of treatment. The patient was very friendly with R. and her husband, with whom she sought to find a business to go into partnership with together. When R. came up with some potential ventures, the patient became frightened and backed off. Finally, R. went into business with another partner. The patient was furious, but when R. invited her to come to work for her, she went along to "prove that she held no hard feelings and so as not to ruin the friendship." All of this is backdrop to the session to be focused on. The patient was progressively getting in touch with the unbearable circumstances of being a dutiful employee for someone whom she felt betrayed her. She had announced to the friend that she was leaving and the friend tried to appeal to her loyalty and sense of fairness (leaving R. in the lurch). The patient then proceeded to discuss an incident in a college English class. She had cried and run out of the class while the instructor was interpreting King Lear's attempts to reconcile with his daughter. The teacher never inquired about what was upsetting the patient. Later in the term, the instructor indirectly tried to broach the incident and the patient failed to pick up on what the instructor was hinting at. In the session, the patient berated herself for being naive and stupid for not realizing what the teacher was talking about.

What is most prominent in this woman's history is the tendency for significant objects in her life to project their own negative affects upon her and then try to cure these alien feelings within the patient. The mother, who was party to a destructive splintering of the family unit and abandonment of her husband, appeals to the patient to be a loving daughter and to "try harder to be a good mother." The father, who because of his weakness and passivity was not able to adequately contend with his wife, attacked the patient for her continued depression and bad moods. The other siblings who were not similarly affected, and chose not to deal with the upheaval in their family, made the patient feel selfish, bad, and crazy for continuing to hold a grudge. The patient's inclination to guiltily absorb the blame (identify with the projections) have an interesting revival in treatment. When the issue came up about the friend deciding without her to purchase a business, the analyst was drawn into the role of taming the patient's fury. In a sense, the analyst was transferentially assuming a similar posture as previous pathological introjects who demanded maturity, understanding, and fairmindedness of the patient.

The analyst's guilt-provoking identification with the patient's primitive superego, is important to trace. The patient, through masochistic emphasis on her own failures and fearfulness in following through on previous business partnerships together with her continually berating herself for having such irrational reactions because of her own procrastination, had succeeded in convincing the analyst that her anger had to be softened in order to relax her. Failing to adequately support the patient's hurt and disappointment even in the face of the patient's conscious dismissal of these feelings as unfair, seriously impaired the patient's capacity to accept and work through significant dissociated self-object-affective units from the past.

The reference to the English instructor who was uncomfortable and therefore circumstantial in dealing with the patient's emotional distress is thus seen as an unconscious communication to the analyst to rectify his previous stance. The patient is consistent in assuming the responsibility in attacking herself for being stupid, thereby masochistically protecting the object from her anger. At the same time, however, she's informing the analyst of her deep pain and of her enduring but frustrated efforts to resolve her resentment so that she could feel good toward those she is close to. A pathological configuration becomes operative if the analyst, for unresolved reasons of his own, cannot tolerate the patient's continued hurt and resentments. If the analyst has not come to terms with ambivalence toward objects in his own life and has not maturely integrated resentments toward these objects, then there is a strong possibility for counterprojective tendencies to be injected into the therapeutic field. A key point of this chapter is that the analyst must continuously sort out, process, and differentiate between what is his and what belongs to the patient. If the analyst discovers himself, as in this case, treating certain constellations of feelings in such a way so as to strongly influence a patient's disposition toward these feelings, then he should be prepared to investigate his ego investment in fostering this line of thinking. Oftentimes, therapeutic errors can be reversed by using the patient's associations about derivative objects (e.g., the English instructor) to reevaluate previously maintained analytic positions. With this fresh outlook, the analyst was able to identify the patient's perception of him as a need-satisfying object who was most available when the patient was agreeable to compromise (e.g., quickly surrendering her bitterness in developing a reasonableness). These qualities of the analyst were predispositions that were triggered by the projective identification of object representations of the patient onto the analyst. Once the analyst put space between himself and the patient and could now observe that the patient was externalizing aspects of her internal object world onto him, managing these feelings in projective form and reintrojecting them, the analyst was able to restore a therapeutic frame where he could once again be supportive and remindful of the patient's prevailing ambivalences. In this case, unlike the work with the previous patient, the patient had already attained an ambivalent level of functioning, but strong guilt feelings interfered with a sustained, relaxed acceptance of this mental state. The therapeutic task here was to integrate the ego ideal with ambivalences and to gradually promote the belief that a solid reconciliation can only follow a greater acceptance and understanding of oneself.

NON-PATHOLOGICAL PROJECTIVE IDENTIFICATIONS
AND THE COALESCENCE OF SPLIT-OBJECTS

Winnicott (1965, p. 32) has suggested that the capacity to be securely independent depends on the existence of a good object in the psychic reality of the individual. Confidence about the present or future is contingent then on the sufficiency of internal relationships even in the temporary absence of external objects. The relative belief in a benign environment enables a maturity and frustration tolerance in the face of transitory states of change, anxiety, and uncertainty. Such an orientation allows for relative freedom from persecutory anxiety and, in more positive terms, "the good internal objects are available for projection at a suitable moment." All of this is predicated of course on the individual introjecting an ego-supportive environment which enables the courage of independence.

Winnicott's optimistic view of an individual's behavior when he is on good terms with his internal objects is closely related to the individual's achievement in harmonizing primitive splits, going beyond black and white discriminations, and establishing hierarchies of importance with such classifications (Volkan, 1976). In times of stress, the primitive splitting threatens once again but the patient's reinforced observing ego faculty allows him to put feelings in perspective within the context of the transference neurosis.

A clinical illustration of this phenomena in operation occurred when an analyst announced to his group that he was moving his practice. The change actually involved half an hour extra traveling time. The population of the group was comprised of people who had worked closely together for over three years, developed a strong sense of group unity and cohesiveness, and had experienced many personal and interpersonal gains by the participation in the group. At first, the analyst's announcement was met with accusations of disloyalty, abandonment, the breaking of an implicit contract, an act of selfishness, and lack of consideration and concern. As the analyst absorbed these attacks and answered them undefensively, the tide shifted to a greater interest in the analyst's realistic reasons for making a move. A third phase was the patients' shifting from benign and charitable understanding, to a continuation of their disturbance and an, anoyance, but now accompanied by a growing acceptance of the analyst's entitlement to make a change that was beneficial to him. A fascinating secondary phenomena at this juncture was that many unverbalized symbiotic contracts were opened up for discussion for the first time, only after the analyst "broke" his end of the bargain and acted independent of guilt, coercion, or the need to fulfill infantile omnipotent fantasies on the patient's behalf. Several of the patients reported experimental behavior that symbolically represented an affirmation that they too were free from a dependent, directed-by-others role. Over a three-month period of working this issue through, virtually the entire membership of the group raised their maturity level of responsibility taking and independent action to their furthest advance during the course of treatment.

If we examine the mutative impact of the potentially traumatic event of the lives of these people, we can draw several significant conclusions:

1. The analyst did not respond retributively of defensively. He did not discourage the flow of negative affect.

2. This holding environment allowed the understandable patient negativity to operate freely without it having to gain new virile forms in the need to defend the propriety of

righteous patient anger. Nor did the patients feel manipulated by seductive-analyst hurt, disillusionment ("How could you say such a thing to a good mother?"), or impatience. This easily could have caused a repression and shallow denial of spontaneous negative reactions.

3. Past history together with working on this current problem with the analyst seemed to fuse together in an ambivalent image of the analyst ("You've helped us—you have now upset us, but we still like you"). Correspondingly, the image of the patients that the analyst projects is "I've enjoyed working with you—I wish I didn't have to upset you, but I've reached a point where I have to make certain changes for myself—if you are upset, I think I can understand and live with that."

4. The severity of what both parties (patient and analyst) have to identify with in terms of the images that are projected onto them, is considerably reduced. Both parties manage to struggle with and overcome bad representations that are imposed upon them by either internal or external sources.

5. The analyst together with the group members use the mutual support system that has been built up and maintained to provide the patients with a sense that the presence of bad feelings does not have to spoil good ones. As the destructive qualities of the environment are slowly tamed by their combining with nurturing, loving qualities over a three-year period, the introjections that are assimilated become compatible with good self-and-object representations within. Once this is initiated, primitive splits are gradually mended and projective identification tendencies lose their pathological roots. A beneficial feedback cycle is set in motion since objects which are the containers for positive projections are more likely to regard the projector with a positive valence.

6. Again, it is important to emphasize to the reader the fundamental significance of the analyst's personality integration, particularly in dealing with stressful and threatening predicaments. Counterprojective tendencies in this case, if left unnoticed would have (a) grievously interfered with

negative projections (with their underlying narcissistic-grandiose base; e.g., you belong to me; you cannot do anything I don't want you to do), and (b) contaminated the voluntary and mature acceptance of painful frustration by possibly introducing obligatory, guilty elements ("what kind of person am I to complain to a person I should be so grateful to, like you").

I would like to close with a poem written by a schizophrenic patient who placed the complexities of the projective-counterprojective identification cycle in a simple perspective.

From Me To You.
I have a little symptom,
It does not go away.
I have a little symptom,
And I will make you pay.
It bothers me on trains
On public busses too,
And long as it keeps bothering me
I'll keep on bothering you.
I'll annoy you in the morning,
I'll annoy you every day.
I'll annoy you 'til my symptom
Has up and gone away.
And after all is said and done
And all annoying's through,
I wouldn't be at all surprised
That you'll have symptoms, too.

REFERENCES

Bibring, E. (1941). Mechanisms of Defense In P. Greenacre (ed.) Affective Disorders. New York: International Universities Press.

Giovacchini, P. (1975). *Tactics and Techniques in Psychoanalytic Treatment-Countertransference Aspects.* New York: Jason Aronson Press.

Grinberg, L. Perturbaciones en la interpretacion motivadas por la contraidentificacion proyectiva. *Revista de Pscoanalisis,* 1957, *14,* 23-30.

Grinberg, L. On a specific aspect of countertransference due to the tient's projective identification. *International Journal of Psycho-Analysis,* 1962, *43,* 436-440.

Grinberg, L. Countertransference and projective counteridentification. *Contemporary Psychoanalysis,* 1979, *40,* (2) 226-247.

Klein, M. Notes on some schizoid mechanisms. *International Journal of Psycho-Analysis,* 1946, *27,* 111-126.

Pruyser, P. What splits in "Splitting"? A scrutiny of the splitting in psychoanalysis and psychiatry. *Bulletin of the Menninger Clinic,* 1975, *39,* 1-46.

Racker, H. Estudios sobre Tecnica a Psicoanalitica. Buenos Aires: Ed. Paidos, 1960.

Sandler, J. & Rosenblatt, B. The concept of the representational world. *The Psychoanalytic Study of the Child,* 1962, *17,* 128-145.

Searles, H. (1976). Transitional phenomena and therapeutic symbiosis. *Countertransference.* New York: International Universities Press.

Spitz, R. Some early prototypes of ego defenses. *Journal of the American Psychiatric Association,* 1961, *9,* 626-651.

Spitz, R. Metapsychology and direct infant oberservation. In: R. Lowenstein, L. Newman, M. Schur, and A. Solnit (Eds.), New York: International Universities Press, 1966, pp. 123-151.

Stolorow, R., & Lachmann, M. The developmental prestages of defenses: Diagnostic and therapeutic implocations. *Psychoanalytic Review,* 1977, *46,* 73-302.

Volkan, V. *Primitive internalized object relations.* New York: International Universities Press, 1976.

Winnicott, D.W. *The maturational process and facilitating environment.* New York: International Universities Press, 1965.

Part II
Innovative Models for Intervention

The chapters in Part II address themselves to some parameters that have been introduced to reverse entrenched pathological processes. Viola Bernstein develops the theme that the group medium offers an unusual opportunity in working with primitive affects in unstructured patients. The interactional intensity of group is identified as the key for breaking through emotional inaccessibility and liberating frozen rage in a safe, nonretaliative setting. The carefully directed group is viewed as the treatment of choice for character problems who resist ameliorative efforts by devaluation, withdrawal, and the smoke screen of rageful affects. In this chapter Viola Furst Bernstein helps us to understand how patients who are not responsive to interpretations benefit from peer feedback and modification of omnipotent fantasies within the group setting. Saretsky's chapter on "The ambivalent search for object constancy" indicates that group is an excellent framework for working out vicissitudes of the rapprochement crisis. Saretsky suggests that group is a particularly valuable vehicle for illuminating separation anxieties, object fixations, and identity formation difficulties and the analyst's optimal contribution in facilitating these processes operates from Mahler's contention that the momentous accomplishment of object constancy is crucial for self-object differentiation. Saretsky presents a group in turmoil whereby individual transactions repeatedly revolve around conflicts between autonomy and symbiotic ties. The author helps us to see this phase in group life as representing something more than resistance and destructive acting-out; instead, we are reminded that this period is a necessary subphase in attaining a more substantial sense of self. June Bernstein in her chapter on "A modern approach to the management of treatment impasses," introduces us to the methodologies employed by Hyman Spotnitz and his colleagues. These paradigmatic techniques are designed to meet the needs of narcissistic patients who have little or no libido available for positive transferences. By fostering a negative transference where aggressive impulses are mobilized and worked through with an object who is perceived as being like the self, severe self-destructive, treatment-resistant defenses are softened. A preliminary framework is thereby established so that therapeutic communication continues on a more motivated, cooperative, and mature level. Finally, Normund Wong's chapter on "Combined treatment approaches with borderline and narcissistic patients" establishes a clear rationale for blending patients with different character styles together. The reciprocal advantages of group and individual treatment approaches with the same individual are illustrated by the very vivid clinical material.

Chapter 7

TOWARD A DEVELOPMENTAL
MODEL FOR GROUP AFFECTS
Viola Furst Bernstein, CSW

In recent years, we as clinicians have been faced with patients who do not fit Freud's descriptions of neurotic patients, and who do not respond to the classical treatment methods which he and his followers espoused, either in individual or group treatment. Such patients are often labelled borderline, character disorderes, or narcissistically disordered patients and a lot of attention is being paid to them because of the difficult treatment dilemmas they pose. One outstanding characteristic of these patients is their effective states. The predominance of rage reactions and other primitive feeling states which are easily evoked in them is characteristic of their general state of ego defectiveness. They present us with affect disorders as well as other symptoms. As our knowledge of psychic growth processes enlarges, especially in relation to the way the ego functions develop, there has been increased investigation into the role of affects as part of ego functioning.

Thinking about affects and drives in relation to other ego functions remains ambiguous and beclouded. Merton

Gill, the eminent psychoanalyst and theoretician, suggested in a *Panel on Affects* (1977) that we need two theories of affects in psychoanalysis; a metapsychology of biological, instinctual drive theory, and a clinical psychology of emotions and feelings. He suggested that there was confusion between the two aspects in Freud's economic theory of psychic energy. I am in agreement with Gill, and this discussion is concerned with the clinical psychological aspects of affects in groups.

Based on clinical data from groups and investigations by psychoanalysts reported in the literature, the thesis of this discussion is put forth that affects demonstrate a developmental pattern of their own, separate from other developments of ego functions. I propose that groups demonstrate developmental patterns of affects, and that the patterning differs among groups. It is, in other words, possible to diagnose the affective level upon which a group functions and arrive at a treatment paradigm suitable to the diagnostic assessment. In the course of demonstrating the foregoing, a distinction will be made between groups which function on a neurotic level, and groups which function on an earlier level, that is, developmentally arrested. Since neurotics have reached the oedipal level of development, an earlier level implies preoedipal development. Groups, like individuals, who function on a preoedipal level of development fall into the borderline, narcissistically disordered, or character-disordered disgnosis. We are, in a word, talking about people who have not developed the highly differentiated ego structures and superego structures of neurotics, but possess immature, somewhat undifferentiated egos and superegos. From a theoretical point of view, there has been a gradual evolution of thinking about how the ego structures come to exist.

Freud based his thinking about ego development on the dual drive theory of libidinal and aggressive drives which are innate in all of us. The drives or component instincts unfold in a given maturational sequence from the oral, anal, and phallic stages to the genital stage, connected with affects and feelings. When he connected psychic development or growth with biological drives, he implicitly evoked a maturational scheme. Maturational growth is defined as the ripening or unfolding of successive stages in an inborn sequence of events. He saw the ego as maturing out of the primordial id with which we are born. In 1939, Hartman, Kris, and Lowenstein noted that there were nondrive related activities of the ego; i.e., cognition, perception, and ideation, which, they felt, was possible because of neutralized energy in the ego. Thus was born the idea of autonomous ego functions. In proposing the existence of neutralized energy in the ego, they made the first step toward recognizing that ego functions may not all arise from the id, as Freud thought. Hartman, in 1939, went on to propose that growth processes of the ego had three aspects: congenital, maturational, and environmental. The congenital aspects were constitutional givens. The maturational aspects were rooted in biological sources from which there is an expected sequence of emerging functions leading to progressively differentiated structures. Environmental influences interacted with the congenital and maturational aspects. Hartman postulated that all three were involved in ego development. Affects are seen in the terms of this discussion as a function of the ego, in which the above-named aspects of growth are involved.

In 1960, Piaget, investigating the development of thinking in children, introduced the idea of developmental aspects of growth processes in the ego. He called them developmental schema, which he defined as the existence of inborn reflexes, innate dormant responses which depend on phase-appropriate stimulation from the environment in order to be activated. What he meant was that when a reflex is ready to be activated, and the mother stimulates the reflex in the infant, the infant's response is established as an internal structure, after repetition of the stimulus response pattern. Piaget traced the developmental patterns of cognition and perception in children. With the introduction of developmental schema existing in the ego, he moved Hartman's postulation of the environmental influences on ego growth to an interactive process between the infant and his environment, the mother. He removed cognition and perception from the drive or nondrive related framework that Freud and Hartman, et al. (1939) functioned in, and opened up a new area of knowledge and investigation.

Rene Spitz (1965) applied developmental thinking to object relations in infants, focusing on the affective component in their development. When he postulated the three psychic organizers which were indicators of developmental achievements by the infant, he saw them as affective in nature. The smiling response at three months, stranger anxiety at eight months, and the acquisition of speech at one year link the establishment of the first love object, the mother, with emotional responses activated by her and established in the infant. The use of speech as the emergence of symbolic function, used to communicate affects on a symbolic level, as well as overall communication on a symbolic level, is congruent with the developmental patterning of affects. Spitz was demonstrating a developmental patterning of ego functions in addition to object relations.

Margaret Mahler (1975) emphasized the importance of developmental processes in her work on the separation-individuation processes in children. As she described the growth of separation-individuation processes, she included the affective component of each subphase. She described the predominant mood accompanying each subphase, ranging from elation to depression, and shades in between. Feeling states became more complex and differentiated as separation-individuation progressed. Mahler was describing important ego structure-building activities which were developmental in nature, and included affects in the development.

Henry Krystal, in 1976, explicitly linked the development and modification of affects to the establishment of self and object representation. He saw a parallel between the development of the subjective world of self and object images and that of affects. He described affects as having a developmental pattern of their own, separate from other developmental patterns. Piaget (1968) was in agreement with him, in commenting that affects have a developmental pattern of their own which parallels that of cognition and perception.

Thus far, theoretical thinking about affects has been traced, beginning with Freud. Freud concentrated on the biological, drive oriented aspects of affects and their maturation. Hartman, in his exploration of ego development and psychic energy, delineated the differences between congenital, maturational, and environmental aspects of ego development. Piaget contributed to our knowledge of the development of some ego functions by defining developmental schema which consisted of inborn reflexes that depended on stimulation from the environment at the phase-appropriate time, in order to be activated and established as a structure and function of the ego. Spitz furthered our knowledge of the developmental aspects of ego functions through his investigation of the development of object relations in infants, using affective responses as indicators of certain developmental achievements related to object relations. Mahler and her associates furthered our knowledge of the developmental aspects of the establishment of the subjective world of self and object, with affective states being part of every subphase of the process of separation-individuation. Henry Krystal explicitly attended to the developmental aspects of affects, seeing them linked to the development of self and object representations and being parallel to but separate from such development. In that, he and Piaget were in agreement, with Piaget commenting on the parallel between affects and cognitive and perceptual developmental patterns.

Affects can be seen to include congenital, maturational, and developmental aspects. The congenital aspects are constitutional in nature, the instensity of the drives. The maturational aspects include instincts and drives and the sequential unfolding of the various stages of drive development. The developmental aspects of affects, or feelings, are the result of the interactive processes between mother and infant, which activate inborn responses. Feelings develop from primitive to mature, complex, and highly differentiated in the interactive processes of mother and infant.

Affects then, can be evoked by inner sensations, biological needs, and tension states. They may also be evoked by thoughts, images events, perceptions, and interactions. They never exist in a vacuum. They may frame an experience or be evoked by one. They lend a sense of reality to existence, a meaning to life, and an orientation in time and space. They are part of every moment, either conscious or unconscious. These functions of feelings contribute to other ego functions and are intertwined with all aspects of functioning on a human, intrapsychic and interpersonal level. We can now look at the developmental aspects of feelings as they are experienced and seen from infancy to adulthood.

Normal development of feelings means that the raw, simple, urgent drive-oriented feelings of the infant become complex and differentiated, increasingly independent of physical need states as he and his mother work and play with each other. The baby learns to use his feelings for information about himself and others, for judgment as to how to behave and what to do. He learns to use his feelings to orient himself in the world, to experience the reality of his existence, and that of others. As he grows up, he develops a wider range of feelings with shading, subtleties and nuances. From the early libidinal drive-oriented emotions he becomes capable of love, respect, gratitude, tenderness, and gentleness. From the early aggressive drive-oriented emotions, he becomes capable of anger, assertiveness, annoyance, irritation, and unhappiness. Global states of raw, primitive, drive-oriented emotions are rare. Responsiveness to ideals, ethics, and esthetics are established and enjoyed as sources of pleasure. The ability to empathize with others is an adult emotional state, as is the increasing use of humor about oneself and others. Self-regulation of feeling states which maintain the stability of the self-image and the positive-feeling tone is an adult attribute. Emotional flooding is not an issue or danger for the adult but is for the child.

The expression of feelings also undergoes change. Increasing ability to articulate one's feelings and use them for communication with others is one change. Along with it is a decrease in the use of somatic symptoms such as stomach aches to express emotions. Verbal expressions replace facial and body expressions of feelings. Infants use nonverbal communications of feelings exclusively, but as adulthood is approached there is a marked decrease in such forms of expression. The developmental aspect of feeling expression is clear if we think of it in relation to childhood states of development. The infant in distress is a red-faced, squalling baby whose hands and feet flail helplessly while it is emitting loud wails of grief. The toddler in distress cries or has a tantrum, throwing himself on the floor, kicking his heels, and pounding his fists while sobbing loudly. A latency age child cries, complains, whines, and nags, or becomes silent and withdrawn. In adolescence, where emotional turmoil is the rule rather than the exception, eruptions in anger, depressive states of poignant intensity, and a range of other intense feelings are familiar to all of us. There are adults who are children in disguise, infants, toddlers, latency aged, and adolescents. Looking at such adults we can see them react and express their feelings in ways which are similar to that of children of various ages.

What is being proposed is that there is a progression of feeling development from simple drive oriented urges and emotions to more finely differentiated complex feelings as the infant grows into adulthood. The intrapsychic functions of feelings have been stated as being for information about oneself and others, for judgment about behavior for oneself and others, for self-orientation in the world, for the establishment of an inner sense of reality as well as a sense of the reality of others. The expression of feelings has a developmental pattern which is shown by a progression from primary motoric discharge patterns in infants to increasing use of verbalization and decreasing use of somatic symptoms. This developmental pattern of expression can be seen as infants develop into toddlers, latency, adolescence, and finally adulthood. We find adults who show arrests in development of the feelings anywhere along the continuum.

It has been necessary to discuss affect development in terms of individual development, both intrapsychic and interpersonal aspects being included. The affective life of the psychoanalytic group is distinguished by its emphasis on the interpersonal functions and meanings of feelings, and by the group as a whole aspect of feelings. That is, groups tend to develop characteristic styles of functioning, which include affective functioning. It is the contension of this discussion that they fall into two categories of affective functioning, developmental arrest and psychic conflict. Following is a sample session of a group operating as developmentally arrested in feelings. There are six people in the group, four women and two men, ranging in age from 20 to 30. The session is one following Evan's telling the group he is gay.

> Adrienne began by saying she had tried to tell Evan she was sorry for what she said last week, and he replied, "shove it." She said that she was afraid of being a homosexual herself; she had a homosexual cousin who had visited her once, and she was so frightened of the woman that she could not sleep. She appealed to Evan for his reaction to her, asking him what he was feeling now about her; she did not want him to be angry with her because it made her feel bad. Evan remained stony, accused her of being a man-hater, and said that was her problem. He did not want to have anything to do with her and was certainly not going to tell her it was all right for her to feel the way she did. Chip sat by as the exchange proceeded, and when the therapist asked for his reaction, seeing how angry he looked, he burst out that Evan was provoking anger as before. With much heat and rage he began telling Evan how angry he made him, how he was sitting there like a judge and how furious he had been last week at his judgmental condemning attitude. Evan, still stony and white, said he was furious with Chip because he too was a homophobe, which enraged Chip some more. The two men looked as though they were squaring off for a fight, being flushed by now, angrily yelling names at each other. The group sat by in silence and the therapist intervened by commenting on how angry they both were, and how silent the group was. This was a momentary interruption, although the therapist hoped it would be a diversion, because Adrienne joined the fray by cursing Evan and calling him a fucking snob too good for the group. She said

she was fed up with trying to reach him, and he could go to hell for all she cared. Susan chimed in by repeating fucking snob and daring him to leave. The therapist said the group felt worried about finding out that Evan was gay, as he worried about telling them, and that they were protecting themselves from the worry by being angry. The therapist joked that gay was not happy for this group right now, and the group laughed out of proportion to the feeble joke. It did serve to calm and divert the group momentarily whereupon the therapist seized the moment to summarize some of the ideas and feelings expressed by the group. In Chip's individual session he thanked the therapist for intervening, saying he felt protected by the activity in a way he never felt in his family. His mother would sit passively by as he and his father quarreled heatedly and he became more and more frightened of his father's violence. Evan related the group reaction to his father beating him up while his mother tried to protect him without success. The group experience was different because the leader was effectively protective.

The raw feelings expressed in this group session were characteristic of the way they were in other sessions. The enormous threat posed by having a gay member in the group was dealt with by mobilizing aggression and directing it towards Evan. The possibility of emotional flooding was present, and the therapist acted twice to avert it, once by trying to contact the anxiety which was unsuccessful, and the second time by being more active and diverting attention to the cognitive activity of the summary. The real threat of physical violence was there, in view of the past experiences of the two men with their violent fathers.

The group is characterized by a great deal of nonverbal communication along with relatively primitive verbal communication. There is also a sense of narcissistic depletion or impoverishment, which is shown by chronically low levels of energy and general inactivity or passivity in their real lives. As young adults, they lack real goals or achievements, although they are intelligent. This group would be diagnosed as a borderline group, both in their emotional and ego development.

A sample session from a neurotic group which functions

on a relatively mature emotional level may serve to illustrate qualitative differences in affects.

> Dan said his mother had died and been buried by the family during the week. His father had telephoned him yesterday to tell him. He fell silent. Margo asked how he was feeling. After a time he said he did not know, it was mixed. He was glad she was finally dead, she had been sick for so long. John said he seemed sad. Dan said it was hard for him to be too sad, she had never been much of a mother to him, being in and out of mental hospitals most of his life. He had to help by taking care of his brothers and sisters. He resented it and her, but he felt sorry for her. June commented that he seemed stuck. She said maybe he needed to mourn with the group since his family was far away and he was alone. Dan began by remembering how pretty his mother had been when she was young. He had been her favorite and she always remembered his birthday, even when she was in the hospital. She had been very playful when he was young, and he recalled the fun he had with her. He began to weep as did several other members. The therapist asked Bud, who seemed tearful, if he was reminded of his mother's death. Bud responded by saying that he was like Dan in that he had had anger towards her initially but when that was over, he was able to feel how much he loved her. Each of the members remembered aloud the death of a parent, and talked about the feelings of loss, abandonment, pain, and anger when it happened. They knew what Dan was feeling, they felt that too. The group was swept together in common feelings, and at the end of the session there was an intense silent communion within the room.

In this group, feelings needed to be uncovered and explored because they were so mixed. Some of them were hidden and some were unconscious. As the members expressed their ambivalence toward the parent, they were able to experience stronger feelings for Dan and to articulate them. The range and subtlety of feelings expressed is characteristic of a neurotic group. The ability to mourn indicates a mature level of development. The way the group handled Dan's need to mourn with them was also adult. They actively identified with him and felt joined in a common experience, another developmental achievement. They had reciprocal relations in the group, yet another indication of mature development. Such a group would fall into the psychically conflicted range of development rather than developmental arrest. Diagnostically, one would find resistances and defenses against anxiety around intrapsychic conflict. One would expect to find some regressive affects as a defense against anxiety or unconscious conflicts. The diagnostic difference between the first and second group would be in the overall pattern of functioning. Neurotic groups maintain a relatively mature level of affective functioning most of the time, so that when primitive feelings emerge, they are regressive in nature rather than developmentally arrested. Overall ego strength in this group is relatively good and can be mobilized to deal with emotional regressions.

There is another category of primitive affects in groups which is evoked by uncovering traumatic material or revealing unconscious fantasies. They are different in that traumatic material will often lead to temporary regressive feeling states in otherwise healthy adults. Infantile fantasies accompanied by infantile feelings expose a pocket of material which has remained in its original state, split off from other development, and still in its primitive form. When the clinician comes upon such a fantasy, it usually stands out in contrast to other aspects of the patient's or group's functioning. It is a specific kind of developmental arrest in a specific area, and treatment techniques would be the the same as for the developmentally arrested group, for that material and time. Treatment techniques have to shift to accommodate the diagnostic assessment of the patient's needs at any given time, the patient being the individual or the group as a patient.

Here is an example of a group session in which an infantile fantasy emerged which was shared by the group.

Eve, an obese young woman, opened the session by talking about her difficulty in paying her fee for treatment. She described her feeling that she deserved to have treatment free because she needed it, and that she resented paying for it. Her feeling was picked up by Frank who said he not only felt that way sometimes, but also felt he deserved to have as much money as he needed to live luxuriously. Donna agreed, saying it was the feeling she had when she took clothing from department stores. Cynthia and John said they had the feeling that they were entitled to be rich and famous, but knew it was foolish. Eva said she did not know it was foolish, she did deserve to have the things she needed, other people had them, why not her? Eva had begun passing candy around when she listened to Frank, and most of the members were eating as they talked. There were resentful silences and simultaneously frightened and sheepish glances toward the therapist. Two people sat hugging themselves and Eva looked like a petulant baby. She said she really did believe what she was saying, and all agreed that they did too. They shared the thought that if only they knew the right word or behavior, they could have everything they wanted and deserved. The therapist verbalized for them the unspoken which was that they had gotten a cruel mommy instead of a good mommy who would give them what they wanted. It was the feeling of the group that the therapist was depriving them in some magical way of the good life, not just money. She had the secret, and if they knew the right button to press, they could make her give it to them.

In this session, there is the emergence of an infantile fantasy which is accompanied by infantile ways of expressing feelings as well as the feelings themselves. They are expressed in body language, feeding, and facial expressions. The verbal expression is also infantile, but not as regressed as the nonverbal expressions. The therapist joined the group in the regression with her use of infantile expressions and indicated empathic understanding of the narcissistic wounding they described. The underlying feelings of rage were explored after the group had been joined by the understanding of the therapist. If it had been seen as a conflictual problem, the rage would have been interpreted immediately, along with other defenses.

In individual treatment, an example of such a regression is an hour in which Mona described her husband's hovering over her as she ate, commenting on how, what, and when she ate in a manner which reminded her of her mother. As she described the childhood scenes with her mother, her voice became a little higher, words were enunciated in a baby-like way, and her facial expressions and gestures assumed the naivete of childhood. Such reliving of incidents often includes recapturing the expressions and feelings which accompany the situation.

I have described three group sessions, one illustrating developmental arrest, one psychic conflict, and one demonstrating the emergence of infantile fantasies accompanied by infantile feelings and expressions. A brief discussion of the basis for a diagnosis of developmental arrest or psychic conflict will serve to clarify the meaning of each category.

Humberto Nagera (1966) defined developmental conflicts as being conflicts between a child's drives and his environment. Anna Freud (1962) has described them as external conflicts, having the same meaning as Nagera's. Environmental interferences with developmental phases can result in developmental conflicts. The conflict between the child and his environment remains as a conflict, and one sees adults who display the same kind of developmental conflicts. This kind of conflict remains as part of the adult's character structure, never having been internalized or resolved, and is often called developmental arrest. Developmental arrest, in other words, means that the developmental stage of ego development has not been resolved enough to be internalized as part of the ego structure, but remains in its infantile, externalized form. With regard to affect development, internalized self-regulatory processes have not been achieved, so that emotional feelings and expressions exist in their infantile forms. For these adults, stimulation from the environment is both necessary and dangerous, leading as it does to impulsive, global reactions of primitive feelings which can evoke punitive reactions from the environment. In addition, they have defects in reality testing because they lack inner awareness and consciousness. Without external stimulation they feel empty and dead, or that they do not really exist. As they are dependent on external stimulation of feelings, their reactions are also immediately externalized, so that these people are in constant conflict with their environment, consequently experiencing the environment as dangerous. In summary, developmental conflicts which exist in adults take the form of developmental arrests in ego structuring, leading to externalization of affect and dependence on the environment for emotional stimulation.

In contrast, internal or neurotic conflicts are described by Nagera (1966) as resulting from "component instincts pushing for gratification and other aspects of the personality opposing such gratification." Neurotic conflicts are frequently remnants of developmental conflicts, in that all aspects have been internalized as part of the internal structure of the psyche.

The neurotic experiences conflict from within himself. He uses external stimulation in conjuction with internal regulatory processes, so that he can regulate his responses to environmental stimulation. The neurotic has achieved a complex structuring of the psychic apparatus, with ego functions differentiated and stable. When the neurotic is in conflict, he displays defenses against anxiety, resistances, and symptoms stemming from the anxiety related to the internal conflict. The neurotic has achieved complex, highly differentiated feelings which are in conflict with each other, and are often unconscious. Unlike the neurotic, the developmentally arrested person lives as though the external world were in some way a part of himself and uses the world as an extension of himself, a substitute for internal structuring. His demands are on the world primarily, whereas the neurotic experiences his demands as being on himself primarily.

In drawing the distinction between the externalizing of the developmentally arrested group and the inner conflicts of the neurotic group, I included the affects of the first as being raw and primitive. The more neurotic group experienced ambivalence as well as other complex feelings which they expressed verbally. There are treatment techniques specific to each diagnostic assessment which will be discussed.

For the developmentally arrested group, their developmental needs are the primary consideration in treatment. As babies grow through their experiences with their mothers, groups can grow through their experiences with the therapist and each other. The therapist of such a group is active. Because such a group has not developed internalized ways of coping with strong emotional states, the group can become overwhelmed or flooded. The therapist tests the emotional temperature constantly and keeps it at tolerable levels by interventions which are geared to the regulation of feelings. It is analogous to the mother of the infant who soothes her infant before he becomes overwhelmed. The therapist may need to help patients find words for their feelings when they are silent, because they have no words for such feelings. These patients have not had mothers who helped them verbalize their feelings in order to communicate with her and others. The therapist assumes this function until they are able to do it for themselves. It is a function of the toddler's mother. It is necessary to empathically verbalize and interpret patient or group feelings. Verbal reflecting of feelings helps the group feel understood and responded to. It lends reality to feelings, helping them with their deficits in reality awareness, a sense of their own reality. Because of the unresponsiveness of the early environment, these patients have an impaired sense of their own reality, a lack of consciousness of inner feelings. In addition, the experience of empathic understanding by the group and therapist enables such patients to form bonds with each other, the group, and the therapist. It is a step toward internalizing good mothering functions that they experience in the group. The therapist needs to actively interpret the underlying feelings as well as the defensive ones, in order to move the group from the rigid attitudes which characterize their emotional functioning. As the more vulnerable feelings emerge, are acknowledged, and accepted, the group begins to soften its stance and one sees the emergence of ambivalence and shades of gray in the emotional tones.

Verbalizing of nonverbal communications in the group is also very important. The original symbiotic tie with the mother eliminated the need for speech. Nonverbal communications are reflective of that symbiotic tie. Thus, verbalizing what is expressed through body language or facial expressions is helpful in dealing with such developmentally fixated expressions. In general, the developmental needs of the group are for emotional regulation, articulation, empathy, responsiveness, establishing group bonds, and communication with words. When the therapist meets these needs, the group can internalize those functions for themselves. It is essentially providing an environmental experience which encourages internalizations, identifications, and ultimately structure-building activities of the ego.

Progress in the group is toward the more neurotic range of functioning, with more inner conflicts being experienced. As conflict with the environment is moved to inner conflict, more inner discomfort and anxiety is experienced. The group begins to deal with issues of occupations, social adjustment, and relationships. These are higher-level issues which require assuming responsibility for oneself and one's behavior. Issues of individuation are implicit in such issues. There is often an increase in energy and more active involvements. The activities are self-improvement activities, in contrast to earlier solitary daydreaming. Things are not as simple as they used to be. The group is able to work on problems in sessions, and there is more direct and lively communication and interaction. It is a new developmental level for the group. Therapeutic interventions take on a more classical interpretive quality, and the therapist is much less active.

With a neurotic, conflicted group, the classical technique is used. The analysis of transference and resistance, both conscious and unconscious, is pursued using the group process. In the group, nonverbal communications are the result of repressed feelings, and they can be brought to consciousness via interpretations. The group has trouble expressing anger and other strong feelings, and needs help in doing so. Structual conflicts on an oedipal level can be brought out and resolved through analytic techniques.

It is true that groups fall into one or the other category of psychically conflicted or developmentally arrested. There is, however, no group which is always on the same level of emotional functioning. Themes appear which evoke higher-level responses in developmentally arrested groups and some which evoke regressive responses in neurotic groups. As we explore the subtleties of development of other ego functions, we can also explore the subtleties of emotional development, using treatment techniques which meet the needs of each group session. If we are aware of the emotional needs of the group as they change, we can diagnose and treat them appropriately. Thus far, I have described normal emotional development, developmental arrest in groups, structural conflict in groups, and treatment approaches for each diagnostic assessment. Treatment approaches for the developmentally arrested are geared toward structure building and internalizations, whereas for the neurotic or psychically conflicted group or patient, treatment is geared toward the analysis of transference and resistances. The question of how affects are related to other ego functions is interesting to consider both on a theoretical and clinical level.

If we consider the functions of affects in relation to cognition, we see that under the impact of strong feelings thinking processes slow up, become speeded up, or fail. These are experienced as racing thoughts, or blanking out, or painfully laborious thinking. Pseudostupidity is symptomatic of emotional stress. Children fail examinations if they are afraid. We forget things we know under stress. Affect may organize or disorganize cognition. Hartman's postulation of the existence of nondrive related ego activities, or neutralized energy available for ego activities has to be qualified to allow for the invasion by affects which are drive related.

Perception, the ego activity which is also a nondrive related function in Hartman's terms, is organized by affects also. The inner self and object images one has, along with the affective tone accompanying the images, serve to organize one's perception of the world, events, people, and things. An example would be Sharon who received a compliment in the afternoon which induced such good feeling that she felt thin and desirable afterward. That evening she played the best game of tennis she played all season. People in love see themselves in a positive way and the world looks rosy to them. Depression makes the world look gloomy and each event seen as confirming the reality of the bad feelings. Perception, an ego function, can be organized by affects, another ego function.

In the same vein, ego functions like reality testing and motor functions are organized by affects. Affects are unlike other ego functions in that they parallel and intertwine with all other ego functions, acting as organizers of other ego functions. It is in a sense a confirmation of Spitz's work on the psychic organizers because he too chose affective reponses as the organizers. Affects have a special place in the psychic functioning of groups and individuals.

SUMMARY

The fact that affects demonstrate a developmental pattern of their own, different from other ego functions, and yet intertwined with all other ego functions, has been discussed in relation to group affects. Developmental conflicts which result in developmental arrests in affects were demonstrated by examples of group sessions and treatment techniques were discussed which are specific for the developmentally arrested group. Groups functioning on a predominantly neurotic level demonstrate psychic conflict in their affective development and functioning and treatment techniques specific for those groups were described. The theoretical evolution from drive-oriented biological thinking to developmental schematic thinking about affects was traced beginning with Freud, and including Hartman, Spitz, Mahler, and Piaget. Henry Krystal, whose work is specifically about the developmental pattern of affects, was discussed.

The role of affects in relation to the ego functions of cognition and perception was also discussed in terms of affects acting as organizers for other ego functions.

BIBLIOGRAPHY

Arlow, J. Jerusalem Congress, Affects and the Psychoanalytic Situation, p. 161, International Journal of Psychoanalysis.

Foulkes, S.H., 1977, Notes on the Concept of Resonance in Group Therapy, 1977, An Overview, Lewis R. Wolberg & Marvin L. Aronson, Editors, pp. 52-68, Stratton Intercontinental Medical Book Corp.

Freud, S. 1923, The Ego and the Id, Standard Edition, 19:3-66 London, Hogarth Press, 1961

Freud, A., Assessment of childhood disturbances, *The Psychoanalytic Study of the Child*, 1962, *17*, 149-158.

Gedo & Goldberg, 1973, Models of the Mind, A Psychoanalytic Theory, U. of Chicago Press, Chicago & London, pp. 47-55.

Gill, Merton, 1977, Psychic Energy Reconsidered, JAPA pp. 581-598.

Green, Andre, Concepts of Affects, Jerusalem Congress, International Journal of Psychoanalysis, 1977, p. 150.

Hartmann, H. 1939, Ego Psychology and the Problem of Adaption. New York, International Universities Press.

Hartmann, H., Kris, E., Lowenstein, R., 1946. Comments on the Formation of Psychic Structure. Psychoanalytic Study of the Child, Vol. 2.

Jacobson, Edith, 1957, Normal and Pathological Moods, Psychoanalytic Study of the Child, Vol XII, 1957, pp. 83-95, Affects & Discharge Processes in: Drives, Affects & Behaviour, edited by R. Lowenstein, 1953, Int. U. Press, New York.

Joseph, Edward, Panel on Affects, Journal of American Psychoanalytic Assn., 1974, Vol. 22, p. 622, Int. Un. Press, New York.

Kernberg, Otto, Object Relations Theory and Clinical Psychoanalysis, 1976, Jason Aronson, New York, pp. 247-258.

Kohut, Heinz, The Analysis of the Self, Monograph Series of the Psychoanalytic Study of the Child, Int. Univ. Press, New York, p. 97.

Krystal, Henry, 1976, Affect Regression, Annual of Psychoanalysis, Vol. IV, Edited by Chicago Institute for Psychoanalysis, pp. 119-130. The Genetic Development of Affects and Affect Regression, 1974, Annual of Psychoanalysis, Vol. II, Int. Univ. Press, New York.

Lagache, Daniel, 1953, Behaviour and Psychic Experience in: Drives, Affects & Behaviour, edited by R. Lowenstein, Int. Univ. Press, N.Y., pp. 120-125.

Lewin, Bertram, Reflections in Affect in: Drives, Affects & Behaviour Edited by R. Lowenstein, Int. U. Press, New York, pp. 23-38.

Limantani, Adam, 1977, Affects and the Psychoanalytic Situation, Jerusalem Congress, International Journal of Psychoanalysis, pp. 171-183.

Mahler, M. The psychological birth of the human infant, Mahler, Pine. and Bergman (Eds.), New York: Basic Books, 1975.

Modell, Arnold, 1977, The Narcissistic Character & Disturbances in the Holding Environment, Presented at American Psychotherapy Seminar.

Peto, Andrew, 1967, On Affect Control, Psychoanalytic Study of the Child, Vol. XXII, Int. U. Press, New York, pp. 30-37.

Piaget, J. 1968, Six Psychological Studies. Vintage Books, New York, pp. 33-35.

Rappaport, David, 1951, Towards a Theory of Thinking, in Organization and Pathology of Thought, California Un. Press, p. 691

Schafer, Roy, 1964, The Clinical Analysis of Affects, JAPA, Vol. 12, #2, Int. U. Press, pp. 275-380.

Spitz, Rene, 1959, A Genic Field Theory of Ego Formation, The Freud Anniversary Lecture Series, New York Psychoanalytic Institute, Int. U. Press, pp. 31-83. 1963, The First Year of Life, A Psychoanalytic Study of Normal and Deviant Development of Object Relations, IUP, New York.

Spitz, R. The evolution of dialogue. Im: M. Schur (Ed.), *Drives, Affects and Behaviour*. Vol. 2. New York: International Universities Press, pp. 174-176.

Tedesco, Castelnuevo Pietro, 1974, Toward a Theory of Affects, Reporter on Panel in JAPA, Vol. 22, #3, pp. 612-625, Int. U. Press, N.Y.

Tolpin, Marian, 1971, On the Beginnings of a Cohesive Self, an Application of the Concept of Transmuting Internalization to the study of the transitional object and signal anxiety in Psychoanalytic Study of the Child, Vol. 26, Quadrangle Books, New York & Chicago, pp. 316-353.

*NAGERA, H. Early childhood disturbances: The infantile neurosis and the adulthood disturbances, International Universities Press, 1966, New York: pp. 39-64.

Wolff, Peter, H. 1967, Language Acquisition and Cognitive Considerations for a Psychoanalytic Theory of Language Acquisition in: Motives and Thought, Psychoanalytic Essays in Honor of David Rappaport, Edited by Robert Hold, IUP, New York, Vol. V, #2-3 Monograph 18/19.

Zetzel, Elizabeth R. 1953, Depression and the incapacity to bear it in: Drives, Affects & Behaviour, Vol. 2, edited by Max Schur, pp. 243-273.

Chapter 8

THE AMBIVALENT SEARCH FOR OBJECT CONSTANCY— THE RAPPROCHMENT CRISIS.
Ted Saretsky, Ph.D.

OBJECT CONSTANCY IN GROUP THERAPY

The group literature seems to be in general agreement that establishing a sense of group cohesiveness is essential for therapeutic change (Shellow, 1958; Taylor, 1958; Wolf, 1949). In keeping with this tradition various investigators have emphasized the necessity for establishing a common aim, a shared commitment and mutual involvement early in the history of the group. Cartwright (1951) has gone so far as to say that only distorted communication occurs if it is conceived as going from I to thou. Communication only works from one member of "us" to another. The particular significance and priority assigned to fostering group cohesiveness seems to be rooted in the philosophy that it is necessary to create a symbiotic union within the interpersonal context of group in order for healing processes to ultimately take over. As the therapist and the other patients slowly become identified as significant others, maladaptive transference potential within each individual becomes stimulated. As these nuclear conflicts are aroused by transactions, experiences, and events during the session, patients begin to reveal their repertoire of habitual solutions and defenses against stress.

Both social psychological studies and clinical experience suggest that under conditions of threat and resulting anxiety, the individual is likely to seek relief by rendering the environment "viable" (Freud, A., 1954; Khan, 1963, 1964). Within the group, patients attempt to change the current situation so that they can reduce anxiety to a more tolerable level. Stereotyped behavior, habits, identifications, transference projections, and introjections, communication patterns, character styles, and favorite roles are all unconsciously designed to induce others to respond in a predictable and familiar way.* The complex, interlocking vectors that emerge in group therapy reflect transference symbiosis. Patients who are susceptible to the projections assigned to them, tend to accommodate to the projections by finding a self-gratifying, complementary dyadic role. A whining, complaining woman will usually succeed in discovering someone who will reward her behavior with scolding and repugnance. A withdrawn man will manage to motivate someone else to try to impatiently break through his aloofness and then give up in frustration. Each of these patterns represent a repetition of pathological nuclear relationships in the past. Interestingly enough, the emergence of these reciprocal transference patterns within the group setting is the very vehicle through which a potentially therapeutic symbiosis can be attained (Searles, 1959). Epstein (1977) has described how the analytic relationship offers the therapist a unique opportunity to facilitate maturation and contribute to egobuilding internal structures by augmenting those roles where the primary family failed. The therapist's

---

*Maladaptive behavior (e.g., masochism, drug addiction) which on the surface is self-destructive and often invites hostility and rejection, can be explained on the basis of secondary gain and the avoidance of an even greater danger.

capacity to address himself to the highest adaptive level that the patient is functioning on, to identify and enourage the growth thrust and to promote autonomy, are vital factors in determining whether or not this "second chance" is an improvement over the first one.

Within the group psychotherapy setting, it is convenient to conceptualize diverse, contradictory, or meaningless aspects of group process in terms of an equilibrium model (Whitaker & Liebermann, 1964). The group situation at any given time can be understood in terms of forces in equilibrium, and individual patient's movements within the session can be seen as successive shifts in equilibrium. The capacity of the group to find means to reduce tension and to restore homeostasis is often pivotal in determining whether a group continues or disbands. Obviously certain methods of coping with group and individual anxieties are progressive and other means tend to fixate patients at early developmental levels. The major purpose of this chapter is to examine tension-reducing mechanisms operative during the middle stages of the working-through process. Picture a group where a majority of the members are in crossroad with regard to moving toward more adult, independent roles. Separation anxiety becomes of paramount concern. The group solution can take the form of collusive resistances, regressive tendencies, rebelliousness, or any of a number of ways, all unconsciously designed to invite the leader to adopt a parental position. The therapist's ability to be part of this primitive tension system and yet to be sufficiently autonomous so as not to yield to the easy temptation to find a constrictive solution, is vital. A conceptual tool that I have found to be extremely valuable in discriminating between destructive and constructive tension-reduction operations in group is the formulation of "object constancy."

The term, object constancy, as it is most commonly used, refers to the capacity to maintain object relatedness irrespective of frustration or satisfaction (Hartmann, 1964; McDevitt, 1975). The degree to which a relationship has relative autonomy from the fluctuations of need states is positively correlated with the security of object constancy (Masterson, 1976). The achievement of this capacity is based on early experience that continuously reassures the infant that the emotional accessibility of the mother figure will remain stable regardless of fluctuations in mood state in either infant or mother. This "good and stable" quality is associated with and probably dependent on the ability to evoke a memory image of the mother, whether she is there or not.

Mahler (1963, 1965), in her pioneering work on separation-individuation conflicts in normal development, indicates that from the 16th through the 18th month, the toddler is faced with a serious dilemma. He goes through a waxing and waning period whereby he realizes his power and ability to physically move away from the mother, while at the same time, he feels an increased need for mother to share with him every new experience. Mahler suggests that during the "rapprochement period," the competent mother provides sufficient encouragement for the progressive mastery of physical skills and greater independence while at the same time be available for the emotional refueling during moments of vulnerability and anxiety. If the maternal attitudes are unintegrated and operate on a pathological level, then we may expect that true internalization and identification processes are interfered with. In relation to "object constancy," counterphobic, impulse-ridden behavior that denies the need for (and very existence of) the mother can develop and clinging, phobic-avoidance mechanisms ("I can't do without mother") seem to predominate.

According to Mahler (1963) then, as acute organismic distress is aroused, the mothering pattern is called upon to contribute a particularly large portion of symbiotic help toward the maintenance of the infant's homeostasis.* Within

*Mahler calls the rapprochement crisis, "a period...during which the resolution of separateness is acute. The toddler's belief in his omnipotence is severely threatened and the environment is coerced as he tries to restore the status quo...the toddler wants to be united with, and at the same time, separate from mother. Temper tantrums, whining, sad moods, and intense separation reactions are at their height." (Mahler *et al.,* 1965, p. 169.)

the group setting, during the maturational crisis of the separation phase, patients seem to need a similar kind of reassurance that help is waiting if it is needed. During periods of extreme anxiety the therapist and fellow members are enlisted as auxiliary egos to overcome the fear of object loss. Successful reminders of the relative permanency of love objects seems to be necessary for new "states of self" to be experienced and experimented with. If the therapist and the group are up to satisfying these frustrated maturational needs, this seems to lay the necessary groundwork for a revitalization of an internal image of a good love object. The "carrying power" of this reliable support system can augment and encourage an interested but tentative ego in the direction of higher levels of functioning, exploration, and self-differentiation.

In the next section of this chapter, I would like to present process notes of a group in transition and turmoil. The group had been in existence for one and a half years and most of the members were just beginning to experiment with breaking some of their infantile ties and functioning more independently. The ambivalence with which the members treat this new-found power suggests that it is just this success that heightens their awareness of dependent attachments toward others. The separation anxiety leads each member to seek security by reaffirming his relations with a significant object (or objects). In another context (adolescence), Peter Blos (1962) called this process a constant cycle of object relinquishment and object finding.

The backdrop to this session was one or more patients being absent for several consecutive sessions. In addition, the therapist had returned from his summer vacation to discover that he had lost a number of his patients.

Someone had asked about Roberta, a patient who was absent the previous week and had not yet arrived. "Is she coming?" Therapist, "I don't know." "Well, is she sick?" Therapist, "She says she is" (slightly sarcastically).

Elements of tension creep into the opening moments of

the group. Collective unconscious fantasies of loss and abandonment begin to manifest themselves.

Irene tells what happened during the previous week's session addressing herself to Mindy, a member who was absent. Irene describes how she asserted herself with her boyfriend who frequently discounts her unhappiness regarding his continued association with an ex-girl friend, on the basis of her "sick jealousy." Irene then confronts the leader with an issue that was discussed the previous week. "Talking outside the group about other members is not so bad."

Irene's compulsion to address herself exclusively to Mindy, the member who was absent the previous week, reflects a possible inability to separate herself from Mindy. The fear that Mindy will feel excluded (or that Irene had an experience that Mindy was not part of) propelled Irene to take Mindy into account. This phenomenon is interesting in view of Irene's minor rebellion (separation) against the therapist in terms of breaking group rules. It would appear that the anxiety engendered in acting independently in one regard arouses anxiety that is relieved by seeking out another secure object-attachment (Mindy) through ingratiation. This ambivalent attitude regarding autonomy is also embodied in Irene's description of her interaction with the boyfriend. She has discovered sufficient ego strength to challenge his need to parade old girlfriends in front of her. The security that she feels in questioning his provocative behavior is temporary however. She offsets her anxiety by allowing herself to be falsely identified as neurotically jealous. So long as the boyfriend is granted this one-up position, Irene can permit herself to keep confronting him with less fear of rejection. During this particular phase in her life, Irene was acting with a greater degree of confidence and less self-blame than ever before (e.g., asserting self with boyfriend and therapist). The anxiety that this independence may have taken her too far causes her to stabilize her relationship with Mindy, the most prominent mothering figure in the group.

Lionel mentions how several weeks previously, the therapist

had overridden his comments. When Lionel confronted the therapist, the therapist had parried him defensively by asking, "Why didn't you speak up sooner?" Lionel tells the therapist that he feels the therapist always has the need to be on top. The therapist acknowledges his defensiveness and need to be right. Lionel says, "It's frightening to challenge someone who needs to be the authority. I'm afraid they'll get angry and withdraw from me." Lionel believes that starting with his mother and father and continuing on to his present relations with his wife and the therapist, the opinions of authority are interpreted as biblical pronouncements, givens, nonhuman, automatic truths, "like commands coming from a loud-speaker." Lionel explores why he is reluctant to inquire, question, or assert. "I guess I'm afraid the other person will only come down harder. Sometimes I would get violently angry but then I'd recede back into myself and get all mixed up."

Lionel's background consists of rigid, controlling parents who were chronically complaining about their health and always seemed overwhelmed by life. Lionel came to feel that even reasonable questioning of their judgments cause them either to become enraged or to withdraw. His transference to the therapist recaptures this memory. "If I tell a therapist that I see him doing something wrong, he won't be able to take it. My observation, in itself, becomes a dangerous piece of information." Lionel typically confused behavior, blank mind and abstract way of talking seems designed to protect relationships from the explosive and disastrous consequences of honest feedback. The therapist's acknowledgement of his own defensiveness ("Why didn't you speak up at the time?") validates Lionel's perception and is designed to provide a "corrective object" experience. Trusting one's own feelings, expressing them, and not having to submit to narcissistic need states of authority are reinforced. The fear of object loss is rectified by the working through. The love object (therapist) supports Lionel's autonomy, hopefully making the object more constant in Lionel's mind (objects are flexible, understanding, accepting).

Doug talks about a suicidal friend whom he saw during the weekend. When the friend felt better and wanted to go home to his mother, Doug felt confused and upset as though he were losing control. "As long as he was dependent on me, I felt the relationship was permanent, that I was important to him. I felt threatened when he started acting as though he didn't need me." Doug then went on to discuss the possibility of his going to California in the near future, to look for work. "Perhaps you (the therapist) will be upset if I go." Doug then goes on to relate a fantasy he had about bringing the suicidal friend to the therapist. At this point, the therapist has the fantasy that maybe the whole group and himself should move to California together.

Doug creates object constancy by making himself important to others. He protects them and encourages their dependency on him thereby guarding against the possibility that they will leave him. The friend's departure comes as a shock and reminds Doug of the tentativeness of all object attachments. Despite his best efforts to control, he can never ensure himself completely against upsetting changes in his life. His mothering attitude possibly represents a reaction formation against the wish to be taken care of. The desire to logically consider California job opportunities is a mature attitude. The prospect of separating from his New York based family (symbolized by the group and the therapist) is anxiety provoking. Will we still remember him if he acts independently? Doug dealt with his friend very caringly and was quite therapeutic. Why the urge to bring the friend in for a consultation? It would appear that unconsciously Doug wants to leave a replacement for himself. In Doug's mind, the therapist will be disappointed. The therapist's need for a loyal son and an appreciative patient will be satisfied by the referral. On another level, Doug's unnecessary dependency on the therapist ("You handle the case; I can't") is a way of offsetting separation fears engendered by the prospect of leaving the group. Doug's identification with the therapist's concurrent fantasy about moving to California with the entire group reflects his own practice, the possible membership turnover, recent absences, and the loss of narcissistic gratification offered by the continued existence of a smoothly working, well-integrated group, the therapist feels threatened.

Doug goes on talking; the group grows silent and seems to withdraw. The therapist has the urge to ask Irwin, a relatively quiet member during this session, how things are going.

The therapist's impulse to be solicitous of Irwin represents another form of ensuring against further object loss. By neutralizing another source of dissatisfaction (expressed by Irwin's non participation), the therapist unconsciously hopes to bind a shaky structure.

The therapist asked the group about their anxiety with regard to Doug possibly going to California. He wonders whether this could have caused the silence. Different members speak about their upset, feelings of loss, and the thought that they wish him well but hope he does not go yet.

The therapist asked Doug whether his gratitude to the therapist and the group interfere with his making a clear decision. Privately the therapist feels grateful for Doug's public acknowledgement of the therapist's helpfulness. The therapist wonders "where will he get a replacement for such an appreciative, hard working patient."

Mindy describes how small mistakes by others get her upset, angry. Someone suggests that maybe this is a projection. "Maybe you feel you have to be perfect in order not to jeopardize relationships." The therapist confirms this interpretation reminding the group of his quick defensiveness with Lionel even though he knows Lionel likes him. "Many of us seem to feel that relationships are very tentative and precious. We feel we have to live up to unrealistic standards in order to get constant demonstrations of love. But we also seem to demand the same thing of others—that they must not disappoint us even in little ways, otherwise we threaten not to love them."

The session ends. Typically, the group remains for an hour after-session. The therapist asked to speak to Irene about arranging a private session. Suddenly, three or four different patients approached the therapist. One member says he cannot make the next private hour. Another member forgot when her next appointment was. "Is it for tomorrow?" (It was for the following week.) Still another member reminds the therapist that they had an appointment together on Friday. The group spontaneously dissolves the post-session as soon as the therapist leaves. This has never taken place before in the two year history of the group.

A group's capacity to conduct alternate sessions in a constructive fashion is testimony to their ability to function effectively independent of the therapist's presence. The disintegration of this tradition represents a denial of this capacity and a regressive reminder of their continued attachment to the therapist. The exchanges with various group members at the session's end reflect the marked ambivalence that is experienced as a result of this dependency.

It might be useful to view the patients in this group as in transition. Each of them seems to be striving to crystallize their own sense of identity independently of parental introjects and current expectations of how they should feel and behave. In order to successfully integrate the separation from a parent-child role, repeated "checking back" seems to be necessary to ensure that the good parent can tolerate such movement. The achievement of individuality rests on the formation of new kinds of relationships with internalized objects (Blos, 1967). Until a patient can rest assured that nothing catastrophic will result if he operates outside the parental sphere of influence, two popular types of behavior can be predicted: (1) The compulsive need to test out and be satisfied that the object will not abandon. (2) A rebellious acting-out ("I don't depend on you at all, your feelings do not matter to me").

In order for growth to occur, the therapist must meet the maturational needs of the individual. In this light, transference can be viewed as a challenge to the therapist to deal with an emotional demand in a more adaptive way than the original parents did under similar circumstances. The therapeutic task is to upset ingrained neurotic expectations of dyadic interaction patterns. If we trace the subtle threads of the aforementioned group process, it can be observed that many of the so-called "resistive patterns" represent experimental attempts to find the optimal personal space and distance in relation to the love object (therapist, group as a whole). The therapist who mistakes this normal transitional phase for chaos, rebelliousness, and acting-out, and deals with these phenomena by being threatened, controlling, or rejecting, misses an important opportunity to support the emerging autonomy of his patients.

OBJECT CONSTANCY IN THE INDIVIDUAL THERAPY SETTING

The current interest in object-relations theory has made formulations about early development the subject of lively controversy. Since many of the fundamental hypotheses of psychoanalysis are based on the presumption of a continuity of mental life, a valid theory of psychic development necessarily involves a great deal of reconstruction and projection back into the subject's early history. This chapter addresses itself to a particular aspect of the structuralization of the self, namely the formulation of the concept of the object, which permits a new economic equilibrium in the face of drive impulses. A theory of object constancy that focuses on preconscious exchanges between very young infants and those who mother them has important implications for the analytic situation, where primitive communication between patient and analyst has become a matter of special interest. A clearer understanding of pregenital phases of the libido and the cathexis of part objects is seen as very applicable to the mystifying swirls of regressive transferential phenomena.

It should be noted that massive group regressions involving most of the members usually takes place only when special extenuating circumstances prevail. Threatening events that seem to be outside of the control of the group members, particularly disorganizing communications from the leader, are chiefly responsible for homogeneous treatment-resistant group behavior. Fortunately, the group as a whole retains a relative stability during most of its life as a result of the support provided by the leader and fellow members. If the leader falters momentarily, other members are adequate temporary replacements as cathected "good" objects. In the two-person interaction of individual analysis, the leader's behavior together with the patient's perception and representation of the leader, can more readily produce an inordinate wish for the absent object. The physical finality of the same object being loved and hated places great strains on the adequacy of the patient's homeostatic system.

In discussing the child's great cultural achievement, that is, his renunciation of instinctual satisfaction by allowing the mother to go away without protesting, Freud (1920) set the stage for the further investigation of such concepts as object constancy, separation-individuation, and emotion refueling.

> . . . This good little boy had an occasional disturbing habit of taking any small objects he got hold of and throwing them away from him into a corner, under the bed, and so on, so that hunting for his toys and picking them up was often quite a business. As he did this he gave vent to a loud, long drawn-out "o-o-o-o," accompanied by an expression of interest and satisfaction. His mother and the writer of the present account were agreed in thinking that this was not a mere interjection but represented the German word *fort* ("gone"). I eventually realized that it was a game and that the only use he made of any of his toys was to play "gone" with them. One day I made an observation which confirmed my view. The child had a wooden reel with a piece of string tied around it. It never occurred to him to pull it along the floor behind him, for instance, and play at its being a carriage. What he did was to hold the reel by the string and very skillfully throw it over the edge of his curtained cot, so that it disappeared into it, at the same time uttering his expressive "o-o-o-o." He then pulled the reel out of the cot again by the string and hailed its reappearance with a joyful *da* ("there"). This, then, was the complete game—disappearance and return . . . (pp. 14-15).

Diatkine (1978) points out that in order for the child to comfortably carry the parents around within himself, the parents must first cathect the baby by empathically giving behavior a meaning which does not as yet have any. This anticipatory illusion enhances the child's capacity to have predictive hallucinations, which organize tension-reduction mechanisms around the supportive availability of the parents. Simultaneous with the establishment of a sense of the continuous reliable object, there develops a relative stability of internal and external experiences. Joseph and Marie Sandler (1978) suggest that in order for an individual to achieve a feeling of safety, he has to gain affirmation and reassurance through interactions with others and with his own self. In order to obtain gratification, the individual negotiates to get others to respond in certain specified ways. The individual's wishes, thoughts, and expectations drive him to assign others certain desired roles. The goal is to experience important subjective aspects of object relationships from the first years of life. This formulation emphasizes not only a wishful aim directed toward an object, but also a wish for interaction (an imagined response of the object).

In the clinical setting, transference is then seen as a testing out of the "role responsiveness" of the object choice (Sandler, 1978). Through his interaction with the analyst, the patient seeks a constantly recurring source of wish fulfillment in the context of a stable object relationship. The patient attempts to actualize his dominant unconscious fantasies by inducing the analyst to comply with the roles demanded of him. This role evocation usually occurs most blatantly when the patient is resistant or incapable of reducing tensions by himself. To the extent that every wish contains an unconscious object relationship, every form of transference represents a symbolic enactment intended to transform the analyst into a reliable gratifying object. Since every wish has an irrational context, one of the tasks of analysis centers around illuminating the prominent fantasies of the self in relation to significant objects. Understanding the complementary dynamics between the self and primary affective objects in a framework that highlights the intention of restoring a pleasant feeling state by solidifying object relationships is of crucial importance in evaluating the analytic process.

Case 2

A hostile patient with a tendency to seize on anything that jarred him in the slightest, began one session by asking the analyst to summarize his current impressions of the patient. The analyst declined, explaining that such an intellectual rehashing seemed like an empty ritual. The patient became frustrated and angry. The analyst inquired whether, aside from the informational aspect of the request, the patient might not be testing the analyst. When the various possibilities of what the analyst might say were reviewed, the patient agreed that practically anything the analyst said would be criticized. The patient then changed the topic and began talking about a recent conversation with his father. When the patient was 4 years old, he was accused by his father of killing a duck. The father screamed at the boy and gave him a bad beating. Later on, when it was discovered that the boy was innocent, the father gave a very begrudging, mild apology. In the most recent confrontation, the patient asked the father how he could abuse a young child like that. The father's response was: "I don't believe in apologizing. I just did it because your mother wanted me to." This triggered off a tirade by the patient. After the early trauma, the patient remembered the father as being superficially benign and nonthreatening, but the patient always felt tense in his presence. The analyst suggested that considering the father's flip-flop from sadism to hypocritical pleasantries, the patient seemed to have become confused about just what to believe. Should the underlying anger or the surface calm be trusted as the prevailing sentiment? In the face of these contradictory messages, the patient could not settle his own feelings and maintained a permanent state of tension and vigilance. The requests for the summary was now seen on one level as an attempt to find out how the analyst really felt about him. On a deeper level, however, the analyst's negative feelings were sought after so that the patient could confidently feel negative counterfeelings. When the patient was capable of inducing a bipolar field of mutual animosity and anger, it was easily preferable to pervasive uncertainty and paranoid suspiciousness.

The father's projected sadism had left the patient with unbearable tensions stemming from actual feelings of righteous anger coupled with a horrible dread that he might indeed be as monstrous as the father's image of him. In this instance, the patient sought relief by attempting to discover the evil feelings of the analyst. The analyst went on to admit that he felt wary of a trap and withheld out of a defensive anticipation of attack. The patient was very relieved after this acknowledgement. He began to recognize his threatening effect on the analyst and saw that he could not very well expect unflustered perfect behavior. He connected this with his own inability to accept his continued anger toward the father despite his perception of the father as trying to be nice. Relating this back to the concept of object constancy, the patient unrealistically expected the analyst to be the same no matter what took place around him.

By conceptualizing patient-analyst movements over the course of successive sessions in terms of a reciprocal desire for object constancy, we can arrive at a view of motivation, conflict, psychopathology, and symptom formation, in which the control of feelings via the maintenance of specific role relationships assumes a crucial significance.

REFERENCES

Blos, P. *On adolescence: A psychoanalytic interpretation.* New York: Free Press, 1962.

Blos, P. The second individuation process of adolescence. *The Psychoanalytical Study of the Child.* pp. 162-186.

Cartwright, D. Achieving change in people: Some applications of group dynamic thought. *Human Relations,* 1951, *4,* 381-392.

Diatkine, R. The development of object relationships and affects. *International Journal of Psycho-Analysis,* 1978, *59,* 277-284.

Epstein, L. The therapeutic function of hate in the countertransference. *Contemporary Psychoanalysis,* 1977, Vol. 13, No. 4, 442-469.

Freud, A. Problems of infantile neurosis: A discussion: *The Psychoanalytical Study of the Child,* 1954, *9,* 24-71.

Freud, S. Beyond the pleasure principle (1920). *Standard edition, 18,* 14-15. London: Hogarth Press, 1953.

Hartmann, H. *Essays on ego psychology: Selected problems in psychoanalytic theory.* New York: International Universities Press, 1964.

Khan, M. The concept of cumulative trauma. *The Psychoanalytical Study of the Child,* 1963, *18,* 286-306.

Khan, M. Ego distortion, cumulative trauma, and the role of reconstruction in the analytic situation. *International Journal of Psycho-Analysis,* 64, *45,* 272-279.

Mahler, M. (1963). Thoughts about development and individuation. *The Psychoanalytical Study of the Child,* 16:332-351.

Mahler, M. On the significance of the separation-individuation phase. M. Schur (Ed.), In: *Drive, affects, and behavior.* Vol. 21. New York: International Universities Press, pp. 161-169.

Masterson, J. *Psychotherapy of the borderline adult.* New York: Brunner-Mazel, 1976.

McDevitt, J. Separation-individuation and object constancy. *Journal of the American Psychoanalytic Association,* 1975, *23,* 713-742.

Sandler, J.J. On the development of object relations and affects. *International Journal of Psycho-Analysis,* 1978, *59,* 285-295.

Searles, H. Intervention and Differentiation in Schizophrenia. *Collected Papers on Schizophrenia and Related Subjects.* New York: International Universities Press, 1965, 304-316.

Shellow, R. Group therapy and the institutionalized delinquent. *International Journal of Group Psychiatry,* 1958, *8,* 265-275.

Taylor, F. The therapeutic factors in group-analytic treatment. *Journal of Mental Science,* 1958, *96,* pp. 976-999.

Whitaker, D., & Lieberman, M. (1964). Psychotherapy through the group process. New York: Atherton Press, 1964.

Wolf, A. The psychoanalysis of groups. *American Journal of Psychotherapy,* 1949, *3,* 525-558.

Chapter 9

A MODERN PSYCHOANALYTIC
APPROACH TO THE MANAGEMENT
OF TREATMENT IMPASSES
June Bernstein

The aim of modern psychoanalysis is not to provide a corrective emotional experience, to offer insight, to reconstruct the past, to afford catharsis, or to repair the ego, although all these things may occur. The purpose of treatment is for the analyst to resolve the patient's resistance to feeling, thinking and remembering everything—and putting it all into words.

What Spotnitz and his colleagues call *Modern Psychoanalysis* is an expansion of classical technique that evolved in response to the impasses that tended to develop in the treatment of preoedipal conditions. Finding that interpretation was not usually effective with such patients, modern psychoanalysts extended the range of their interventions. They regard a most significant contribution to technique as being the emphasis on the role of emotional communication, especially in the analyst's interventions.

Freud's writings have provided the source for two lines

of development of psychoanalytic technique. In one, described by Sterba in 1934, the analyst helps the patient to dissociate the reasonable part of the ego from the drives and defenses that arise in the transference. The analyst and patient together examine the events of the transference in a state of affective detachment. This procedure is reminiscent of Wordsworth's definition of poetry as emotion recollected in tranquility. Sterba's approach derives from Freud's structural theory and is the preferred one in psychoanalytic ego psychology. However, it requires that the patient have a reasonable ego accessible to intellectual conviction.

Strachey, writing in the same year (1934), put the emphasis on the emotional interaction between analyst and patient rather than on intellectual insight or the therapeutic alliance. In describing the conditions necessary for a mutative interpretation he said: "A mutative interpretation can only be applied to an id-impulse which is actually in a state of cathexis . . . a charge of energy originating in the patient himself." Since the id-impulse must be directed at the analyst within the transference, the analyst is "exposing himself to some great danger . . . deliberately evoking a quantity of the patient's id-energy while it is alive and actual and unambiguous and aimed directly at himself." Thus, a mutative interpretation is neither given nor received in a state of affective tranquility.

In such a situation, the patient's reasonable ego is not likely to be available. Freud (1912) noted how, under the influence of transference resistance, the patient is "hurled out of all reality," how "logical connections . . . become matters of indifference to him . . . ." He said: "The patient ascribes, just as in dreams, currency and reality to what results from the awakening of his unconscious feelings; he seeks to discharge his emotions regardless of the reality of the situation."

Under such circumstances, the effectiveness of interpretations tends to be particularly impaired and the use of emotional communication is most crucial.

Emotional communication is a communication given

from within the transference-countertransference interaction, rather than an interpretation from outside it. According to Margolis (1978), it is "a form of exchange between people which conveys information, transmitted and received emotionally rather than intellectually, concerning their conscious and unconscious feeling states." Thus, a patient who has been expressing self hatred may be told, "You're despicable!" rather than being informed that he suffers from low self-esteem. The emotional communication is used to promote further verbalization and to resolve or mobilize resistance rather than to offer insight. If the patient believes that he is unloveable, the conviction will be activated in the transference. The patient will believe the analyst does not find him worthwhile, that he is boring and unwanted in the here and now. By agreeing with him, the analyst accepts his perception and offers him the opportunity to examine it at some distance from his own ego. Meadow (1974) says:

> To tell him he is not in touch with reality, as we do when we interpret his projection as belonging to relationships of the past, denies his emotion. Telling him he deserves our hatred accepts his projection. Asking him why the analyst is so mean also accepts his projection. Feeling accepted, the patient can learn to say: "I don't deserve your hatred and if you were a decent person you would treat me better." (p. 93)

Modern analysts believe that every transference provokes a reciprocal countertransference. The analyst's willingness to experience and tolerate the feelings that the patient induces, without acting upon them, is an index of his ability to work with the emotional force of the countertransference. Treatment impasses may occur when the analyst resists having, or letting the patient have, some unpleasant feeling.

Freud considered negative transference an obstacle to treatment. He dismissed as untreatable those patients who were incapable of forming a positive transference. Freud (1912) observed that patients enter treatment with certain conditions for loving. These conditions are bound to infantile imagos in which the patient's libido is regressively invested.

The analyst meets the patient's requirements for loving when the infantile prototypes are reactivated in the transference. But for Freud, if the withdrawn libido cannot be reanimated and redirected toward the transference figure, the patient is not a suitable candidate for psychoanalysis. Freud says: "Where the capacity to transfer feeling has come to be of an essentially negative order, as with paranoids, the possibility of influence or cure ceases."

Later psychoanalysts found that these patients, in whom the conditions for loving cannot be met, either run away from treatment themselves, or induce the analyst to get rid of them. They cannot find the right object, and they prefer no relationship at all to the kind of relationship they characteristically have. Their resistance to forming and maintaining a relationship may first be expressed in the difficulties they make about the simplest arrangements for coming. They attempt to give up treatment before it begins. The modern analyst tries to make the patient comfortable enough to state all his objections to coming: "It's too far. There's no parking. The time isn't right. The fee is too high."

The analyst deals with these objections in two ways. He accepts them at face value; that is, he does not interpret their unconscious defensive significance, and he explores them in order to get the patient to expand on them more fully. How does the patient get here? Can he take public transportation? Is there a parking lot nearby? What fee would he like to pay?

A patient who asks about the analyst's credentials may really want to know whether the analyst is a person with whom he can have a relationship. The analyst who answers the question without further investigation may be foreclosing an opportunity to discover what kind of object the patient needs. If the patient inquires, the modern analyst explores the request to clarify how the patient views the relationship.

One new arrival wanted to know whether the analyst was familiar with Gestalt therapy. When the analyst asked what he should know about it, the patient explained that his mind was in fragments and he needed someone who was interested in making things whole. He thus gave his presenting problem and told what he wanted from treatment. The patient is still defining the object he needs. At present he wants someone who will help him to feel an emotion and is explaining what the analyst would have to do to enable him to have one. His usual form of discourse is highly idiosyncratic and incomprehensible, but the need to instruct the analyst involves him increasingly in secondary process thinking.

A successful and apparently forthright businessman asked if the analyst had been trained in any specialty. What he wanted to know was how he should begin. Would the analyst structure the interview or just let him flounder around? He wished to know about the analyst's training so he could cooperate with it. Asking him to tell the story of his life was sufficient to get him started.

It is important to explore the patient's questions to discover what kind of object will meet his conditions for investing his psychic energy in the task of psychoanalysis.

Since narcissistic patients have serious difficulties in forming intimate relationships, treatment begins at a frequency the patient can tolerate. Patients have been known to start treatment on a once a month basis. Others may ask to be seen several times a week, but indicate by lateness or missed sessions that they are seeing too much of the analyst. Spotnitz (1969) recommends that the patient be kept in a mild state of object hunger so that he will work most productively in sessions.

Some narcissistic patients arrive in treatment in an essentially objectless state. They demonstrate by self-absorption and withdrawal that they have not yet cathected objects as a means for reducing tension. Their main requirement seems to be a need for insulation. For the person who defends against emotions by sensations of deadness, numbness or emptiness, the analyst provides ego insulation to protect the patient from overstimulation and the consequent necessity to employ even more radical defenses.

Overstimulation is dangerous to such patients because the tension it generates is not discharged in interaction with the outside world. Instead, it is turned back onto the patient's own psyche or soma. Originally Freud (1914) saw narcissism as the withdrawal of libidinal cathexis from the outside world and its reinvestment in the self. In 1917 he described how in melancholia the self is attacked in lieu of the abandoned object. In 1920, with the introduction of the dual drive theory, the self is seen as the original object of both libidinal and aggressive impulses. Since that time there has been increasing recognition that it is the disposition of the aggressive, rather than the libidinal drive that is the nuclear problem in narcissistic disorders. Modern analysts believe that what is needed to help a patient move from narcissism to object relations is an object that can be perceived as being like the self. Spotnitz and his colleagues facilitate conditions which promote narcissistic transference by limiting their responses to the patient's direct attempts at contact. Spotnitz (1969) describes how he begins treatment by providing a neutral, nonstimulating atmosphere in which the patient will feel comfortable enough to form a relationship with the analyst. Spotnitz times his interventions to the patient's attempt to contact him. His responses are not only cued by the patient, they also mirror the patient's style of contact. Meadow (1974) says: "Contact functioning replaces the subjectively determined timing of classical interpretation with what might be called 'demand feeding', in which the timing and type of communication are what the subject asks for. When the analyst responds to a question with a question, a devaluation with a devaluation, the subject is incontrol of the quantity and type of stimulation that he receives." According to Spotnitz (1976) " . . . when the analyst is guided by the patient's contact functioning, and responds in kind, it promotes the development of transference on a narcissistic basis. The patient is permitted to mold the transference object in his own image. He builds up a picture of the therapist as someone like himself—the kind of person whom he will eventually feel free to love and hate." An object who can be hated or loved like the self can be used as a substitute for the self, and may be the first step in acquiring object relations.

Although in 1912 Freud spoke only of the patient's

buried love emotions, toward the end of his life he became increasingly aware of aggressive impulses. Eventually he said that all of psychoanalysis would have to be reformulated in terms of understanding the aggressive drive as separate from the libidinal drive. According to Spotnitz and Meadow (1976), modern psychoanalysts have used this as their starting point.

Many modern psychoanalysts use Freud's early energy concepts, but emphasize in preoedipal cases the bottled-up aggression rather than dammed-up libido. Spotnitz and Meadow offer examples from published case histories to support the thesis that patients protect their object and defend themselves against recognizing their destructive wishes. They report on a patient (Reik's) who said: "Instead of knowing that you want to kill someone else, you wipe yourself out."

The inability to find acceptable and adequate methods for the discharge of the aggressive drive is often considered responsible for narcissistic disorders. Because libidinal energy is tied up in object protection it is not available for other purposes. According to Spotnitz (1969), libidinal energy "is overwhelmed as the organizing force of the mental apparatus."

The infant first discharges tension in random, unfocused movement or in somatic conversions. Gradually he learns more adaptive ways of discharging energy, culminating, if all goes well, in the establishment of object relations and a structured psychic apparatus. The narcissistic patient, however, still presents the problem of energy discharge. Because his psychic structure is incomplete, it is useless to appeal to his ego with intellectual insight. In modern psychoanalysis the aim is not insight, but discharge of thoughts, feelings and memories into words — a process of psychic ego development and integration.

Narcissism may be viewed as a form of self-attack. Such narcissistic defenses as autism, ego fragmentation, depression, and somatization are methods of turning aggressive impulses against the self in order to protect a valued object. The objectless state is, paradoxically, employed to protect the object from the feelings the patient would have were he to acknowledge the object's reality and importance. Spotnitz (1976) suggests that such patients experience too much stimulation and too little discharge, and that the analyst must support the defenses until the patient has developed the ability to engage in the rapid, verbal discharge of all feelings, particularly negative ones. Until that time the analyst insulates the patient from experiencing more feeling than can be dealt with in the session. Encouraging the emergence of hostile feelings at too rapid a pace may lead to psychosis.

Freud (1950) suggested in his "Project For A Scientific Psychology" that discharge of energy is the first requirement of human life. Objects are acquired in association with drive reduction. Every infant who survives the crib has acquired some rudimentary object. It was Freud's (1915) hypothesis that the first object was indistinguishable from the self. Furthermore, he speculated that hate might precede love and be the older form of relating: "At the very beginning, it seems, the external world, objects, and what is hated are identical." When in 1912, Freud emphasized the patient's conditions for loving, he had not yet formulated his theories about aggression and the death instinct. At present it appears that conditions for hating may be even more crucial in the treatment of narcissistic patients. Modern analysts find that the narcissistic defense (self-attack) can be mitigated by resolving the patient's resistance to expressing hatred in undisguised verbal form. Such a resolution of resistance releases libidinal energy that is otherwise tied up in protecting the object (Spotnitz & Meadow, 1976). To facilitate the expression of both love and hate, the modern analyst does nothing to interfere with the spontaneous development of transference.

Although the oedipal-level patient reactivates infantile imagos of real objects, the narcissistic patient creates an object in his own image, blending self and introjects from the undifferentiated state. He externalizes early self and object impressions from the period before ego boundaries are formed. Such a narcissistic transference fulfills the patient's conditions for having a relationship.

Narcissistic patients are treated on the couch. The immobility this imposes, like that of dreaming, allows the patient to freely verbalize aggression without fear of actually harming the analyst. Face to face treatment inhibits the development of transference and substitutes nonverbal communication for speech. The couch permits a more desirable control of regression by what is said rather than nonverbal cues or reliance on familiar reality. Verbalization is ego building, whereas discharging feelings in gestures and facial expressions circumvents the ego. Restricting both patient and analyst to speech permits greater range and flexibility of verbal expression. Most patients become freer to express all their feelings if they do not have to "face" the analyst while doing so. Face-to-face treatment keeps the patient oriented to the social realities, but social reality has already failed to resolve the patient's resistances.

Early in treatment, emotional communication is used to make the patient feel understood and to facilitate narcissistic transference. Instead of confronting the patient with reality or correcting his distortions, the analyst joins the patient behind the stone wall of narcissism. In essence modern analysts follow the procedure recommended by Anna Freud (1946) for the treatment of children:

> Did he come to his appointment in a cheerful disposition, I was cheerful too...I followed his lead in every subject of talk...I did nothing but follow his moods and humours along all their paths and bypaths...if he were serious or depressed I was the same (p. 9)

The patient is justified in experiencing any emotion in the presence of the analyst without being contradicted. If the patient feels uncomfortable or frightened and the analyst tells him he has nothing to fear, it inhibits the expression of the feeling without dispelling it. Therefore it may be preferable not to contradict the patient who says, "You hate me," or "You think I'm terrific," but to explore further. A patient, who commented that the analyst was yawning the week before, was asked, "Why did I yawn?" and not, "Why did you think I yawned?''

In describing the treatment methods developed by Spotnitz and his colleagues, Meadow (1969) says:

> They reflect the feeling of the patient as a way of joining him in his type of verbal contact—answering his questions with a question of the same type, agreeing with him in his hopelessness and feelings of inadequacy, and by devaluating the person of the analyst that he has overevaluated, thus bringing the analyst down to the patient's own ego level where he is not too powerful to criticize. (p. 19)

She also says:

> In classical psychoanalytic interpretation, the psychoanalyst brings the unconscious reason for the maladaptive response to the attention of the patient's rational ego; in psychological reflection, the psychoanalyst agrees with the subject's maladaptive distortion so that it may be examined as in a mirror. (p. 20)

Thus, a patient who repetitively attacks himself may be "joined" by being told he is even worse than he realizes, that he is hopeless. Or the analyst may "mirror" the patient by saying that the patient is doing fine, the problem is that the analyst may not be adequate. In the first case, the analyst joins the patient's feelings by agreeing with him. In the second, the analyst mirrors the patient by describing himself as inadequate like the patient.

Whether mirroring or joining, the analyst limits these responses to requests from the patient for some feedback. Modern analysts call this *contact functioning* because it relies on the patient's contacting rather than on the analyst's desire to say something. It puts the patient in control of the amount and type of stimulation he receives.

Patients may have been over- or understimulated in the past, and they may require a similar or different experience with the analyst. They will indicate what they need by the amount of contact they seek from the analyst.

Thus, the patient who wants to fight can get a fight. Patients are relieved to discover that the analyst can be as rude, silly, coarse, or argumentative as they are. One patient threatened to bash in Spotnitz's head. Spotnitz, who by this point had plenty of negative feelings to employ for emotional communication, retorted, "No you won't, because I'll bash yours in before you get off the couch!" (Spotnitz & Nagelberg, 1960). The patient declared solemnly: "If you can take what I've dished out here and give it back to me, you're my friend for life." (Spotnitz, 1976, p. 112) This patient found just the person he needed for a long-term object relationship, someone who could hate and be just as vicious as he was. When the patient creates an object in his own image, it does not necessarily mean that the analyst is perceived as a nice fellow. Most narcissistic patients have a low opinion of themselves.

The ability to offer emotional communication depends on the analyst's willingness to have countertransference feelings. Unacknowledged, unfelt countertransference is much more likely to be impulsively acted out by the analyst. If the analyst blocks a feeling, the patient may block it too. A treatment impasse is often solved by the analyst resolving his own resistance to having some feeling, or to letting the patient have it. Each transference resistance is likely to provoke a corresponding countertransference resistance. The first resistance is resistance to transference. Neither the patient nor the analyst want to have emotional relationship at all.

After the patient's conditions for having a relationship have been worked through, and a relationship has been established, the patient may find the whole situation too valuable and potentially precarious to allow his inevitable negative feelings to emerge. Usually, establishment of a narcissistic transference is followed by a period of resistance to having any negative feelings for the newly found, selfconfirming object. Idealizing transference has been described by Kohut (1971), and he has emphasized its curative aspects. Modern psychoanalysts would agree that the "syntonic feeling of oneness is a curative one, while the feeling of aloneness, the withdrawn state, is merely protective." (Spotnitz & Meadow, 1976.) However, this benevolent transference and its corresponding countertransference does eventually become an impasse to experiencing the full range of feelings.

The modern analyst does not interpret the latent negative transference, but he does work on resolving the patient's resistance to expressing it himself. The patient who is trying to maintain the status quo may nonetheless indicate in disguised ways that he is dissatisfied. Why does the patient not simply say, ''I suspect the treatment is no good and won't help me at all.'' Usually the patient attacks himself in some devious and disguised way that also implicates the object. This is due, partly, to the lack of discrimination between self and object. Among narcissistic patients, it must be remembered that any attack upon the object is also an attack upon the self. It is also true that self-attacks, stories of failure, and assertions of hopelessness are attacks on the unhelping object. The depressive characteristically attacks the object by attacking himself; the paranoid believes the object outside is attacking him. In both cases treatment impasses occur when the patient inhibits his own expressions of rage against the analyst in order to save a valued relationship.

In a case study provided by Meadow (Spotnitz & Meadow, 1976), a series of impasses are described along with their eventual resolution. The patient, a withdrawn schizophrenic girl, was first helped over her initial resistance, which was to avoid treatment altogether and to evade contact with the analyst.

Meadow helped the patient remain in treatment by providing a neutral nonstimulating environment and by respectting her need for distance. Her resistance to transference was supported by the analyst who reflected back her style of contact. During the first period, the patient was self-absorbed and seemed unaware that the analyst was in the room with her. Under such circumstances, modern psychoanalysts ask one to three object-oriented questions. These are questions designed to take pressure off the ego by directing attention to something, or someone, external. Questions about neutral subjects discussed by the patient counter introspective tendencies and provide ego insulation for those patients who are unable to talk about themselves without increased anxiety, defensiveness, and withdrawal. Modern analysts are willing to discuss any topic with the patient, no matter how apparently trivial or removed from the reasons for which the patient sought treatment.

Meadow occasionally called attention to herself (as object) by asking what she might be doing to make the patient want to stay away from her or come late to sessions. According to Meadow (1978), caution was used in introducing herself as a transference object before the patient had spontaneously turned her attention to the analyst as an object of interest. She believes that the introduction of transference, or any other subject not initiated by the narcissistic patient is experienced as an intrusion. It was done in this case rarely, and with dramatic emphasis. The patient's usual response was to blame herself for lack of progress in treatment. This narcissistic defense both saves the object and eliminates it as a real presence.

Meadow finally joined her patient by agreeing that the patient was not getting much out of treatment. She then mirrored the patient's self-criticism by asking her to help her understand why she, Meadow, was not doing a better job. These interventions supported the patient's perceptions of failure but were experienced as intrusive. As a result the patient externalized the attack. She vigorously blamed the analyst, not for the failure of the analysis, but for her intervention which made a demand on the patient. The rare and dramatic use of this technique resolved a major impasse—repetitive self-attacking and ignoring of the object. It precipitated the first undisguised expression of the patient's covert negative feelings toward the incompetent analyst who was not helping her. Resolving the resistance to expression of the negative narcissistic transference permits the otherwise withdrawn patient to attack an object, thus externalizing the self-attack.

As this patient moved from self-attack to observations

on the object, she improved. As a further resistance she resisted being influenced by the analyst. Meadow noted the secondary gain in keeping the analyst helpless to help her. The patient expressed the rejection of all outside influence by a session of complete silence. Neither patient nor analyst said anything. Following this, the patient reported a sense of relief. She had been afraid that she would be forced to do what the analyst wanted. Such a transference may reach an impasse when it serves as a resistance to expressing awareness and desire for the analyst's benevolence.

As the patient increasingly directed her aggression outward, she also began to cathect the analyst with libido, and to want things from her. When the analyst became valuable to her as an omnipotent mother, she reverted, when frustrated, to the defense of self-attack. This time Meadow emotionally joined the self-attack in an ego dystonic way. Since the patient's ego was no longer so fragile, and a firm transference had been established, Meadow was able to use some of the negative feelings the patient had induced in her. She demanded to know how the patient could expect anyone to care for such a cold and unfeeling person. The patient was amazed and relieved to discover she had inspired such strong feeling in the analyst. It made her feel real, cared for, and understood. She began to thaw. Confronting her with emotion had given her a new model with which to identify.

The emotional communication that Meadow used is an example of what Spotnitz (1963) calls the *toxoid response,* in which the feelings that the patient characteristically induces in others are fed back to him. As the patient progresses in treatment, the analyst puts him under increasing strain and exposes him to a greater range of emotions.

The patient not only needs to be able to hate the object, he needs, at various points in treatment, to be able to tolerate being hated, without recourse to self-destructive maneuvers. He needs to be hated by a real person, not by a conspiracy or by a delusional object. Because the paranoid was hated by a parent during his formative years, he is apt to create an omnipotent object who hates him in the transference. Some paranoids defend against this by believing they are particularly valued. Kohut, the Chicago group, and modern psychoanalysts agree that narcissistic patients need to have their infantile omnipotence confirmed by an idealized object. But since they need to be able to experience a full range of feelings in order to mature, they must also eventually have the experience of being frustrated, disliked, and even hated, without being devastated. Modern analysts are willing to be bad objects as well as good ones.

In the epilogue of her case, Meadow's patient says that the most important thing the analyst did was to overcome her desire to leave. Meadow attributes the patient's impulse to leave to her having been an unwanted child.

Fairbairn (1954) describes how the schizoid defense is employed by patients who believe that their libidinal attachment is unacceptable to the object. These are the patients who would literally rather die than ask for help.

Rosenfeld (1971) reports on a narcissistic patient who dreamt of

> . . . a small boy who was in a comatose condition, dying from some kind of of poisoning. He was lying on a bed in the courtyard and was endangered by the hot midday sun which was beginning to shine on him. The patient was standing near to the boy but did nothing to move or protect him. He only felt critical and superior to the doctor treating the child, since it was he who should have seen that the child was moved into the shade. (p. 174)

Rosenfeld confronted the patient with the meaning of the dream:

> I showed him that even when he came close to realizing the seriousness of his mental state, experienced as a dying condition, he did not lift a finger to help himself or to help the analyst make a move towards saving him, because he was using the killing of his infantile dependent self to triumph over the analyst and to show him up as a failure. (p. 174)

Rosenfeld notes in his commentary that the patient's

response to interpretation, even when momentarily effective, is ultimately, to become detached and sleepy, to drift away from the consulting room and to avoid closer contact with the analyst. Thus, although the analyst understands the dream and offers a brilliant interpretation, the patient is unable to profit from it. Even when the reasonable part of his ego awakens momentarily, it is not stable enough to form a reliable alliance. The patient reacts to the narcissistic injury of a correct interpretation by resorting to the comatose condition he describes in the dream. Kohut (1972) describes how narcissistic rage arises in response to injuries to self-esteem. This patient appears to defend against expressing rage toward the analyst, by further withdrawal.

Spotnitz and Meadow (1976) believe that the manifest content of a dream may be a disguised expression of preverbal wishes. To understand the hidden meaning of the dream, they recommend concentrating on the manifest content as well as on the associations. The manifest content expresses symbolically, primary process thoughts and feeling states that cannot be put into words. The associations consist of material that is preconscious and thus capable of being expressed through secondary processes of thought and language. Associations usually reveal the preconscious defenses against the wish expressed by the dream. The patient dreams what he cannot state openly or reveal in his associations. The modern analyst's aim is to get the patient to say what he wants in adult language instead of merely dreaming it. The dream may be used to understand what the patient wants from the analyst and why he can not get it. Rosenfeld's patient reveals his wish to be taken care of without having to lift a finger. His defense against such a regressive and infantile desire is to feel critical and superior, and to die rather than ask for help. The superficial feeling of triumph is really a pyrrhic victory since the patient expects to die. He will attack his own body if he is neglected by an uncaring object.

One might assume that he wants the doctor in the dream to take responsibility for him, but does not wish to ask or to be exposed to too much warmth or probing. He may want an object who is cool and remote, like himself. Any such hypothesis would have to be confirmed by finding out from the patient why he does not advise the analyst.

In the process of externalization, paranoid patients divest themselves of the feeling and self-concepts their egos are too weak to tolerate, thus indicating that confrontation is likely to have a negative therapeutic result. They reactivate an infantile image that is valuable to them. An object that persecutes or neglects is better than no object at all. In treating the analyst as a personification of the early, uncaring mother, they preserve the original relationship. It may have been a deficient relationship, but it is the only one they had and they cannot relinquish it.

To help this patient discharge feelings into words instead of discharging them against his body or mind, the modern analyst might draw attention to the object by asking why the doctor in the dream does not take better care of the patient. The dream expresses negative narcissistic transference in disguised form. The patient is resisting telling the analyst how much he hates him for not taking better care of him. When the patient has been trained to verbalize his feelings freely, the analyst may respond to such dreams by asking ego-oriented questions. Why does he want the boy to die? If the patient protests that he does not want that, it is simply what happens in the dream, he is asked why he dreamed it. It is, after all, his dream. Why does he choose to dream this rather than something else? Finally the patient may be asked "Do you hate me so much that you would rather die than see me win?" The last intervention conveys the analyst's interpretation in the form of an emotional communication. It invites the patient to describe the transference to the analyst instead of subjecting him to the narcissistic mortification of having the analyst tell it to him.

How one responds to the dreams depends on where the patient is in treatment, how close to the surface the dream appears to be, and what contact the patient makes. If the patient tells the dream without further comment, and without asking anything about it, the analyst may remain silent. If the patient does make some request relating to the dream, his form of contact—hostile, polite, distancing, placating—may provide a clue for the analyst's response.

Inverventions are aimed at helping the patient to talk rather than to understand. According to Spotnitz (1967): "Any type of intervention that helps the patient say what he really feels, thinks, and remembers without narcissistic mortification is designated as a maturational communication.

The modern analyst evaluates his interventions on the basis of the patient's reaction to them. If the patient responds to a brilliant and correct interpretation by threatening to leave treatment, feeling suicidal, or decompensating, the interpretation is not judged effective. Only if the patient responds with progressive communication, putting more feelings, thoughts, impulses, and ideas into words is the intervention considered successful. One patient, with a paranoid character disorder, had been complaining for years how difficult it was to have a relationship with a woman. Homosexual material had been presented in disguised form throughout treatment. Asked why he did not have a relationship with a man, the patient discussed the merits of the question in a reasonable way, but the following week could not remember anything about the session. He also wondered how much longer he should continue treatment. This was a clue that he was not ready to consider the issue of homosexuality. The intervention had led to increased defensiveness.

The paranoid is only an apparent exception to the rule that the narcissistic defense protects the object. It is true that he reactivates a bad infantile object. However, although he projects the aggression, it is still being directed at himself. The bad object persecutes him, he does not persecute the object. Why doesn't the patient harm the object, instead of vice versa? The fantasy of persecution is on some level a wish that the self rather than the object be harmed. Nightmares are a form of paranoid persecution. One patient, who dreamed that the analyst was choking him, asked plaintively: "Why can't I dream that I am choking you?"

The paranoid's suspicion of the object, often mixed with

criticism and contempt, may be genetically linked to identification with a critical and contemptuous parent. The patient alternates feeling criticized with being critical himself.
Relinquishing the critical attitude would mean giving up the
critical mother. The paranoid is unable to do this because he
would rather have an object that hates him than no object at
all. The object is saved through what Kernberg (1975) calls
projective identification. Kernberg also notes how the patient
devalues the object. Apparently the patient can only maintain
the relationship by regarding it as expendable and unimportant. The patient saves the analyst from his rage by making
him insignificant. One patient confessed he would feel no
sense of loss if the analyst died. His pattern with women was
to leave them if they became too important to him because he
feared being devasted by rage and self-hatred if they rejected him. He was able to sustain a relationship with a
woman analyst only by not taking her too seriously.

The paranoid, by his defenses, is able to maintain some
distance from his objects, which the depressive is unable to
achieve. The depressive's object attacks him from inside the
self, and he entertains killing himself in order to get rid of the
critical introject. The paranoid's strategy allows him to
disgorge the toxic introject by projecting it outside himself.
In the alternation between paranoid and depressive defenses,
patients who achieve some progress on the continuum from
narcissism to object awareness begin to see the object, rather
than themselves, as the cause of their distress. Paranoid patients achieve progress when they acknowledge that they want
the object, rather than themselves, to suffer.

However, the aim of treatment is not merely to provide
for discharge of aggressive feelings while in a regressed state
of narcissistic transference. That is a first step in redirecting
energy. Eventually it is hoped that the patient will be capable
of making constructive use of aggression without attacking
either the self or the object. The goal of treatment is to permit
the patient to feel and think everything and to accomplish
what he wants to in life. The method the analyst uses to
achieve this goal is to resolve the patient's resistance to saying

everything.

The patient who repetitively attacks the analyst may be avoiding positive feelings. In such a case the analyst works eventually on the resistance to loving.

Each transference is a resistance to the next higher-level form of transference. A narcissistic transference is ultimately a resistance to seeing the analyst as a separate person. Negative transference operates as a resistance to having positive feelings for the analyst. Aggressive feelings may be used to block libidinal ones.

Repetitive communications are one of the most common and frustrating treatment impasses. In 1920 Freud proposed that the compulsion to repeat was an instinct "beyond the pleasure principle." Patients in psychoanalysis used the treatment to recreate experiences from the past. They obliged the analyst to treat them as their early objects had done, apparently not for the purpose of gratification or pleasure, but because: "All instincts tend toward the restoration of an earlier state of things."

It is possible that the conservative nature of this instinct operates in the interest of maintaining an introjected object. Thus, new patterns of adaptation, although apparently desired, threaten the loss of an object. The analyst himself, once the relationship has become valuable, becomes an object to be preserved. Maintaining the status quo may then become a formidable obstacle to progress.

It is possible to use the feelings aroused by the countertransference to understand the patient and to provide the impetus for the kind of emotional communication the patient needs to progress in treatment. Patients in the status-quo phase may literally put the analyst to sleep by repetition and avoidance of feelings. The therapist needs to experience the feelings the patient induces in order to help the patient put them into words. The analyst is called upon to make a range of emotional communications so that the patient will be able to experience the whole gamut of human emotions with him. The range of subjects discussed should include whatever can be talked about between two people. As the patient puts everything into words, he expands the domain of the ego until "where id was, there ego shall be." At that point the patient may seek and profit from understanding. Eventually both patient and analyst should be able to say everything.

REFERENCES

Fairbairn, R.D. *An Object Relations Theory of the Personality*. New York: Basic Books, 1952.

Freud, A. *The Psychoanalytic Treatment of Children*. New York: Imago, 1946. Repr, 1965

Freud, S. The dynamics of the transference (1912). *Standard Edition, 12*, 123. London: Hogarth Press, 1974.

Freud, S. On beginning the treatment (1913). *Standard Edition, 12, 123*.

Freud, S. Remembering, repeating, and working through (1914). *Standard Edition, 12, 147*.

Freud, S. On narcissism: An introduction (1914). *Standard Edition, 14*, 69.

Freud, S. Observations on transference love (1915). *Standard Edition, 12*, 159.

Freud, S. Mourning and melancholia (1917). *Standard Edition, 14*, 239.

Freud, S. Beyond the pleasure principle. *Standard Edition, 18*, 7.

Freud, S. Analysis terminable and interminable. (1937) *Standard Edition, 23*. 211

Freud, S. An outline of psychoanalysis (1940). *Standard Edition, 23*, 41.

Freud, S. Project for a scientific psychology (1950). *Standard Edition. 1*, 283.

Kernberg, O. *Borderline Conditions and Pathological Narcissism*. New York: Jason Aronson, 1975.

Kohut, H. *The Analysis of the Self*. New York: International Universities Press, 1971.

Kohut, H. Thoughts on narcissism and narcissistic rage. *The Psychoanalytic Study of the Child*, 1972, *27*, 360-399.

Margolis, B. Narcissistic countertransference: Emotional availability and case management. *Modern Psychoanalysis*, 1978, *3*, 2, 133-151.

Meadow, P.W. The relative effectiveness of two educational techniques used in the extinction of maladaptive responses with block learning. *Dissertation Abstracts International*, 1969, *21*, 2.

Meadow, P.W. A research method for investigating the effectiveness of psychoanalytic techniques. Psychoanalytical Review, 1974, *61*(1), 79-94.

Meadow, P.W. *Theory of the technique*. Unpublished lecture. New York: Center for Modern Psychoanalytical Studies, 1978.

Rosenfeld, H. A clinical approach to the psychoanalytic theory of the life and death instincts: An investigation into the aggressive aspects of narcissism. *International Journal of Psycho-Analysis 1971, 52,* 169-177.

Spotnitz, H. The toxoid response. *Psychoanalytic Review,* 1963, *50,* 611-624.

Spotnitz, H. The maturational interpretation (1967). In: E. Hammer *(Ed.), Use of Interpretation in Treatment.* New York: Grune & Stratton, pp. 107-109.

Spotnitz, H. *Modern Psychoanalysis of the Schizophrenic Patient.* New York: Grune & Stratton, 1969.

Spotnitz, H. *Psychotherapy of Preoedipal Conditions: Schizophrenia and Severe Character Disorders.* New York: Jason Aronson, 1976.

Spotnitz, H. & L. Nagelberg. A preanalytic technique for resolving the narcissistic defense, 1960, *Psychiatry 23,*193-197.

Spotnitz, H., & P. Meadow. *Treatment of the Narcissistic Neuroses.* New York: Manhattan Center for Advanced Psychoanalytic Studies, 1976.

Sterba, R. The fate of the ego in analytic therapy. *International Journal of Psycho-Analysis,* 1934, *15,* 117-126.

Strachey, J. The nature of the therapeutic action of psychoanalysis. *International Journal of Psycho-Analysis,* 1934, *15,* 127-159.

Chapter 10

RATIONALE FOR THE HETEROGENEOUS GROUP—COMBINED TREATMENT FORMAT OF BORDERLINE AND NARCISSISTIC PATIENTS.*
Normund Wong, M.D.

Introduction

It gives me great pleasure to contribute to this monograph on the treatment of borderline and narcissistic patients. I have been asked to focus on some clinical issues pertaining to the treatment of borderline and narcissistic patients in a heterogeneous, combined group format. As the main point of this chapter I will present the hypothesis that this approach is one of the most complete and effective treatment means of conducting reconstructive therapy with these vastly complicated and troubled patients who require extensive treatment and occasional periods of hospitalization.

Before proceeding further, I wish to define what is

---

*This chapter was first presented at the 1979 AGPA Annual Conference as part of a Symposium on Clinical Vignettes of Change in Borderline and Narcissistic Patients in Groups.

meant by a borderline and narcissistic disorder. I am in essential agreement with the descriptions of these conditions offered in the draft of the American Psychiatric Association's DSM 111. The borderline personality disorder requires the presence of at least five of the following eight characteristics: (1) impulsivity or unpredictability in at least two areas that are potentially self-damaging; for example, spending sex, drug or alcohol abuse, overeating, or physically self-damaging acts; (2) a pattern of unstable and intense interpersonal relationships; (3) inappropriate, intense anger or lack of control of anger; (4) identity disturbance manifested by uncertainty about several issues relating to identity; (5) affective instability; (6) problems tolerating being alone; (7) physically self damaging acts; and (8) chronic feelings of emptiness or boredom. Although comprehensive, the definition fails to take into account quantitative differences among borderline patients. Toward that end, I find Grinker's classification of borderline patients into four groups clinically useful. Patients in Group I are closest to the psychotic border, whereas those in Group IV most closely resemble neurotics. A structural, dynamic understanding of the borderline personality is also essential and I agree with the conceptualizations offered by Kernberg (1975) and Masterson and Rinsley (1975).

The descriptive diagnosis of the narcissistic personality disorder in the DSM III is as follows: The narcissistic personality possesses a grandiose sense of self-importance or uniqueness; preoccupation with fantasies of unlimited success, power, brilliance, beauty, or ideal love; exhibitionistic features; responses to criticism, indifference of others or defeat with either cool indifference or feelings of rage, shame, emptiness, humiliation or inferiority; and presence of at least two of the following reactions in response to disturbed interpersonal relationships. The narcissistic patient may show lack of empathy, a sense of entitlement, or expectation of special favors without assuming reciprocal responsibilities; and interpersonal exploitiveness or relationships which characteristically vacillate between the extremes of over idealization and devaluation.

Some significant theoretical differences exist between two principal authorities on the definition of narcissistic personality. Kernberg and Kohut would both make the diagnosis of narcissistic personality largely on the basis of the transference manifestations. Kohut feels that the diagnosis of narcissistic personality is warranted when specific resistances in the transference neurosis allows the discernment of one of two transference or transference-like responses, namely the idealizing transference and the mirror transference. Kernberg sees the denial of the existence of the therapist as an independent, autonomous human being as one of the major characteristics of the narcissistic personality. Although he regards most of these patients as suffering from an underlying borderline organization, Kohut feels that borderline patients are not narcissistic personality disorders, although they indeed suffer from disorders of narcissism.

In order to illustrate my points I will refer to three clinical examples where variations of the combined individual-group treatment approach were utilized, describing the finding encountered with each of these modifications. Let me hasten to add that only the last of the three treatment approaches was carefully conceived in advance and successfully implemented. The other groups represent a combination of inexperience and the lack of available technical knowledge at that time. However, it was only from these earlier groups that the third format emerged. Because of space constraints, only the most germane data about the patients and their course of treatment will be presented.

ILLUSTRATIONS

Case 1
Dr. D., a 43-year-old academically prominent specialist, had been in and out of individual treatment for 15 years with chronic complaints of anhedonia, suicidal preoccupations, and occasional gestures following the termination of

homosexual love affairs, and chronic depression and bouts with alcoholism. A brilliant researcher and writer, she could not maintain a clinical practice because of her erratic personal life, which sometimes incapacitated her for months. Moreover, she conveyed the feeling to her patients that their medical problems and challenges interested her more than their suffering. Because of inherited wealth and her academic salary, she was able to sustain herself through these regressive periods and continue with psychiatric treatment. She had seen five therapists over the course of her life, but the longest she had stayed with any therapist was three years. This therapist felt that he had done all he could for her in individual therapy and referred her for group, stating that she needed to work on her social skills and interpersonal relationships. She continued seeing him on a biweekly or monthly basis she deemed necessary.

Case 2

Mr. M., a 27-year-old law student and holder of two masters degrees was referred for group therapy by his psychiatrist, who felt that he needed more support than could be offered by the therapist alone. Mr. M. was informed that he had to learn to get along better with his peers and teachers. He had been in psychotherapy for three months on a weekly basis for depression and inability to study after the recent break-up with his girlfriend. Similar reactions to disrupted relationships had been noted in the past.

Case 3

Miss J., a 24-year-old school teacher, was referred for help by her internist because of long-standing somatic symptoms, difficulties with authority figures at work, and her inability to maintain heterosexual relationships. Although she was bright, articulate, and attractive, her relationships usually ended in bitter arguments wherein the man was usually devalued and thrown out. Following two years in individual therapy she was placed in combined treatment with the same therapist for six years.

Over the course of treatment all three patients described were diagnosed as having a borderline disorder with prominent narcissistic pathology.

COURSE OF TREATMENT

Group I: Dr. D.

Of the three patients described, Dr. D., the first patient, benefited least from group therapy. Her group met weekly for one and a half years and disbanded because of geographic moves by three of its members, but mainly because the group was unable to provide a therapeutic milieu to benefit its members. On the surface this group had much in common. All five members were articulate and well educated. Two were physicians, one was a nurse, the fourth a college professor, and the fifth a college graduate and wife of a successful executive. All were considered borderline patients, but none had been sufficiently impaired to warrant psychiatric hospitalization. In the group setting the members of the group recapitulated the problems which had brought them into therapy. They remained alienated from one another, exhibited little group altruism, were highly distrustful of the motives of one another, and throughout most of the sessions exhibited projective identification, denial, and intellectualization. Group ambiance varied from depression to overt hostility. Two of the patients were in combined individual and group treatment with me, one was in group therapy solely, and the remaining two patients were in individual treatment with different therapists while being in the group.

I will focus most of my remarks about this group on Dr. D. as she represented the most difficult and least improved patient in the group. Much of her difficulty will highlight the weaknesses of the combined group format in which she was placed. The brightest member of the group, Dr. D. was intellectually sheathed in a suit of armor. She rendered all the members impotent with her premature intellectualized insights, know-it-all attitude, and presumably level-headed advice and complex interpretations for the other members.

At all times, she viewed herself as the senior member and the personification of reason and objectivity in the group. She harangued the group in a subtle devaluating manner for being her intellectual and psychological inferiors and therefore of little help to her. Even the group therapist was useless to her, for none of his interpretations seemed to change anything. She was older than he, a full professor, and a national authority. She had seen the most senior psychiatrists in the city, yet none had been able to affect her in any way.

Her agenda in the group was quite clear. From her family history and defensive maneuvers in the group she was acting out the negative transference with her father, who had failed to rescue her from the clutches of the aggressive, devouring mother who engulfed the patient and never gave her sufficient self-worth and security to individuate and to gain self-esteem. In fact, Dr. D. only remained in the city because of mother, who was now chronically ill and, like the patient, would not heed any outside professional advice.

Father had long since died. Dr. D was openly ambivalent toward mother, hating but desperately needing her. Dr. D.'s homosexual relationships were complex. In her partners she sought the good mother she had lacked. Simultaneously, she attempted to repudiate her need for mother because of the danger of engulfment and thus she unconsciously chose younger women whom she could dominate much as mother dominated her. Unknowingly, she still identified with mother and, hating the traits of dependency and clinging in herself, she would project these onto her lovers. Inevitably the relationships would disintegrate and Dr. D. would feel torn assunder. With the flight of each partner she felt she had lost part of her own self. Following repeated encounters and the loss of physical attractiveness with increasing age, she relentlessly pursued her professional career, hoping to gain the much needed praise and adoration she never experienced from her parents. All her professional success, however, were temporary and insufficient. She would lapse back into bouts of depression.

Dr. D. entered the group hoping to find the admiration

and approving attention to which she felt entitled. She ignored the men in the group, chose a young woman physician, Dr. L., as a love object and idealized her from the beginning as she had done with previous lovers. The impairing relationship between these two became intense, ambivalent, and eventually errupted into stormy, protracted tirades characterized by accusations and demands.

Drs. D. and L. were in individual therapy with outside therapists but communication between the group therapist and the individual therapists was spotty and irregular. The group was split. The other group members felt left out, angered, and at times amused by the pairing situation. Initially they assumed the role of spectators at a love feast but soon became a jeering audience watching two gladiators going for the jugular. The intensity of the desperate hunger, loneliness, fear of loss of self, and chronic anger and frustration most pronounced in Dr. D. and Dr. L., but also present in a lesser degree in all the members, impeded the development of group norms such as altruism, interpersonal learning, instillation of hope, and cohesiveness. In this group of all borderline patients the members viewed themselves as chronic losers. Via their professional facades they attempted to gain a partial identity and acceptance but no members dared to take a risk of exposing their personal lives in the group, fearing attack and ridicule from the others. The common group tension was repeatedly interpreted as a manifestation of the desperate attempt to hide the neediness and fear each member had of becoming dependent upon a "dog eat dog" group.

After a year and a half this group disbanded. The two physicians, D. and L., were planning to move out of the city, and another member's husband was transferred to a job out of state. The remaining two members of the group, in combined individual and group therapy with the group therapist, refused to join another group.

Dr. D.'s mother died shortly after the group broke up and she was able to accept a position in another city. Of all the members, she was the least improved. She remained chronically angry and depressed, proving to herself through her protracted individual and group experiences, that the external world, like her mother, was cold, unsympathetic, and undependable.

Group II: Mr. M.

Mr. M., the law student, was placed in a group of seven patients composed of four females and three males. In the beginning the therapists diagnosed all the patients as having neurotic or character disorder problems. The two resident therapists received weekly supervision and I frequently observed the group on video tapes.

Mr. M. entered the group four weeks after its inception. One patient was still being seen by one of the group therapists, and another continued to see his outside individual therapist intermittently. Fresh from their group dynamics training, the two neophyte therapists were eager to start a group and were pleased to have Mr. M. as a patient. Intelligent, articulate, and sophisticated, he would lend a touch of class to the group. Feeling uneasy with their first group, the therapists adopted a silent, analytic manner, ready to interpret to the group whenever the occasion arose.

Mr. M., still hurting and feeling rejected by his girfriend, saw the referral for group therapy as yet another narcissistic trauma. Although he was in his last year of law school, he was running into more, rather than less, difficulty. Playing upon his good looks and smooth talk, Mr. M. sought solace from the women in the group. It readily emerged in the group that he had been close to his mother and was always involved in a relationship with a woman, usually older and more mature than he. His relationship with men was polite but distant. As expected, his relationship with father had been chronically dissatisfying.

Sensing his insatiable oral needs, the women members became uneasy and then repelled by Mr. M. He became attracted to and yet frightened by Mr. K., a macho-appearing member who revealed homosexual leanings and later proved to have an underlying borderline disorder. Mr. M. himself started to entertain homosexual fantasies and showed increasing anxiety in the group. During the initial months he continued to present the facade of the golden-haired boy on the pinnacle of success who had suddenly tripped. In his repeated attempts to explain what had occurred to him and brought about his downfall, Mr. M. irritated the group and they were unable to empathize with his plight.

The therapists themselves were puzzled at their lack of empathy and only upon viewing the patient on tape was it evident that Mr. M. exhibited an emptiness and an "as-if" quality in persistent role playing. There was a clear defect in his identity. Over the ensuing meetings he vacillated in his attempts to identify with one and then another of the group members. He desperately sought to "get inside" people as though to anchor himself. Experiencing little support and gratification from the group, he grew increasingly depressed and anxious. He sensed that he was getting nowhere. He pouted and withdrew into silences. Upon breaking these, he would deliver scathing and paranoid attacks upon the members. No one, and nothing in the group, seemed to be helping. On several occasions Mr. M. contacted the therapists outside of the group and requested emergency appointments. His intense dependency needs, depression, and chronic rage created marked discomfort in the therapists. In the group he avoided the glances of the therapists and was increasingly preoccupied with homosexual thoughts. He insisted on returning to his former therapist. During that visit he wound up crying and rolling on the floor in regressed fashion. His therapist then referred him for individual care with another psychiatrist and over the next few weeks Mr. M. was in combined therapy.

The 20th group session was his last. As a farewell he launched into a diatribe, denouncing each member and the two group therapists, pointing out in detail all their weakness. With unrelenting fury he complained how each person in the group had ignored his needs and, in fact, how they were persecuting him. Upon reviewing Mr. M.'s course in the group, the student therapists expressed disbelief and shock that Mr. M., who seemed so ideal a group member and so

strong, could decompensate before their eyes in a group setting, rendering all the members and the therapists helpless.
This was their first encounter treating a narcissistic patient
with an underlying borderline disorder.

Group III: Miss J.

Miss J. was one of eight members in a newly formed,
close-ended group in which all the members were in combined
treatment with the same therapist. Two had been in individual treatment less than one year. The other six had been
in therapy two or more years with me prior to which they had
seen at least three or more therapists. Four of the members
were borderline personalities, one of whom manifested pronounced narcissistic pathology. One patient was a narcissistic
character. The remaining three patients exhibited character
disorders; one was a hysterical personality, another a phobic
individual with severe obsessive-compulsive features, and the
third member, a chronic depressive character. Two members
dropped out of this group after two years of treatment and
the remainder of the patients terminated as a group after six
years. Another borderline patient was added to the group
three years after its inception and she remained with the
group until it terminated.

It was decided in advance that this group would be
heterogeneous in its membership and would include several
borderline patients. All the members were to be seen in combined treatment with the same therapist. This approach
would be used throughout the life of the group. Individual
sessions would range from a minimum of one visit per week
to a maximum of four sessions per week. The patients
selected for this group were of good intelligence, had held
responsible positions, and were highly motivated to join a
group. They were in many ways similar to the members of
Group I, which I have described as being well educated and
articulate. In marked contrast to that group, however, this
group was very successful and cohesive and the majority of
the members indicated that they were definitely improved.
Follow-up studies with the group are now in the 11th year and

consist of semiannual interviews with six of the group members. Improvement has been maintained in the majority of these patients five years after the group terminated.

Miss J. took to this group like a duck to water. Aggressive and determined to be the leader, she quickly took charge of the group. She became the group interpreter, established the norm of letting everything hang out for the group and also adopted a Scotland Yard, probing attitude. The anticipated defensiveness or animosity created by such an approach was counteracted by the personalities of the three nonborderline patients, in particular the narcissistic patient who was, by profession, an entertainer. He bid his time. The group members had a low level of anxiety and were not susceptible to guilt and were themselves aggressive individuals. In addition, this group had been carefully prepared during individual sessions to expect personal confrontations. Initially, some members even viewed Miss J. as a "ringer" who had been put into the group to keep them on track and to stimulate them in what was perceived as a laboratory setting in which they were to learn about themselves and how they reacted with people.

Although this illusion about Miss J. was to fade, the group did not lose track of their task which was reinforced in the individual sessions. The members saw through Miss J.'s defensive maneuvers after the second year and pointed out to her how she protected herself by focusing on others in an aggressive fashion. In part she came to realize that her open attacks upon the other patients represented a disavowal of the hated parts of herself which she projected onto people. These she feared and had to actively control. In turn she was able to experience how she was used by other borderline patients in a similar manner.

Miss J. shared her job difficulties with the group and saw them reenacted. Although never fired from any position she came perilously close to being dismissed by outraged supervisors and being scapegoated in the group because of her attitudes. Her labile temper and sense of chronic emptiness usually followed on the heels of an exhibitionistic action which would intrigue the group, and temporarily allay her sense of hollowness and loneliness. A physically attractive person, she displayed her sex in unabashed fashion, wearing blouses with low, plunging necklines and displaying her legs to advantage whenever she dealt with the male group members. In the group she flaunted her sexual escapades with prominent men in the community and described how she could seduce and humiliate them.

Although her appearance, behavior, and affect might easily lead one to diagnose her as a hysterical personality, a more malignant underlying disorder was present. She was unable to separate from a cold, very masculine, and controlling mother. She suffered severe somatic symptoms and had marked identity problems. During her treatment course she demonstrated drastic changes in her manner of dress, hair styles, make up, speech mannerisms, and personal opinions. In her own words, she was desperately seeking to find "the real Miss J."

The group confronted her with her chameleon attitudes and chronic rage; the individual therapy provided her the safety and opportunity to work through her identity diffusion and the resolution of her grandiose self. She was able to learn through therapy that her acting out in the group and destructive social relationships on the outside represented at one level a flight from the Oedipal situation and, on a more regressive plane, the need for an idealizing male parent who was missing from her life. Her father died during her course of therapy, but had divorced her mother when the patient was very young. During the last year of therapy Miss J. was finally able to maintain a solid relationship with a professional man whom she later married. Over the course of her therapy she ran through a total of 25 lovers with destructive results.

The glue of the individual sessions held this group together, allowing her heated interchange between its members, the emergence of projective identification, splitting, and a vast range of intermember and therapist-member transferences. The transference phenomena included a transference neurosis with one patient, and merger and idealizing transferences at different times between others. Most of the time the individual and group sessions were synchronously interwoven. Upon the termination of this group after six years, many members continued to communicate via occasional phone calls, lunch, or dinner engagements. However, they maintained the group norm of confidentiality. There was no sexual acting out between male and female members so far as I could tell from follow-up interviews, although the members regarded one another with affection and respect after the group terminated.

DISCUSSION

No matter how carefully group therapists select their patients, compose their groups, and establish therapeutic group norms, they find that each group has its own personality which determines, to a great extent, how successful and beneficial the group will be for its members. To be sure, the better trained and more experienced the therapist, the better will be their results.

When we are specifically asked to propose a research design to test out a hypothesis—such as: do borderline or narcissistic disordered patients do better in a homogeneous or heterogeneous group, better with combined individual and group therapy or in group therapy alone, better with separate individual and group therapists, and the various modifications of this format—we come to grief. Much depends on the personality and ever-evolving technique of each group therapist as well as the composite personalities of the members of each group. It is truly difficult to talk about control groups and control situations when we deal with such a large number of variables in testing out a complex hypothesis. Well-known research studies have shown that there are many similarities among respected therapists of different schools and techniques and wide variations in the techniques of people who espouse the same treatment orientation. I introduce these preliminary considerations prior to making the following personal observations about my experience with patients suffering from borderline and narcissistic conditions.

I have drawn some conclusions for the patients described in the three preceding groups which I believe to be valid under the conditions described. Whether or not the reader is in agreement with my approach will depend on his or her own personality, theoretical orientation, and the type of patients in groups.

In the case of Dr. D., who exhibited prominent borderline and narcissistic pathology, placement in a homogeneous group of borderline patients where the majority of the patients were in combined individual and group therapy, albeit with a number of individual patients, did not work out. Of the three groups which I have described, I considered this format to be the least beneficial. In particular, I felt that Dr. D. was the patient who gained the least from the group.

Her group appeared to be homogeneous by conventional grouping standards and in regard to common conflicts. At its inception all the members expressed motivation to join the group. Why then did Dr. D. derive such little benefit from her treatment? First, it is significant to note that Dr. D. paired in the group with Dr. L., another woman physician but who was also a member in individual treatment with an outside therapist. Both saw their individual therapists infrequently, providing little opportunity for the objective distancing and emotional refueling necessary to sustain them when suffering repeated narcissistic injuries in the group setting. Throughout the life of the group Drs. D. and L. engaged in a pairing relationship, creating a split and preventing the development of group cohesion. Furthermore, on closer examination Drs. D. and L. paired on the basis of a twinship transference which was not effectively handled in the group. The acting out continued in the group and, although the pair was not extruded from the group, they were, in essence, scapegoats upon whom the other members could displace their conflicts and avoid doing their personal work.

Second, a major obstacle to constructive therapy in this group which prevented growth in Dr. D. and Dr. L. was the lack of clarity in regard to the individual goals. All the patients in the combined individual and group format were expected to engage in a therapy which would stress personality reconstruction. This was not the same aim of the two individual therapists treating Drs. D. and L. They were operating on the premise that therapy would be supportive with the goal of personality repair rather than reconstruction or reorganization. If personality reconstruction is to be the major therapeutic objective, the following conditions must be satisfied before the patient moves into the group: The patient should have established basic trust in the therapist; the patient should have demonstrated that he or she possesses sufficient reality testing and a sense of reality which can be depended on when expectable regressions to primitive states occur; and there should be an existing therapeutic alliance developed from the individual work. These conditions were not fulfilled with Dr. D.

Third, a major defense mechanism employed by borderline patients is splitting, and having two or more therapists treating these patients separately in two different modalities tends to invite splitting even more. Under this arrangement, I have noted that countertransference difficulties arise frequently between patients and their therapists and also between the therapists themselves. In particular, the boundaries of confidentiality may become fuzzy, to the disadvantage of the patients. The issues of what properly can be conveyed by the individual therapist to the group therapist, and perhaps to peers in the group, and what is to be kept confidential in the group and away from the knowledge of the individual therapist are only a few of the items which may arise and promote resistance.

In order to deal with the problems engendered by splitting as well as the other primitive ego defenses utilized by the borderline patient, the two or more therapists must conscientiously meet on a regular basis to discuss the patient's treatment. In practice the lack of time and presence of counter-transference problems mediated against frequent meetings. Where splitting becomes a problem, one often sees the operation of primitive idealization as well. Therefore, the individual therapist tended to become the idealized good, magical object and the group therapist the all bad, persecutory object.

I will now proceed to the case of Mr. M. and discuss the many problems posed in his treatment. Perhaps the most glaring error in his management was the lack of diagnostic understanding of the patient by his individual and group therapists. An accurate diagnosis of the borderline or narcissistic patient is the cornerstone for successful therapy. Even when the diagnosis is well established there is considerable controversy about the role of group therapy in the treatment of these patients.

Not all group therapists would agree that the narcissistic patient or borderline patient is best treated in the group setting, or that such a patient is good for the group. Yalom (1975) states that "the narcissistic patient generally has a stormier time of it in group therapy than in individual therapy." In his book he points out that the price paid by the group which dealt with a narcissistic patient was enormous; that other members were neglected and many important isues were left untouched. Horner (1975) has found in her experience that the narcissistic personality disorder as delineated by Kohut has not responded well to group treatment. She believes that "the group has been nonproductive for the patient at best, and destructive for both the patient and the group at worst." Other group therapists contend that, although group therapy may be effective in confronting a patient with the pathologic aspects of his narcissism, the group does not provide the opportunity to allow the narcissistic patient a good enough one-to-one relationship with the therapist. Without such a relationship, the patient is unable to progress from the position of narcissistic fixation and entitlement. In addition, through his behavior the narcissistic patient is likely to become the focus of negative transferences from other group members, be scapegoated, and eventually be excluded from the group.

Some therapists regard patients exhibiting excessive narcissistic manifestations as unsuitable for group therapy on the basis that they are too disruptive, interfere with culture building, and prevent group cohesion. Group therapists who adhere to the "group as a whole" approach often voice this opinion, recognizing that the narcissistic patient does not respond well to situations where he is afforded little opportunity for recognition of his uniqueness. In such cases, he may attempt to overidealize the leader but frequently becomes enraged and withdraws from the group.

The combined individual and group approach can frequently overcome the aforementioned difficulties. In individual therapy, the transference reactions are allowed to develop without intrusion. Here the therapist can convey to the patient a sense of constancy, empathetic awareness, and security—the very feelings the narcissistic patient has lacked in his life. It is a rare group, indeed, which early in its life can give the patient the feeling of acceptance and stability and, later, the adaptability to satiate his immense oral needs. No doubt, in the beginning, the narcissistic patient is readily welcomed to drain off the primitive anxieties for the group. To the inexperienced group leader, the narcissistic patient is seen as the initiator of self-disclosure, catharsis, and universality. It is usually in the second stage of group formation, described by Yalom (1975), that the group and the narcissistic patient come to grief. This stage is characterized by conflict, dominance, and rebellion. If the group leader does not properly understand and handle the narcissistic patient, he may bolt, the group may remain in chaos, or it may dissolve.

Thus, Mr. M. experienced both his individual and group therapies as repeat situations in a life-long succession of empathic failures with people whom he sought to idealize, to whom he could exhibit, and with whose aid he might develop a cohesive self. The individual therapist was seduced by Mr. M.'s exhibitionistic display early in treatment and responded by referring him to a group in the belief that he possessed a basically sound identity or cohesive self. The group could have helped him look at his interpersonal behavior and provided him with feedback and support to rectify his environmental deficits. However, the group therapists saw in him only the manifestations of late adolescent turmoil which they treated with interpretation and attempted to foster his independence. They misunderstood the meaning of his aggressive reactions, pervasive anxiety and capacity for paranoid thinking when narcissistic supplies were lacking. He was not helped with the setting of boundaries to modulate his emotions as they evolved. In response to Mr. M.'s rage and devaluation of them, the therapists became angry, withdrew, and became even more withholding.

Countertransference problems invariably arise when treating narcissistic patients. Kohut (1971) states that the analyst who works with narcissistic patients,

> . . . must, furthermore, be aware of the potential interference of his own narcissistic demands which rebel against a chronic situation in which he is neither experienced as himself by the patient nor even confused with an object of the patient's past. And finally, in specific instances, the analyst must be free of the active interference by archaic fears of dissolution through merger.

When a therapist is aware that his countertransference reaction is becoming too intense, placing the patient in concurrent group and individual treatment is usually of mutual benefit. This is especially true if the narcissistic character possesses an underlying borderline personality organization. Much is demanded of the group therapist and group members in terms of understanding the potential countertransference reaction which may be induced by the patient's narcissistic transferences. Nevertheless, the lack of regular and meaningful communication between the group and individual therapists negates all the potential benefits to be derived from the combined approach. Once again, they are in the situation of the six blind men describing an elephant and worse still, the patient senses the fragmentation and lack of empathic understanding.

The third group, in which Miss J. was a member, attempted to maximize the strengths of the combined format and to minimize its potential weaknesses. There was an in-depth understanding and careful pregroup preparation of each patient. Communicational gaps were minimized as the group therapist was also each patient's individual therapist. What was observed in the group was studied and worked with in the individual sessions; similarly, the individual sessions helped to overcome blockages in the group.

I have found that the borderline and narcissistic patient feels far more supported in a group setting knowing that the same therapist will be able to see him later in an individual session who will be aware of recent events and who can clarify the often fantastic and distorted perceptions stirred up in a group. If left untouched, these perceptions can cause patients to flee the group.

The emotional burden placed on the therapist resulting from the patient's continual devaluation and projective iden-tification can also be considerably eased by the combined treatment method. Potential countertransference problems can be minimized. His therapeutic task is lightened when the therapist is able to confront the patient in an individual ses-sion with a particular piece of distorted reality and then in the group have group members again point out the distortion. The confrontation is more readily accepted and the border-line patient's sense of reality tends to be much improved. When there are separate therapists treating the patient with different modalities, the work on a particular item or area is often lost or the therapeutic progress is much delayed. All too often patients seek support for the anxiety engendered by their psychopathology rather than expressing support to explore the illness unless they are confronted repeatedly and consistently with their denial. Confrontation must be done in a supportive manner in order not to be con-strued as a parental demand or attack by the overly sensitive patient.

When the therapist sees borderline patients in both the individual and group setting, the transference is better handled as there is opportunity for distancing and dilution. Patients frequently experience a dyadic relationship as too stressful. Very primitive regressive reactions may occur in intensive individual therapy unless there is the opportunity for reality testing and support which is found in a group setting. I specifically refer to borderline patients who are in reconstructive therapy but whose egos are too weak for conventional analysis. In a group the terrified reactions of the borderline patient or idealized transferences of the narcissistic patient toward the therapist have the opportunity to become modified through the eyes of peers, and the sense of reality and reality testing may be improved when perceptions of other patients are shared. The support gained from the group usually makes it less frightening for the patient to discuss his or her feelings about the therapist in individual therapy and also educates the patient about the significance of the transference.

Being subjected to distorted perceptions by the patient, frequent denigration and primitive idealization can play havoc with the therapist who is unaccustomed to encountering intense and often uncomfortable feelings which are aroused in the course of working with the borderline and narcissistic patient. Unlike the psychotic individual who may also evoke primitive emotions in the therapist, the borderline patient is in much better contact with reality and his or her projections cannot be ignored or accepted with the same tranquility and technical neutrality which we often experience working with psychotic patients. The therapist's ability to regress and empathize, utilizing concordant identification (Racker, 1968), is severely taxed when he or she realizes that the borderline patient may leave a highly complex and successful task momentarily to come for therapy and then seemingly disorganize, spewing forth very primitive emotions and regressed thinking, only to quickly reorganize and return to the former task once the session is over. The incongruity of such behavior in the face of mutual denial from the borderline patient promotes a different mental frame of reference in the therapist as contrasted to working with a psychotic patient or a better integrated patient in analysis. When such a patient is worked with intensively and frequently in individual therapy, the combined group and individual approach is of particular help. This is especially true when the borderline patient has an underlying narcissistic or infantile character makeup. One finds that the individual sessions go far better when these patients are also seen in a group setting. The therapist has far less "luggage" to encumber him or her in performing the arduous, demanding work with these patients because peer members in a group lend considerable support to the therapist. The patients also benefit. The oral deprivation and aggression typical of the infantile and narcissistic character are readily confronted by the group and the borderline patient must learn to express and deal with these needs in a more adaptive way. Spotnitz (1976) has referred to the group experience as "first-rate training" for these borderline patients.

In a group setting among peers the borderline patient has the opportunity to find different identification models whereas the narcissistic patient may form mirror transferences. It has long been recognized that one of the mechanisms for change in individuals in therapy is the identification with and internalization of the therapist's attitudes and values. This is often related to a corrective emotional experience. However, in a group both healthy and pathologic identifications may be made by patients with other group members. In any event, what occurs in the group may be observed by the therapist in vivo and dealt with either in the group or the individual setting. The advantage from having the patient in concomitant therapy is that such identifications may be observed in a therapeutic and supportive environment as opposed to acting-out, destructive behavior where the patient seeks to identify with individuals on the outside in order to gain relief from anxiety or from loneliness.

Prior to attaining this stage of identification a patient often projects onto various group members different parts of his or her personality. In practice, members of the group may choose to allow this identification to occur or may reject them. If rejected, the borderline patient will select another individual and tend to make that group patient a total embodiment of one fragmented aspect of his or her personality. Thus, the therapist engaged in concomitant therapy also has the opportunity to observe first-hand the fragmentation which occurs within the borderline patient and to see the patient's struggle to keep separate or to integrate these different fragments or internal objects through multiple identifications.

Where a patient shows outstanding narcissistic pathology, the combined individual and group approach is invaluable in helping both therapist and patient understand and appreciate the changes occurring. During these changes, the therapist can function as the stabilizer, integrator, and anchor upon whom the patient can depend. Both healthy and unhealthy identifications in the group setting may be expected to occur and there will be excessive swings as the patient struggles to evolve a whole and constant self. The therapist who can observe the patient individually and in the group setting is at an advantage in understanding and dealing with the evolving facets of the patient's emerging identity.

REFERENCES

Kohut, H. *The analysis of the self.* New York: International Universities Press, 1971.
Racker, N. *Transference and countertransference.* New York: International Universities Press, 1968.
Spotnitz, H. *Psychotherapy of preoedipal conditions.* New York: Jason Aronson, 1976.

Part III
Harnessing the Analyst's Creativity
through Counter-Transference
Workshops

Saretsky's chapter on "Innovative Approaches to Supervision" follows in the tradition of Edward Tauber's trailblazing article on countertransference phenomena published back in 1952. In this article, Tauber made the observation that countertransference reactions of the analyst to his patient and the supervisor to the supervisee, had been largely characterized as an interference to the ongoing task of improving the technical expertise of the analyst. Tauber suggested that valuable insights could be gleaned regarding the prevailing treatment issues by monitoring the ebb and flow of transference-countertransference processes within the supervisory setting. Saretsky has extended this valuable contribution by indicating a variety of techniques whereby the supervisee can be helped to overcome his blind spots and persisting technical mistakes. Working from the premise that except in the case of the inexperienced analyst, errors in interpretation are potential reflections of countertransference tendencies, Saretsky proposes a supervisory framework designed to more carefully examine these lapses. This approach, which includes role-playing and shared group fantasies, has not only proven successful in breaking deadlocks, but has also frequently led to the supervisee's feeling freer to trust their intuition, use their preconscious reactions to therapeutic advantage, and become more resourceful in employing their technical skills.

Chapter 11

INNOVATIVE APPROACHES TO SUPERVISION WITH ADVANCED THERAPISTS
Ted Saretsky, Ph.D.

The material presented thus far in this book makes it quite evident that the real personality of the analyst is a significant variable in determining treatment progress. The analyst's empathic nature provides a "holding environment" scaffolding until such time that a working alliance is established. Once having met the challenge of being a "good enough mother" and providing a "container" for projective identifications, the analyst can begin to use interpretive techniques and work through conflictual vicissitudes with a patient who is positively motivated and reasonably receptive and trusting. The analyst's sense of timing, his intuition, and his theoretical grasp of personality dynamics must all be harmonized, carefully integrated, and effectively communicated to get the patient to take progressive steps. In working with difficult patients, however, it has been suggested that many analysts are temporarily deprived of their ordinary good sense and adaptive capacities by regressive processes mobilized in narcissistically threatening predicaments. Induced countertransference reactions arouse ego-alien affects that must be reperceived and reintegrated before effective, helpful use can be made of these awarenesses. The inadequacy of cognitive processes alone in clarifying therapeutic enigmas, is, at first, terribly frustrating. It has already been noted that there is a great temptation to distance oneself intellectually by finding mechanical formulas to apply to confusing patient phenomena or by turning to seductive gimmicks that create a great stir, thereby overcoming feelings of passivity and helplessness.

The importance of good supervision in this context cannot be overemphasized. In describing his own approach, Spotnitz (1969) describes the supervisory process as a kind of affective-cognitive education that is designed to supplement areas that have not been worked through in training analysis:

> In addition to reporting the feelings and thoughts verbalized by the patient he is treating, the student is helped to report his own reactions to these thoughts and feelings. He is very much inclined to fear such reactions in himself, and he is also afraid to base his interventions on such emotional understanding of the patient. Thus the student requires a great deal of help in recognizing and understanding the feelings that the patient induces in him. It is important to get the student to communicate all thoughts and feelings, his own and the patient's; but the student is not supposed to act on his thoughts and feelings. He is supposed to carry out the directions of the supervisor at such time as the student has become comfortable with these directions, and can carry them out easily as expressions of his own personality.

> The purpose of helping the student recognize and report his feelings and thoughts is to get him to experience his own resistance. The student experiences much self-opposition to becoming aware of his thoughts and feelings about the patient, particularly those that are realistically provoked by a patient's dangerous or threatening behavior and communications. Moreover, the student experiences much reluctance to comply with the directions of the supervisor; that is, he has to contend himself with a great deal of resistance to the supervisor. Surprisingly enough, this is desirable, because through the process of analyzing and resolving these resistances the student

develops the feelings and thoughts that will enable him to relate to the patient in a way that will promote his recovery.

The principle of resolving resistance rather than trying to overcome it in the supervisory situation is the same principle that is applied in the treatment of the patient. The supervisor operates on the assumption that if he is successful in clearing away whatever obstacles there are to the student therapist's understanding of the patient, to having the right feelings for the patient, and to providing him with the proper interventions at the right time, the student will acquire the ability to treat the patient spontaneously without assistance. It scarcely needs saying that the development of the ability to administer effective treatment spontaneously is the ultimate goal of supervision (p. 208).

Spotnitz draws a parallel between the maturational needs of children and the administration of therapeutic dosages of feelings from analyst to patient. Just as the wise mother shields her child from overexposure to intense negative feelings and provides support and encouragement for independence and mastery, so the analyst should be sensitive to ongoing patient needs. In order for the analyst to provide interventions that meet deficits arising from development failures, he must first be capable of experiencing a wide range of feelings. Spotnitz's main thesis is that the feelings that the analyst is found to be resisting in supervision can provide important information about blind spots with regard to therapeutic impasse. Spotnitz distinguishes between subjective and objective countertransference reactions. Objective countertransference responses have to do with feelings aroused in the analyst (confusion, disgust, helplessness, loss, etc.) that are realistically induced by patient behavior. Spotnitz's orientation is to identify these emotional trends and understand their origins in the analytic interplay in order to facilitate helpful interpretations.

The supervisor must use himself as a catalyst in the service not of "analyzing" his student but of developing in them those ego functions essential for analyzing (Isakower, 1957). Ekstein and Wallerstein (1958) see the supervisory process as a new "experience of growth" which is self-limited according to the nature and degree of those irrational attitudes and resistances which operate in either student or teacher. They see this as an analogous process to the psychotherapeutic situation whereby we work with patients in a mutual endeavor to help them to independence and new insight.

There is one common drawback, however, to the typical dyadic supervisor-supervisee relationship. Leichter (1962) has noted that students have a tendency to be parent bound and project an omnipotent authority image onto their supervisor. The very nature of being a relative beginner or even of being an experienced analyst presenting confusing, difficult cases frequently arouses infantile regressive trends in the trainee. This dependent tendency can interfere with spontaneity and intuition and make the student feel "stupid" and confused. A common derivative of regression is its opposite, i.e., identification with omnipotence. By incorporating the supervisor's wisdom and understanding in unrealistic fashion, the supervisee can place additional pressure on himself to see more than he is actually capable of. An insecure analyst or an analyst who is too heavily invested in being in control cannot possibly be free to use his inner resources creatively.

In light of these potential pitfalls that Mintz (1972) has emphasized the special advantages of group supervision. Besides the broad-based support system provided by sharing common experiences with others, Mintz reminds us that supervisees also benefit by being more receptive to feedback from peers. An observation that has been made in the group therapy setting is that, although the leader is considered the most significant and influential member of the group, fellow patients are experienced with considerably less ambivalence and resistance. With this in mind, Mintz (1972) has conducted experimential group workshops for mature therapists over the past decade and reports considerable success in helping therapists discover unrecognized emotional conflicts in themselves that lead to treatment problems.

Our theoretical knowledge, our subliminal perception of cues from the patient's behavior, and our intuition teaches more than we are consciously aware of. In effective supervision, this knowledge comes to consciousness and can be utilized fully after the personal projections, identifications, repressions, and other defenses inevitably evoked in the therapist have been identified (p. 471).

Mintz has devised several techniques for elucidating the interface of the patient-analyst impasse.

1. The presenting analyst is asked to role-play his patient by imitating the patient's characteristic maneuvers and talking as the patient talks. Most often, responses are evoked from the group that are similar to how the analyst ordinarily feels. The analyst can now identify with the patient's feelings, and the group with the analyst's feelings. With this added dimension, unrecognized transactional elements are quickly brought to the fore and can be more objectively discussed. The technique of identifying with the patient can also enable the analyst to distinguish between his own anxieties and those belonging to the patient. As an illustration, Mintz describes a borderline patient who fantasized that he is entering a long dark tunnel "leading to a place unknown." The analyst was confused about how deeply to probe the unconscious meaning of this fantasy for fear of precipitating a psychotic break. Mintz requested that the analyst imagine himself entering a long dark tunnel and report his feelings. The analyst took this symbolic trip, experienced some anxiety, but concluded by reminding himself that he was an analyst in a supervisory group. Reminding himself of who he was helped the analyst to interpret the patient's shared fantasy as a communication of his relative readiness to proceed to explore his suppressed anxieties. Mintz indicates that aside from greater empathy, the presenting analyst can benefit by seeing how another analyst would work on the same case. By role-playing the patient, and letting other members of the group try to "treat," the analyst is introduced to a broader repertoire of approaches and is made more aware of any technical rigidities that might be operative.

2. The presenting analyst is asked to speak his mind to an

empty chair, representing the patient, for five minutes. The instructions encourage a no-holds-barred approach. "Don't act responsible. Tell the patient what you're really feeling." Not only does this technique cathartically clear the air and reduce buried resentments, but it also seems to pinpoint the underlying resentments that may be coloring the management of the case in question.

> One patient constantly martyred herself by endlessly reciting the irrational, seemingly unprovoked angry behavior by her husband. When the analyst acted out his inner feelings, he unleashed an angry tirade toward the innocent patient that was incongruous with his typical reaction to her niceness. He then realized that her platitudes, detachment, insecurity, and insensitivity to his feelings were experienced as hostility that he previously found very difficult to assign to such a weak, ingratiating person. When this insight was brought back into the treatment setting, the patient was shocked to discover the provocative nature of these traits, and felt very dissociated from the underlying hostility. In the working through process, the patient's recognition of these subtle negativisms made the husband's outraged behavior more comprehensible, and provided the patient with a much sharper perspective of her role in the relationship (p. 473).

3. Everyone in the group is asked to spend several minutes in free fantasy about the patient. Mintz cautions us not to consider these associations as necessarily valid. However, she is impressed by the common themes that emerge which may be an indication of the primary transference-countertransference point of friction. The creativity and intuitive powers of the group provide new approaches and a fresh incentive to return to the challenge of working with the difficult patient.

4. Although it is not required, the analyst is encouraged to think of parallels in his own early family life that may cause him to misidentify the patient with a member of the analyst's family or an unacceptable aspect of the analyst's own personality. One analyst reported beginning work with an anorexic adolescent and thinking he should really request

an additional session each week with the family. He found himself strangely reluctant to make such a request of the parents. In the group, he realized that he identified the weak, submissive, withdrawn father with his own father. He came to see that behind the father's recessive role in the family, there was considerable anger. In anticipation of tapping into that anger, the analyst's inclination was to masochistically assume an untenable treatment situation without asking the parents to share in the responsibility. Not only did this understanding make it easier for the analyst to request the extra session, but it also hit at a core dynamic (a rebellious reaction to the mother's need to control) in the identified patient's presenting symptomatology.

Finally, Robert Langs (1974) has written extensively on the analyst's contribution to serious disruption to the therapeutic alliance. "Indeed, in my supervisory experiences, such human and technical errors are the single largest cause of negative and adverse reactions in patients during therapy. These regressions are often difficult to resolve and cause major disturbances in the therapeutic alliance, especially when they go undetected and unanalyzed. As we shall soon recognize, it follows from this finding, that the appearance of regressions in the patient and disruptions in the therapeutic alliance should alert the therapist to reassess his interventions — or failures to intervene — his general attitude toward the patient, and other aspects of his therapeutic stance for countertransference difficulties." (p. 310) Langs indicates that on the basis of presented material, he is able to predict the occurrence of regression with something like 90-95 percent accuracy. "The therapist's contribution proved to be the crucial day residue and context for the patient's reactions." (p. 311)

In order to offset disturbances in the therapeutic alliance, culminating in acting-out, regression and intensified symptom formation, Langs uses the supervisory experience to establish two major principles:

The necessity to remain vigilant to maintaining adequate boundaries and limits in relationship to the patient. Langs conceptualizes the space between analyst and patient as a clear field and a well-defined structure. Any impingements or boundary infractions must be seriously reviewed and thoroughly worked through. Langs suggests that the patient's reaction to more flagrant violations and deviations of the usual procedures are frequently experienced as incestuous seductions and aggressions. They may stimulate wishes for sexual fusion, create a paranoid apprehension of being tempted and used, and induce the realistic anxiety of being in the hands of an incompetent. The patient's dilemma in these cases is to deal with both a traumatizer and a supposed therapeutic ally, as one and the same person. Conflict, mistrust, defensiveness and feelings of betrayal are a natural outgrowth of analytic errors. Since the patient often has trouble in identifying the origin of these critical reactions, let alone having the confidence to express them, it is the analyst's responsibility during periods of impasse, to carefully monitor his contributions.

Langs suggests that the supervisory experience can be valuable for discovering through subjective awareness and feedback, the analyst's indirect disguised and derivative antitherapeutic communication. He believes that regression of all kinds, especially acting out against the therapy, must be recognized as possible indicators of countertransference problems or errors in technique. Langs recommends acknowledging errors to the patient in an appropriate therapeutic context. Additionally, Langs indicates that the nature of the patient's realistic and transference relationships to the analyst as it relates to his actual experiences with significant past figures and the patient's repressed fantasies and conflicts about them, may assist the analyst's in understanding the unconscious meaning of the analyst's improper response. "In all, the outcome is based on an interaction between the behavior and intra-psychic fantasies of the therapist and those of the patient on every possible level." (p. 33)

Liberman (1978) has described how the qualitatively distinctive feature of the patient's communication requires from the analyst an ideally optimal empathic response. This hierarchically preferable participation of affects combines from the analyst an ideally optimal empathic response. This hierarchically preferable participation of affects combines with a capacity to use rationality in the service of interpretation. The desired result of this "optimal empathy" is a furthering of the analytic task by helping the patient to give a name to predominant emotions and moods. Lieberman believes that the analyst's communications are richest and most effective when he is in a state of empathy because his interpretive messages take into account the language of the patient. The ensuing intervention evokes "feeling" formulations and creative phases in the patient never before uttered or even considered. Through the instrumentation of the analyst's affective responses, a newly created syntactic mood language is developed in the patient. Supervision is an excellent vehicle for strengthening the analyst's skill in employing his affective modulations to technical advantage. If the supervisor and fellow supervisees can help the analyst to detect vague, subtle, and often unnoticed attitudes and mood states within himself, he will be in a far more advantageous position to identify with and resonate to the patient's style of presentation.

The mutually self-corrective attitudes of a supervisory workshop can be particularly helpful in detecting countertransference interferences. Since no analyst can see everything, group feedback can direct attention to deviations from a therapeutic frame. Some of the more common manifestations of regressive tendencies by the analyst include:

1. Chronically depressed, anxious, or elated feelings during or after analytic hours with certain patients.

2. Changing a patient's appointment frequently, letting the hour run over, being late in arriving for the patient, setting too low a fee, not asking directly for money when it is due; not raising the issue of late fees but instead waiting for the patient to bring it up; not questioning absences.

3. Frequently feeling bored, withdrawn, impatient, disappointed.

4. Encouraging acting out (e.g., promoting a divorce,

supporting over aggressive behavior against authority figures, padding insurance forms, suggesting an affair, colluding with truancy, drug use).

5. Continuously reassuring the patient, trying too hard to be liked, letting the therapist's ego get in the way of attending to the patient's feelings; using the patient to impress colleagues with (the patient's status, attractiveness, wealth, progress).

6. Noticing a frequent tendency to be unnecessarily abrupt, hostile, sadistic, sarcastic, gossipy, contemptuous, pessimistic.

7. Finding that one's mood state is overly dependent on a patient being happy, satisfied, improved, cooperative, accepting interpretations.

8. Worrying about losing the patient, being afraid of letting the patient go, being reluctant to acknowledge that one can not work with a particular patient.

9. Consciously soliciting praise, gratitude, appreciation, affection.

10. Becoming personally affronted by temporary negative transferences, reproaches, accusations. Unusual defensive behavior, becoming argumentative, guilty, obsessional with regard to a particular patient.

11. Asking favors of a patient (mailing a letter, borrowing a cigarette, accepting gifts except under very special circumstances).

12. Dreams about a patient; patients' dreams where the therapist is represented as himself.

An interesting phenomena that has been commented on by many recent investigators of the supervisory process is that countertransferential attitudes are significantly more apparent through interactional presentation than through self-reflection. In the same way that projective identification enables the analyst to empathize with the patient's split-off feelings, supervisory group members become containers for the analyst's projected identifications. The transference-countertransference cycle is reversed so that now the group has empathic contact with countertransference reactions toward the presenting analyst and the analyst empathically identifies with the patient. When this complex process is monitored and explored, many relevant factors that would normally interfere with the therapeutic task, become readily apparent.

Some concrete illustrations might be helpful at this point.

1. Something as basic as the style of presenting may be isomorphically representative of a key structural issue that is sabotaging treatment progress. In working with beginning analysts in particular, there is tendency to present verbatim accounts of their sessions to the supervisor. Every remembered detail is reported in an unselective manner which largely excludes the student analyst's own train of associative thinking. If the supervisor consistently reinforces this manner of presentation, many important training objectives will be lost. On a more subtle level, the supervisor's willingness to accept uncomplainingly a passive, undiscriminating, blow-by-blow description of a session may serve to obfuscate the hidden relationship between the latent conflicts in the session proper and the student analyst's way of presenting them. In a supervisory session with three group therapists in training, therapist A was talking about her group in a rather reluctant fashion. "There is nothing terribly interesting to report. For the past three weeks everything has been quiet. No problems — nothing special." After a bit more prodding, she then went on to describe a couples group session where, in successive fashion, three different wives put down their husbands for a lack of involvement, for being too passive, and for not being responsible enough. Therapist A had been presenting for about fifteen minutes when I found myself growing increasingly withdrawn and restless. I intervened at this point and asked the other members of the supervisory group what they were feeling at that moment. Their reactions being similar to mine, I threw out two questions: Why were we bored? If we were bored, what function did this serve for therapist A?

In answer to question one, the general consensus was that therapist A was showing her resistance toward presenting, by being very obsessive, not focusing on any specific problem, talking in a dull, unenthusiastic manner, not pausing to offer her own feelings while the events she was describing were happening, etc.

Question two was interpreted as therapist A's "conscientiously" grinding out an "authentic" account of what supposedly happened during the session. Her self-righteous attitude was unconsciously conveyed by the diligent reporting (without sparing a word), which put the burden on the supervisory group to focus on the important things. After all, hadn't she done her duty by providing us with such a thorough picture?

The net result was a counterresistance by the rest of the supervisory group and myself. We were being asked to be involved and active in relation to material that A was not really taking responsibility for herself but only seeming to do so. In her defense, therapist A based her reluctance to present on the fact that she was the only one in the supervisory group who currently had an ongoing group, so that although on the one hand she welcomed the opportunity to be special and to get frequent chances to receive supervision, on the other hand she resented having to be the responsible one all the time.

The supervisory group proved to be very helpful by showing therapist A the striking parallel between her associations and those of the patients in her group. Her in-depth, first-person awareness of the dynamics of passive hostility toward feelings of unfair responsibility enabled her to more sensitively appreciate the husband and wife interactions from both sides of the fence (as the "resentful" giver and as the "manipulative" exploiter).

The point that I want to emphasize here is that supervision can be a more meaningful experience if certain presentation rituals are repeatedly explored as potential resistances to learning. Why is one patient focused on more than another? Why does a particular supervisor spend an excessive amount of supervisory time referring to individual patients and neglecting the total group? Why not spend a supervisory hour exploring all those segments of the session which the supervisee had not intended to talk about? Ask the supervisee to name the members of his group, whom did he name first? Whom did he name last? Whom did he block on—why? Is there a difference in the therapist's involvement in both the group and in the supervisory experience if he is encouraged to focus on the decision-making processes involved or in his interventions, as they unfold? What role is the therapist structuring for himself and his patients by his remarks? Is he fully aware of the effect on patient expectations of didactic remarks, authoritative "father knows best" statements, seductive "I am more like you than like them" vibrations to adolescent groups, etc.?

2. This next example further confirms the viewpoint that supervision, like the analytic process itself, is a system that can only be comprehended on a transactional level. Much of the value of the supervisory experience comes from the student's dawning recognition that clinical phenomena can be most valuably viewed in their dynamic and adaptational contexts and become units in a behavioral pattern in which both parties play instrumental roles (Fleming & Benedeck, 1966).

I had just been appointed director of group therapy at a large local agency. One of my functions was to supervise three workers in group therapy. During the first two sessions, I felt there was a definite resistance to my approach. The workers did not seem receptive to the use of current group process for the understanding of their cases, there was a strong reluctance to sharing personal thoughts and feelings, and a general tightness and lack of spontaneity in the air. Feeling the force of these negative reactions, I found myself becoming more didactic and "lectury" than I usually am, thereby cutting off more freewheeling individual participation. I approached the third session with some irritation and apparent counterresistance (I arrived ten minutes late).

Worker A began to present the first session of a mothers' group, where she served as a cotherapist (her partner was not able to come to our meeting because of a conflicting schedule). She described the early part of the session as revolving around themes of despondency and futility. Questions such as, "How long will it be before we see improvement?," "How long do we have to be here?" alternated with frustrating stories by parents overwhelmed by how to deal with their problem children. Worker A said that she tended to take a somewhat passive role in relation to her cotherapist, who met many of the questions with lengthy, literal answers ("Group therapy takes time, maybe two years to work," etc.). She also observed that several of the women seemed to take a more optimistic view of the progress they had made through individual therapy, and the cotherapist interpreted this as an avoidance of their real disappointment in being unable to handle their children better. All of this was reported in a matter-of-fact monotone, with no apparent resentment or strong difference of opinion on the part of the presenter.

After about ten minutes of this, workers B and C began to press worker A about whether she wasn't perhaps quite angry at the cotherapist. They challenged her surface placidity and were skeptical regarding her seeming contentment with the passive role. The behavior of workers B and C was in sharp contrast to the way they had acted in the past. They were much more "off the cuff," spoke more aggressively, showed a greater degree of perceptiveness, and managed to create a sense of aliveness in the room. The only qualifying factor I felt was their need to glance at me, apparently to reassure themselves that they were on the right track.

About this time, I made my first few interventions. I suggested that there seemed to be a number of separation problems operating simultaneously. (1) The patients' surface complaints ("How long do we have to come?") reflected early reactive defenses against dependency on the therapist and other group members. (2) The manifest content of the patients' disappointments in being able to handle their children properly also suggested an overidentification with those children and an inability to see them as separate individuals with their own feelings and preferences. By binding the children to them and then feeling trapped by guilt and anger, the patients had put themselves in a paradoxical straitjacket. (3) By not being assertive in the group, worker A was subordinating herself to the male cotherapist. Her fear of individuating was rationalized by a pseudodeference to his maleness ("I don't mind his taking over; men are more active and I'm more passive.") I wondered whether she was not appeasing her dread of being independent by abdicating masochistically to his superior wisdom while secretly feeling competitive and hateful toward him. (4) The male cotherapist's minimization and perfunctory handling of apparent gross misstatements on the part of the patients encouraged an unnecessary dependency. By focusing on pathology and emphasizing their frustration and disappointments, the cotherapist was widening the gap between himself (health, in control) and them (sick, helpless) and was discouraging the development of genuine autonomy and interdependence.

After some discussion, I drew the group's attention to what was happening in the room (the new freedom of interaction and participation). I wondered whether this did not represent a constructive way of disengaging from the old passive, frightened, symbiotic-dependent attitude toward me. The furtive glances were interpreted as "I wonder how far we dare go."

Suddenly, worker A remembered a dream she had prior to the group session. "I was hugging the cotherapist and felt very close to him right after the session. Then I had a feeling of self-disgust." I told worker A that she had spontaneously hugged me after our last session but that I drew back inside, not trusting what looked like a warm, friendly overture. Worker A's associations to this were, "I guess I'm a very envious, ambitious person, but I don't like to show it. I keep the aggressive side of myself under wraps. I want to look feminine to disarm people. I want to get what wisdom I can from people so that I play dumb—sweet, reasonable, and quiet. I think the dream means that I make myself part of people, I blend in with them to steal from them, and then I feel shitty into the bargain."

Now worker B told about her previous experience as a cotherapist: "We worked for two years without ever discussing the fact that I was black and he was white. I think my speaking up today was my way of showing you [the supervisor] that I didn't want this to happen again. I want to be able to confront you but I guess I'm afraid of you. You know so much."

Worker C began to get restless and distracted. " I çan't stand talking about other people when they're not here. You [workers A and B] aren't being fair criticizing them when they're not here." I interrupted at this moment and paraphrased what was being said in separation terms ("We shouldn't be separate people who can talk and act as we please"). The ghost of the others — the parents — always has to be hanging over us. In response to this, workers A, B, and C commented on the fact that it was not so much that they felt guilty about discussing an absent member, but that they felt an impassable gap in approaching him when he was present. There was a consensus that Mr. X was "hard to talk to." to." (But if we can't talk straight to colleagues, how can we talk to patients or expect them to talk to us?)

Now the conversation began to drift away from the business at hand. The previous Tuesday, these same workers had both timidly and provocatively (by asking at the last moment) approached the administration about getting time off for anti-Vietnam demonstrations on Moratorium day.

"We should really unionize here but there's too much dissension. We can't get together, we're not organized or militant enough." I began to interpret this content in terms of our original case discussion. The issue, as I saw it, was what conditions have to operate in order for children (workers) to feel strong enough to deal sensibly with parental authority (administration). Is it possible to ask for what you want and say what you feel without manipulating, ingratiating, or feeling self-righteously exploited? These comments led worker A to wonder out loud if she could differ publicly with her

cotherapist, even (G-d forbid) in front of the group. Workers
B and C chimed in at this point and said they were going to
take a chance with me right now. "What you have to say is
good but you sometimes sound as though if we don't accept
it, we're no good—stupid maybe. I wonder whether we didn't
stay quiet to punish you and make you feel stupid." I
responded by saying there were certain times when "I felt
very much alone as if I was making a speech to an empty
house." As an aside, I mentioned that it did not feel that way
today. "As a matter of fact I'm feeling a lot of contact today,
like I'm really being myself and it feels good." Workers A, B,
and C now began to share in-group secrets with me. It turned
out that I had been given as a sop to them. "The administration here has a traditional analytic approach. They don't
want group therapy, they only give it lip service. They
brought you in to shut us up. Their intake policies are
ridiculous as far as group therapy is concerned. They
eliminate nine-tenths of the patients and see group as a place
to cut down on the waiting list or get rid of unwanted patients." I related these comments to the silent war that
existed between us during the first two sessions, and I
also questioned whether this did not have significant implications for understanding some of worker A's problems in dealing with her group more effectively. Apparently I was seen as
an extension of the workers' helplessness and futility, coming
around to stimulate interest in group, while the truth was,
from their point of view, I was foiled from the beginning. I
now saw the worker's passive resistance as a suspicious (but
somewhat realistic) refusal to bite at something fresh because
beneath it all they knew that there was no chance of success.
The facts about the administration policies I had not known
about, but I was aware of having succeeded a rather prominent group therapist, as director of group therapy at this
agency. I suppose I had a fear of not being able to live up to
his reputation and thereby disappointing the workers. My insecurity must have conveyed itself in the form of trying to
control, giving aggressive, enlightening, rock 'm-sock 'm interpretations, and generally trying to compete with an ego

ideal that I could not possibly match. My ambivalent attempt to fuse with this personified ideal (my predecessor) found life in my unsuccessful attempts to get the supervisory group to merge with me, to follow my style, to submit themselves to my pronouncements, and thereby validate my worth and my identity. The supervisory session ended with a short didactic discussion of the conflict between wanting to lose oneself in the protective omnipotence of another compared to the loneliness of a positive, independent stand.

An approach that emphasizes participating leadership and free but measured use of the process emerging during the supervisory session, helps to dispel the omnipotent parental transference image, leading to increased empathy, responsiveness, perceptivity, and intuition. A new experience for growth as a professional is only attainable if analyst and supervisor engage in a mutual endeavor to cooperatively and independently manage the vicissitudes and complexities of the learning process to reach for new insights.

REFERENCES

Auerback, A. (Ed.), New York: Ronald, 1959, pp. 99-123.

Ekstein, R., & Wallerstein, R. *The teaching and learning of psychotherapy.* New York: Basic Books, 1958.

Fleming, J., & Benedeck, T. *Psychoanalytic supervision.* New York: Grune & Stratton, 1966.

Isakower, O. *Problems of supervision.* Unpublished report to the Curriculum Committee of the New York Psychoanalytic Institute, 1957.

Langs, R. *The technique of psychoanalytic psychotherapy,* Vol. 2. New York: Jason Aronson, 1974.

Leichter, E. Utilization of group process in the training and supervision of group therapists in a social agency setting. Paper presented at the AGPA Conference, New York, Feb. 11, 1962.

Lieberman, D. Affective response of the analyst to the patient's communications. *International Journal of Psycho-Analysis,* 1978, *59,* 335-41.

Mintz, E. Group supervision: An experimental approach. *International Journal of Group Psychiatry,* 1972, *28,* 467-479.

Spotnitz, H. Trends in modern psychoanalytic supervision. *Modern Psychoanalysis.* 1969, *2,* (1) 201-217.

INDEX

Affective states
  affective life of the group,
    172-182
  and level of ego development,
    166
  emotional flooding, 170
  Gill, 166
  Hartman, Kris and Lowenstein,
    167
  Krystal, 168
  organizing function of affects,
    181
  Spitz, 18
Analyst
  active participation, 78
  basic assumptions of, 129
  containing quality of, 137
  difficulties of, 121-122
  Freud, 202
  independent status of, 22
  as maturational object, 93
  pathological transitional status
    of, 23
  positive contributions of, 121
  reality status of, 23
  role in group, 202
  Sterba, 202
  Strachey, 202
Analytic situation
  area of illusion, 10
  bipersonal field, 76
  good-enough mother, 79
  holding environment, 79
  Jacobson, 59
  Mahler, 59
  maternal container, 79
  Modell, 10
  parataxic field, 58
  relating to and using the object,
    11, 21-22
  setting the frame and offering
    the medium, 9-10

Analytic situation (Continued)
  therapeutic regression, 80-81
  transitional phenomena, 10
  Winnicott, 10, 21

Borderline states
  in combined treatment, 224-244
  definition of, 224
  and the fear of merging, 43
  Kernberg, 34
  Liff, 43, 44
  and masochism, 42
  self-destructiveness and, 32
  splitting and projective identifi-
    cation, 91
  symptoms of, 36-37, 56
  treatment approaches to, 65-70
Countertransference
  and the analyst's identity, 109
  as compensation for feelings of
    helplessness, 49
  complementary identifications,
    134
  constructive utilizations of,
    68, 85-86, 220
  ego ideals and, 122-124
  Epstein, 103
  and group psychotherapy, 140
  Herman, 68
  Kernberg and, 84
  parallels in the mother-child
    interaction, 118-120
  positive, 135
  projective identification and,
    125
  Racker, 118, 134
  supervisory workshops, 248
  and the totalistic approach, 85
  transference-countertransference
    binds, 48